Gc 1/3/12.

Please return or renew this item STO  **East Sussex**
by the last date shown. You may
return items to any East Sussex
Library. You may renew books
by telephone or the internet.

0345 60 80 195 for renewals
0345 60 80 196 for enquiries

Library and Information Service
eastsussex.gov.uk/libraries

Car Repair Manual

FIESTA

Compiled and Written by
DAVID PENN

Ford Fiesta

from 1976

Fiesta Base 957 cc Saloon	Fiesta S 1117 cc Saloon
Fiesta L 957 cc Saloon	Fiesta Ghia 1117 cc Saloon
Fiesta Ghia 957 cc Saloon	Fiesta S 1300 cc Saloon
Fiesta L 1117 cc Saloon	Fiesta Ghia 1300 cc Saloon

The Editor would like to acknowledge the help from the following
companies in the preparation of this repair manual:

Ford Motor Co. Ltd
Champion Sparking Plug Co. Ltd
KL Automotive Products Ltd
Sound Service (Oxford) Ltd
Radiomobile Ltd

Autodata Car Repair Manual for the Ford Fiesta

Compiled and Written by David Penn
Edited by Tony Stuart-Jones
Layout and paste-up: Mandy Way/Anne White
Composing: Sajan Neal/Simer Bharji

Published by Autodata Limited
St. Peter's Road, Maidenhead, Berkshire, SL6 7QU. England

ACRM 266

ISBN 0-85666-014-0

Printed in England

Introduction

You are reading one of the best accessories that you could purchase for your car. Whether you are a keen do-it-yourself enthusiast or just eager to cut the cost of motoring, this repair manual will guide you through all the stages of various mechanical repairs - from a simple oil and filter change; fitting new brake shoes; checking the hydraulics; tuning the engine; dealing with the electrics; or even removing and overhauling the engine - all the knowledge and information you are likely to need are here!

The easy-reference contents page and individual chapter headings will guide you to the appropriate section dealing with the part of your car to be checked or repaired. The clear line-drawings will show you what fits where giving you all the confidence to tackle a job for the first time. Each chapter contains easy-to-follow repair sequences with a comprehensive Technical Data section included at the end. If problems occur that can't be solved easily then turn to the special Trouble-shooting chart to be found at the end of the appropriate section.

A large proportion of this manual is devoted to routine and preventative maintenance with a complete chapter covering the servicing of your car - indeed, a money saver in itself!

Tools are of obvious importance to the do-it-yourself car owner and, like this repair manual, can be termed as a good investment. Purchase wisely, not over-spending but just purchasing good quality tools needed for a certain job and building up your equipment as you go. Tools required for general servicing aren't that many but it will be the wise do-it-yourself motorist who invests in a good jack and axle stands or wheel ramps. Some of the operations shown in this book require special tools and, in many cases, they can be hired locally. If specialist knowledge is required then we state as much. If it is possible to manage without special aids then we tell you how. Sometimes a little ingenuity can save a lot of time and money.

Now you can be the expert and the cost of this repair manual will be easily recovered the first time that you use it.

Jack Hay

Editor

Brief History

FEBRUARY 1977

Fiesta introduced in the U.K. Three-door 'hatchback' body style available in four versions, Base, L, S and Ghia. Transverse mounted engine with separate combined gearbox/final drive (transaxle) unit driving front wheels through unequal length driveshafts. Three engine options available, 957 cc low compression, 957 cc high compression and 1117 cc high compression, based on the original 105E Anglia/Cortina three bearing crankshaft engine. Ford 'sonic' idle single venturi (1V) carburettor. McPherson strut type coil spring front suspension, coil spring rear suspension with transverse axle tube, panhard rod and trailing arms. Self-adjusting front disc/rear drum dual circuit brakes and self-adjusting cable operated clutch.

SEPTEMBER 1977

1300 cc S and Ghia models introduced, with Weber twin venturi (2V) carburettor with equal length driveshafts incorporating an intermediate driveshaft. 1300 engine has five bearing crankshaft and based on the Escort Sport unit. Larger 7.5 in dia clutch fitted with final drive ratio raised to 3.842:1. Both models have stiffened suspension with a rear anti-roll bar.

SEPTEMBER 1978

957 cc HC engine available to special order only and LC engine dropped on L models. L and S models now have rear wiper/washer system as standard. S models now have radio as standard.

OCTOBER 1978

Limited edition Fiesta 'Kingfisher' model available with 1117 cc engine and full equipment specification including sun roof.

MARCH 1979

Millionth Fiesta produced. 3100 special replicas produced with Black or Silver paintwork and full equipment specification including stereo cassette player, head restraints and check upholstery.

APRIL 1979

957 cc and 1117 cc models now fitted with 'g' valve in braking system to conform with EEC regulations. Brake fluid level warning light now fitted on all models.

Quick Reference Data

GENERAL DIMENSIONS

Length
    with bumper overriders. . . . . 142 in (3.609 m)
    without bumper overriders . . . . .140.4 in (3.565 m)
Width . . . . .61.7 in (1.567 m)
Height. . . . . .51.8 in (1.314 m)
Wheelbase . . . . .90 in (2.286 m)
Track
    Front . . . . .52.5 in (1.334 m)
    Rear . . . . 52 in (1.321 m)
Turning circle (between kerbs) . . . . .30.5 ft (9.3 m)

ENGINE

Firing order . . . . 1 - 2 - 4 - 3
Valve rocker clearance (engine cold)
    1.0 LC/1.0 HC/1.1 HC
        Inlet . . . . 0.009 in (0.22 mm)
        Exhaust . . . . 0.023 in (0.59 mm)
    1.3 2V
        Inlet . . . . 0.010 in (0.25 mm)
        Exhaust . . . . 0.022 in (0.55 mm)
Spark plug
    Type - 957 cc/1117 cc . . . . Motorcraft AGRF 22
    Gap . . . . 0.030 in (0.75 mm)
    Type 1.3 . . . . AGR 12
    Gap . . . . 0.024 in (0.6 mm)
Distributor points gap
    Motorcraft . . . . 0.025 in (0.64 mm)
    Bosch . . . . 0.016-0.020 in (0.4-0.5 mm)
Dwell angle . . . . 48 - 52°
Static ignition timing
    1.3 2V . . . . 6° BTDC
    All others. . . . . 10° BTDC
Idle speed
    1.1 HC . . . . .750-850 rpm
    All others. . . . . .775-825 rpm
Fuel octane requirement
    LC engine . . . . .90 minimum (2-star, UK)
    HC engines. . . . . .97 minimum (4-star, UK)

CAPACITIES

Engine oil -
    Oil change (inc. filter) . . . . 5.75 pt (3.25 litres)
Gearbox . . . . 5 pt (2.8 litres)
Cooling system . . . . 8.8 pt (5.0 litres)
Fuel tank. . . . . 7.5 gal (34 litres)
Cooling system (inc. heater) . . . . 9.27 pt (5.27 litres)

CHASSIS
    Alternator drive belt tension . . . . 0.5 in (13 mm) on longest run

TYRE PRESSURES - lb/in^2 (bar)	Normal		Fully laden	
	Front	Rear	Front	Rear
135 SR/12	27 (1.9)	27 (1.9)	31 (2.2)	31 (2.2)
145 SR/12	23 (1.6)	26 (1.8)	26 (1.8)	28 (2.0)
155 SR/12	23 (1.6)	26 (1.8)	26 (1.8)	28 (2.0)

Contents

Pass the MoT

Once a year, the MoT test falls due for vehicles, three years old or more (UK only). The test fee paid to the garage covers the cost of carrying out the inspection whether the vehicle passes the test or fails, so it makes sense to ensure that you get the maximum value out of the inspection by carrying out your own pre-test check beforehand.

In this way, you can possibly save yourself the cost of a failure certificate by putting right any likely reasons for failure. Bear in mind that an 'official' tester will more than likely follow a different criterion when examining the same component as the DIY owner, but, by just being aware of what checks the tester will make could avoid a needless failure certificate. Even a simple item like a brake light or one of the screen washers not working could 'fail' the test.

All the items that will come under the tester's scrutiny are included in this repair manual in one way or another although it is obviously not compiled specifically for passing the test. However, if you work your way through the check list below, and turn to the appropriate page number referred to, you will have the information required either to check or to service the relevant components.

LIGHTING EQUIPMENT, STOP LIGHTS, REFLECTORS, INDICATORS . . . . **Pages 127, 128**
All external lights must be in working order - including the headlamp main and dipped beams - and visible from a reasonable distance. Light lenses must not be damaged or missing. The indicators must flash at the correct rate - between one and two flashes per second - and the panel warning lights must also be functioning. Headlamps must be correctly aligned.

STEERING . . . . **Pages 14, 89**
Check for excessive play in all the steering components from the road wheels to the steering wheel. Check the tightness of all nuts and clamp bolts. Check for any unusual stiffness in the steering operation. Examine the steering box for oil leaks.

WHEEL BEARINGS . . . . **Pages 89, 105**
Raise and support the vehicle and check for bearing roughness by rotating the wheels. A worn bearing will either be heard or felt at the tyre as the wheel turns. A slack front wheel bearing cannot be adjusted and will have to be replaced, but the rear wheel bearings are adjustable.

SUSPENSION . . . . **Pages 14, 89, 105**
The vehicle will have to be raised and supported to check the suspension. Using a suitable long lever or screwdriver to give leverage, check for excessive play in all the suspension joints. Check the condition of all shock absorber units - looking for fluid leakage and the security of the upper and lower mountings. Check the damping operation of the shock absorbers with the car on the road, by bouncing it at all four corners.

BRAKES . . . . **Pages 13, 111**
Check the operation of the brakes and the handbrake. Check for brakes pulling to one side and ascertain the cause. Check the condition of the flexible brake hoses looking for signs of cracking and for corrosion on the rigid metal pipes - especially around the rear axle. Check that the brake servo - if fitted, is working properly. Remember that the testing station now uses a 'roller brake tester' to check the efficiency of each wheel.

WHEELS AND TYRES . . . . **Page 16**
Check the condition of the tyres - the tread depth, the side walls, both inner as well as outer, and that they are inflated to correct pressure (The latter may affect the brake tests). Don't forget to check the condition of the spare tyre. Check the condition of the wheel rims for dmage or distortion.

SEAT BELTS . . . . **Page 18**
Check the seat belts for security and the fabric for chafing or obvious damage.

GENERAL - WIPERS, WASHERS, HORN, EXHAUST . . . . **Pages 16, 128, 134**
Both the windscreen wipers and washers should be working efficiently. The horn should also operate clearly. Check that the exhaust system does not leak or make an excessive amount of noise. The best way to check for a leaking exhaust is to place a gloved hand over the end of the tailpipe with the engine idling and listen for the 'hiss' of any leakage.

CORROSION . . . . **Page 18**
Check the body panels for any damage or corrosion on the vehicle likely to render it unsafe.

NOTE: The above check list is only a guide so that the keen DIY owner can check his or her Fiesta before submitting it for the MoT test. Although it is based on the official MoT check list at the time of publication, it is only a guide and should be treated as such.

Service Schedule

WEEKLY OR WHEN REFUELLING

- Check battery electrolyte level
- Check tyre pressures, including spare
- Check operation of all lights
- Check engine oil level
- Check coolant level
- Check windscreen washer level

EVERY 6,000 MILES (10,000 KM) OR 6 MONTHS – STANDARD SERVICE

- Check brake fluid level
- Check transaxle oil level
- Inspect brake pads and linings
- Check operation of rear brake self-adjust mechanism
- Lubricate handbrake linkage and check adjustment
- Inspect all brake lines and hoses for leaks or damage
- Inspect front suspension/steering linkages
- Check tyre pressures and condition
- Check level of battery electrolyte
- Clean and check battery terminals
- Check generator belt tension and condition
- Check coolant level
- Check and adjust valve clearances
- Change engine oil and filter
- Clean spark plugs and adjust gaps, or renew
- Renew distributor points
- Lubricate distributor, clean cap, coil HT leads
- Check dwell angle and ignition timing
- Clean out fuel pump filter
- Lubricate throttle linkage and check cable adjustment
- Check carburettor idle and mixture setting
- Check generally for oil, water, fuel and exhaust leaks
- Check levels in all washer reservoirs
- Check adjustment of washer jets
- Lubricate all locks, hinges, catches, etc.
- Carry out road test and check general condition of car (brakes, clutch, steering, gearchange, instruments, controls, etc.)
- Check tightness of alternator mounting bolts
- Check tightness of manifold and exhaust

EVERY 18,000 MILES (30,000 KM) OR 18 MONTHS – EXTENDED SERVICE
As for Standard Service above, plus the following additional items:

- Clean crankcase emission valve and oil filler cap
- Renew air cleaner element
- Change brake fluid completely

EVERY 36,000 MILES (60,000 KM) OR 3 YEARS – MAJOR SERVICE
As for Extended Service above, plus the following additional items:

- Clean and repack front wheel bearings.
- Renew all brake cylinder seals. Examine all flexible hoses and renew if necessary.

OTHER ITEMS

Every 2 years the cooling system should be drained, flushed and refilled with fresh anti-freeze mixture

MIDWAY SERVICE

If the vehicle is used under severe operating conditions, covers a very low annual mileage or its use includes a high proportion of short journeys, the following service is recommended between scheduled services.

- Check engine oil level (or change engine oil and filter, if required)
- Check coolant level
- Check windscreen washer reservoir
- Check brake fluid level
- Check battery electrolyte level
- Check tyre pressure and condition, including spare
- Check distributor points gap (or dwell angle) and ignition timing
- Check carburettor idle and mixture settings
- Inspect brake system for leaks and hoses for chafing
- Check for evidence of oil, water, fuel or exhaust leaks
- Check operation of all lights, controls and instruments
- Carry out road test and check general condition of car

Routine Maintenance

INTRODUCTION . . . . [1]

There is little doubt that the more knowledge you have about your car, the more equipped you will be to put things right if and when they go wrong. Certainly tackling the servicing or routine maintenance yourself will give you the opportunity of getting to know your car, at the same time saving yourself a lot of money.

The aim of this particular section is to guide the owner through the maze of service items to be found in the major service. You will see that on a previous page we have a Service Schedule which lists all the relevant checks at the appropriate intervals. This schedule does not necessarily list the items in the order that they should be tackled or checked. To save yourself time it would be better to divide the larger service into three or four sections. For example, all the under-bonnet operations could be tackled first - from topping up the various fluid levels to tuning the engine (covered in the next chapter). Then, perhaps, the brakes can be checked along with other items to be checked under the car. Finally, you might end up with tackling the lubrication side of the service. finishing up with light lubrication of the door locks and hinges.

It is worthwhile first reading the ROUTINE MAINTENANCE and TUNE-UP chapter thoroughly before actually starting to service your car so that you are aware of the work entailed and the tools and parts that you are likely to require beforehand. You can refer to the Service Data at the end of this chapter for details of all the lubricants that will be needed.

Apart from carrying out specific service operations, a certain amount of inspection and checking will be required. Remember that a fault, such as an oil leak, spotted now could save you a major, costly overhaul or replacement at a later date.

If you wish just to refer to one particular service item, then simply check the headings at the top of this page and turn to the appropriate check or operation.

ENGINE OIL & FILTER . . . . [2]

Checking Oil Level (Fig. A:1)

It is essential that the engine oil is maintained at the correct level. The oil level should be checked at least once a week and always before a long run. Ensure that the car is standing on level ground when checking the oil. The oil level should be maintained at the upper mark on the dipstick and must never be allowed to fall below the lower mark (Fig. A:1). Top up if necessary with the recommended grade of oil - see Service Data for a list of specified lubricants. Add oil through the filler tube in the rocker cover after removing the filler cap.

The approximate quantity of oil required to raise the level from the lower to the upper mark on the dipstick is 1.25 pt (0.75 litre).

Do NOT overfill as this may result in oil leaks and increased oil consumption.

Changing Engine Oil/Filter

The engine oil and filter should be changed at the recommended intervals or more frequently under severe operating conditions.

The most severe type of operation, and that which gives rise to a sludge formation (mayonnaise) inside the engine, is light engine loading, slow speeds and short journeys where the engine never reaches normal operating temperature. High speeds over long distances are generally kinder to the engine. Modern multigrade engine oils contain additives which go a long way towards preventing sludge formation, but even these have certain limitations.

The oil should be drained when the engine is warm. Place a tray under the drain plug - an old 5 litre oil can with one side cut out is ideal for this - then undo the plug and drain out the oil. Clean the plug and fit a sealing washer. When the oil has finished draining, refit the plug and tighten it to a torque of 18 lb ft (2.5 kg m).

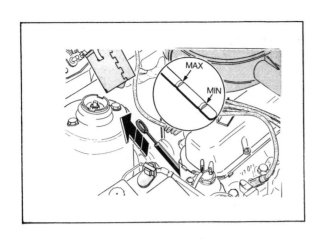

Fig. A:1 The location of the engine oil level dipstick

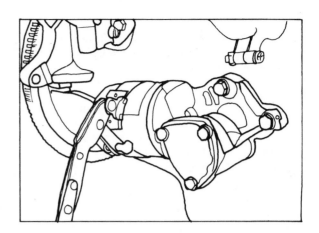

Fig. A:2 Using a strap wrench to undo the oil filter cannister

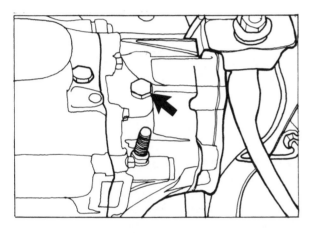

Fig. A:3 Location of gearbox oil filler/level plug

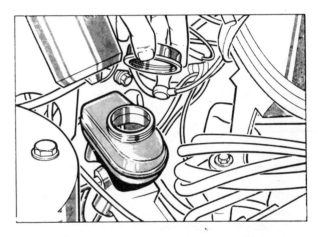

Fig. A:4 Checking/filling brake master cylinder reservoir

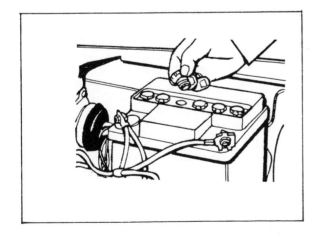

Fig. A:5 Remove cell caps to check/top-up battery electrolyte level

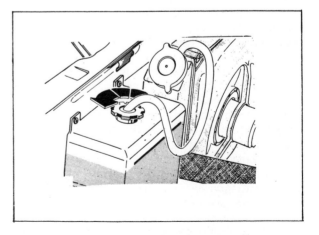

Fig. A:6 Check that the expansion bottle water level is up to the mark

The oil filter element is of the throw-away cannister type and is screwed into an adaptor on the underside of the oil pump housing. The filter should be replaced every time the oil is changed.

A strap wrench will be needed to unscrew the filter cannister (Fig. A:2), alternatively, the cannister can be speared with a screwdriver to undo it although this is a somewhat messy way.

A drip tray should be placed under the filter as a quantity of oil will be released when it is removed. Unscrew the old cartridge from the pump housing and discard it. Clean the mounting face on the pump flange. Wet the seal on the new cartridge with clean engine oil and check that the seal is correctly located in its groove. Screw the cartridge on to the threaded adaptor by hand until the seal just contacts the pump housing, then further tighten ¾ turn.

Refill the engine with the correct quantity and grade of oil - see Service Data. Start the engine and check the filter for signs of leakage - stop the engine immediately if any leaks are present as this indicates that the cartridge is not sealing correctly. If all is well, stop the engine and re-check the oil level after waiting a few minutes.

GEARBOX . . . . [3]

Check/Top-Up Oil Level (Fig. A:3)

The gearbox oil level should be checked only after the vehicle has been standing on level ground for some time, as foaming of the oil during use will cause the level to rise and give an incorrect indication of the lubricant content.

The combined filler/level plug is on the front of the gearbox casing (Fig. A:3). The oil level is correct when the oil reaches the lower edge of the plug hole. If necessary, top up with the specified grade of oil (see Specified Lubricants in Service Data).

Lack of oil in the transmission can only result from a leak and the cause should be established and dealt with.

BRAKE FLUID. . . . . [4]

Checking Level (Fig. A:4)

Check that the brake fluid is up to the MAX mark or above the MIN mark on the master cylinder reservoir. If topping up is necessary, clean the area around the filler cap before unscrewing it. Use only the specified type of brake fluid to top up. Check that the vent hole in the filler cap is clear before refitting the cap.

It should be noted that brake fluid will damage paintwork if allowed to come into contact with it. Any spilt fluid must be wiped (or washed with cold water) from the affected area immediately.

The fluid level in the reservoir will drop slightly over a period of time as the disc caliper pistons move outwards to compensate for pad lining wear - this is normal. However, if the fluid level falls excessively, or requires frequent topping up, this indicates a leak in the braking system and steps should immediately be taken to establish and deal with the cause.

Replacing Brake Fluid

The brake fluid should be changed completely every 12 months. Use only the specified type of fluid to refill the system. See Service Data for specifications. Refer to the BRAKES chapter for the bleeding procedure.

Brake Hydraulic Components

Periodically, all hydraulic pipes, hoses and unions should be checked visually for chafing, leaks or corrosion. Any component which is damaged or suspect should be renewed immediately.

As preventive maintenance, at 36,000 miles (60,000 km), all fluid seals in the braking system should be replaced and all flexible hoses examined and replaced if necessary. At the same time, the working surfaces of the pistons and bores of the master cylinder, wheel cylinders, and any other hydraulic components should be examined and new parts fitted where necessary.

The procedures for replacing the seals in the various hydraulic components of the braking system are fully described under the appropriate headings in the BRAKES chapter.

BATTERY . . . . [5]

Electrolyte Level (Fig. A:5)

The level of the battery electrolyte should be checked periodically, and distilled (de-ionised) water added if the level in any cell is below the separators, or the bottom of the filling tube on trough fill type batteries. In some cases, the battery case is translucent to allow the level to be checked without the need for lifting the vent cover. Do not over-fill the battery. It is good practice to run the car immediately after topping up the battery, especially in cold weather to ensure thorough mixing of the acid and the water and so prevent freezing.

If the battery is found to need frequent topping up, steps should be taken to find out the reason. For example, the battery may be receiving an excessive charge, in which case the charging system charge rate should be checked. If one cell in particular needs topping up more than the others, check the condition of the battery case. If there are signs of an electrolyte leak, the source should be traced and corrective action taken.

NOTE: The electrolyte level should not be topped up within half an hour of the battery being charged, other than by the vehicle's own charging system, lest it floods.

Battery Connections

To ensure good contact, the battery cables should be tight on the battery posts. If the battery posts or cable terminals are corroded, the cables should be disconnected and the terminals and posts cleaned with a soda solution and a wire brush. When reconnecting the cables to the battery posts, a thin coating of petroleum jelly (not grease) should be applied. The battery earth strap and the engine earth strap should also be checked for proper connection and condition.

COOLING SYSTEM . . . . [6]

Coolant level (Fig. A:6)

The radiator coolant level should be checked at least weekly and topped up as necessary. Check the level when the engine is cool. If the system is at normal operating temperature, allow it to cool first. Muffle the pressure cap with a thick cloth to protect the hands against escaping steam and turn the cap slowly anti-clockwise to the first stop to release the pressure in the system before completely removing the cap. The coolant level in the expansion tank should also be checked weekly.

The coolant level should be up to the bottom of the radiator filler neck and between the MAX and MIN marks on the expansion tank. If the level in the system has fallen appreciably, suspect a leak in the system; check the hoses and hose connections first.

NOTE: *When the system contains anti-freeze ensure that the specific gravity of the coolant is maintained.*

Anti-Freeze

Because of the properties of anti-freeze in lowering the freezing point and raising the boiling point of the coolant, it is recommended that an 'All Season' type anti-freeze is used permanently in the cooling system to afford maximum protection against both freezing and overheating. The presence of a corrosion inhibitor in most anti-freezes will also help to prevent corrosion and the formation of scale in the system.

During the winter months an anti-freeze mixture MUST be used in the system to protect against frost damage. The concentration of the anti-freeze solution will depend on the degree of protection required and dilution should be carried out in accordance with the anti-freeze manufacturer's instructions. As a guideline, a 45% solution will remain fluid down to $-32^{\circ}C$ ($-26^{\circ}F$).

Before filling the system with anti-freeze solution, inspect all hoses, hose connections and cooling system joints. Tighten or renew where necessary. After adding the anti-freeze, run the engine up to normal operating temperature and check for leaks. A label should be attached to the radiator to record the date of filling.

The anti-freeze concentration in the system should be checked periodically and in any case before the beginning of the winter season or before travelling to a colder climate. The specific gravity of the coolant should be checked using a suitable hydrometer and brought up to the required strength as necessary. The specific gravity of a 45% concentration solution should be 1.065 providing no other additive is in the coolant.

The cooling system should be completely drained, flushed and refilled with a fresh mixture of anti-freeze and water, at least every two years or as recommended by the anti-freeze manufacturer.

Checking System For Leaks

The hoses, hose connections and system joints should be checked periodically for leaks especially before the beginning of the winter season or when filling the system with anti-freeze.

Examine each hose in turn, looking for deterioration, indicated by cracks, separation of the layers, swelling, or excessive softness of the rubber. Also inspect them for chafing damage due to contact with other components. Replace any hoses which are suspect.

Check that the hose clips are secure and in good condition. Tighten or replace as necessary.

Draining And Refilling

Full details of the draining and refilling procedure are given under the appropriate heading in the COOLING SYSTEM chapter later in this manual.

BRAKES. . . . . [7]

Brake Adjustment

The design of the system is such that adjustment to the front pads and rear drum brake linings is automatic with no provision for periodic manual adjustment.

Handbrake - Adjustment (Fig. A:7)

1. Jack up the car and support it, referring to the jacking information contained later in this chapter. Release the handbrake and check first that the handbrake cable follows its correct run and is properly located in its guides.
2. Loosen the cable adjuster locknut and turn the adjuster to slacken the cable (Fig. A:7).
3. Turn the adjuster to tighten the cable until all slack is removed. A change in cable tension will be noticed when all slack has been removed and the handbrake levers at the brake backplate just begin to move.
4. After the handbrake levers have just begun to move, turn the adjuster three more full turns in the direction necessary to tighten the cable. Secure the adjuster with the locknut. Grease the cable at the points arrowed in Fig. A:10.

NOTE: *When adjustment has been complete the machined section of the threaded adjuster rod must not protrude beyond the locknut.*
5. Lower the car to the ground.

Checking Front Brake Pads

Check the pad thickness for wear by measuring the distance between the face of the pad backing plate and the pad contact face. When this dimension is reduced to or approaching 0.060 in (1.5 mm) the pads must be replaced.

NOTE: Whenever one or more brake pads require replacement, BOTH pads at BOTH front brakes must be replaced, to maintain even braking balance.

If the pads are not being replaced, ensure that sufficient lining material remains to allow the car to run until the next service check.

The procedure for replacinng the brake pads is fully detailed in the BRAKES chapter of this manual.

Checking Rear Brake Linings

Check the rear brake lining wear by removing the rubber inspection plug from the brake carrier plate (Fig. A: 8). It may be necessary to scrape any lining dust away from the brake lining and edge of the brake shoe with a screwdriver or similar tool to reveal the amount of brake lining left. An inspection lamp will be necessary to see inside the drum. This job can be done without jacking up the rear of the car.

If the linings are approaching or worn to the minimum wear limit of 0.060 in (1.5 mm) they should be replaced.

Brake linings should be replaced in axle sets, i.e. BOTH shoes at BOTH rear brakes to maintain even braking balance.

If the linings are not being replaced, ensure that sufficient lining material remains to allow the car to run until the next service check.

The procedure for replacing the rear brake linings is fully detailed in the BRAKES chapter of this manual.

JACKING PROCEDURE . . . . [8]

Jacking Points

Refer to Fig. A:9 for the jacking and support locations beneath the body. It is important that only these positions are used when raising the car, otherwise damage could result.

When raising the complete vehicle, always lift the rear end first. When jacking the rear of the car on the axle beam, a U-shaped wooden block should be made up to prevent the jack head touching the panhard rod and handbrake cable.

When using axle stands to support the car at the sill jacking points, use only square head type stands with wooden cushion pads on top. Only use three legged stands, making sure one of the legs points outwards from the car. Take care when fitting a stand forward of the axle trailing arm that the pad does not touch the trailing arm.

Always raise the rear of the car by lifting it under the axle tube and always raise the front of the car by placing the jack so that its pad lifts the main engine/gearbox longitudinal support member.

When working underneath the car, always fit stands, referring to Fig. A:9 for the correct locations. Never rely on a jack alone, except when wheel changing.

ALTERNATOR DRIVE BELT . . . . [9]

Adjustment (Fig. A:11)

Correct tensioning of the alternator and water pump drive belt is important to ensure efficient operation of both the cooling and charging systems.

When the belt is correctly tensioned, a total deflection of 0.5 in (13 mm) under moderate hand pressure should be possible at the midway point on the longest belt run between the two pulleys (Fig. A:11).

If adjustment is required, slacken the alternator mounting and pivot bolts. Move the alternator towards or away from the engine as necessary until the correct tension is obtained - avoid over-tightening. Apply any leverage necessary to the alternator drive end bracket only using a soft metal or wooden lever. Retighten the alternator mounting bolts and then recheck the belt tension.

The condition of the drive belt should be checked periodically. If it is nicked, cut, excessively worn, or otherwise damaged the belt should be replaced. If the belt is noisy in operation, check for misalignment of the pulleys.

To replace the belt, proceed as for adjusting, but press the alternator fully towards the engine and detach the belt from the pulleys. Fit the new belt, ensuring that it is not twisted, and adjust the tension as described previously. Do NOT attempt to lever a new belt onto the pulleys as this can easily cause damage to the belt or pulleys.

NOTE: The tension of a new belt should be rechecked after approximately 100 miles (160 Km) use.

DISTRIBUTOR. . . . . [10]

Lubrication

Lubrication of the distributor should be carried out at the same time as the engine oil change.

Unclip and remove the distributor cap and pull off the rotor arm from the central spindle.

Apply one or two drops of clean engine oil to the felt wick in the end of the cam spindle (Fig. A:12).

Lightly smear the spindle cam with high melting point grease (Fig. A:13). Use a screwdriver or similar instrument to distribute the lubricant uniformly around the cam surface. When the cam is rotated a small fillet of lubricant should be built up on the back of the points rubbing block.

Avoid over lubricating. Carefully wipe away any surplus lubricant and check that the contact breaker points are perfectly clean and dry. Refit the rotor arm and distributor cap. See TUNE-UP chapter for details on contact breaker inspection and replacement.

STEERING & SUSPENSION . . . . [11]

Ball Joints And Bushes

Check the steering and suspension ball joints for ex-

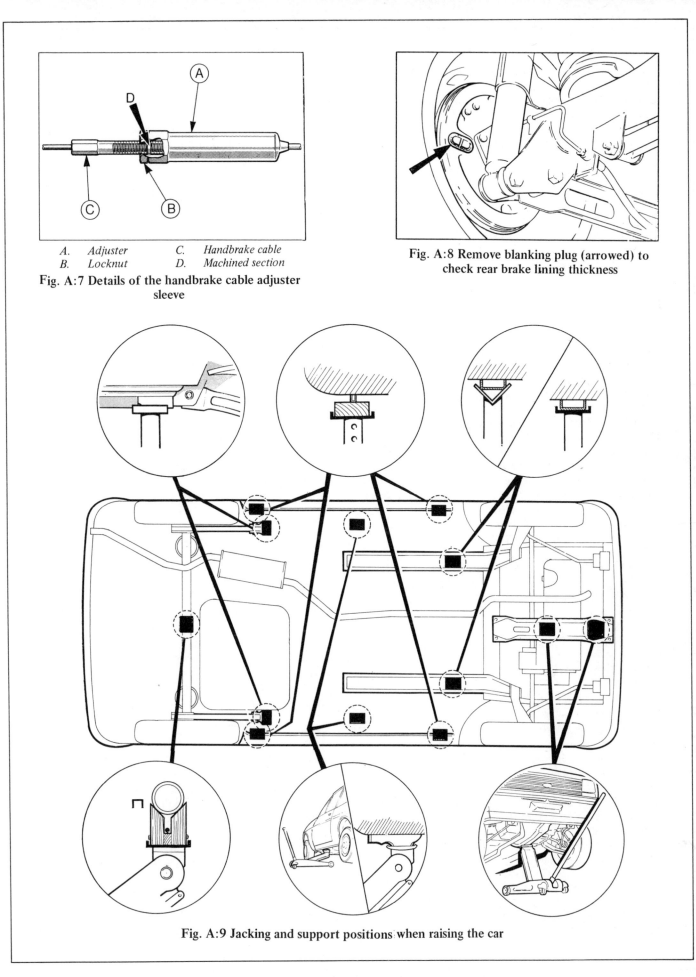

A. Adjuster   C. Handbrake cable
B. Locknut   D. Machined section

Fig. A:7 Details of the handbrake cable adjuster sleeve

Fig. A:8 Remove blanking plug (arrowed) to check rear brake lining thickness

Fig. A:9 Jacking and support positions when raising the car

cessive movement indicating wear. There is a ball joint at the outer end of each lower suspension arm and one at the outer end of each track rod. All of these joints are sealed for life and non-adjustable.

Check the condition of the dust cover at each ball joint as, if damaged, this will allow dirt to enter the joint and accelerate wear.

Check for wear or damage at the track control arm inner pivot bushes and the tie bar rubber mountings.

Check the condition of the front suspension strut top mountings and shock absorber units as detailed in the FRONT SUSPENSION & STEERING chapters.

At the rear of the car check the condition of the various rubber bushes and shock absorbers.

Steering Rack Unit

Check the security of the steering unit mountings. The unit is attached to the front body crossmember by two semi circular clamps.

Check the condition of the convoluted bellows at each end of the steering unit rack housing. If the bellows are torn or otherwise damaged they must be replaced and the unit refilled with lubricant (see STEERING chapter). If the bellows are in good condition, but evidence of leakage is present, check the bellows securing clips for tightness. If leakage has occurred it may be necessary to top up the unit with lubricant. The unit should, ideally, be removed from the car to carry out this operation, but it should be possible to inject oil into the unit in-situ with a syringe after loosening the bellows at one end.

Front Wheel Alignment

The checking and adjustment procedure for the front wheel alignment is fully described under the appropriate heading in the FRONT SUSPENSION chapter, and reference should be made to it for details.

WHEELS & TYRES . . . . [12]

Tyre Pressures

The tyres should be checked and adjusted to the recommended pressures where necessary at least once a week. Check the pressures when the tyres are cold as tyre pressures may increase by as much as 6 lb/in^2 (0.4 kg/cm^2) when hot. The recommended inflation pressures are given in Service Data.

Incorrect inflation pressures will cause abnormal tyre wear and may result in premature failure. There is an average loss of 13% tread mileage for every 10% reduction in inflation pressure below the recommended figure.

When checking the pressures, ensure that the dust caps are refitted to the valves as, apart from keeping out dirt, they also provide a second seal to the valve.

The tightness of the wheel nuts should be checked at the same time as the tyre pressures.

Tyre Inspection

The tyres should be checked periodically for wear or damage.

Check the depth of tread, preferably with a proper tread depth gauge. In the UK the minimum permissible tread depth is 1 mm, but tyres should be replaced before this level is reached as road holding and resistance to punctures will have been affected long before this point.

Check the tyre casing visually for cuts in the casing fabric, exposure of ply or cords, or the presence of lumps or bulges. If any of these conditions are present, the tyre should be discarded.

Abnormal tyre wear may be caused by improper inflation pressures, wheel imbalance, misalignment of front or rear suspension, or mechanical irregularities. When rapid or uneven tyre wear becomes apparent, the cause should be established and dealt with as soon as possible.

Fins and feathering on the tyre tread surface are an indication of severe wheel misalignment. This condition takes the form of a sharp 'fin' on the edge of each pattern rib, and the position of this indicates the direction of misalignment. Fins on the outboard edges are caused by excessive toe-out, whereas fins on the inboard edges of the pattern ribs are caused by excessive toe-in. Finning on the nearside front tyre only may be due to severe road camber conditions and cannot be eliminated by mechanical adjustment. In this event, frequent interchanging of the affected wheel to even out tyre wear is the only solution.

Some mechanical defects which could be a cause of abnormal tyre wear are: loose wheel bearings, uneven brake adjustment, distorted brake discs, excessive looseness or damage in the suspension, loose steering connections, or bent steering arms.

Wheel Balancing

Imbalance of the road wheels may cause wheel tramp, vibration in the steering or abnormal tyre wear.

To obtain maximum ride comfort and tyre life, the balance of the road wheels should be checked periodically. Since specialised knowledge and equipment are required for this operation, the work must be entrusted to an authorised Ford agent or tyre specialist.

EXHAUST SYSTEM. . . . . [13]

Checking

The exhaust system should be checked periodically for leaks and security. It is a good practice to spend a few minutes checking the system whenever work is being carried out under the car.

Check the alignment of the system to ensure that none of the suspension points is strained.

Inspect the exhaust pipes and silencer boxes for damage, corrosion or signs of blowing. The latter is best checked with the engine running at a fast idle and a gloved hand placed over the tailpipe to pressurise the system. Badly rusted components can be detected by tapping the pipes

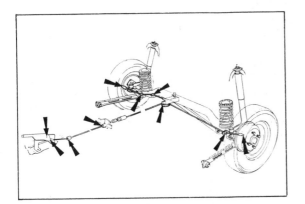

Fig. A:10 Lubricate the handbrake cable at
the points arrowed

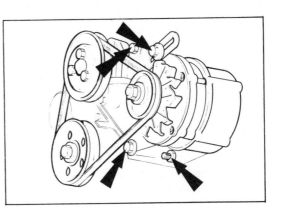

Fig. A:11 Slacken alternator mounting bolts
arrowed to remove/adjust drive belt

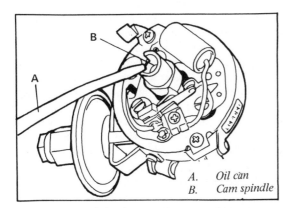

A.   *Oil can*
B.   *Cam spindle*

Fig. A:12 Apply a few drops of oil to lubricate
distributor spindle

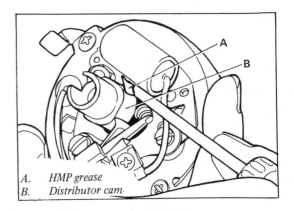

A.   *HMP grease*
B.   *Distributor cam*

Fig. A:13 Smear the spindle cam with a light
coating of HMP grease

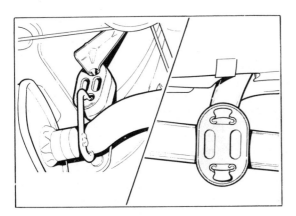

Fig. A:14 Check the condition of the exhaust
system mounting rubbers

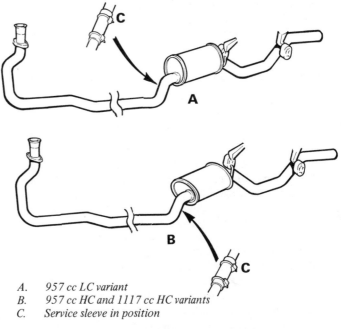

A.   *957 cc LC variant*
B.   *957 cc HC and 1117 cc HC variants*
C.   *Service sleeve in position*

Fig. A:15 Details of the exhaust system on
variant models

and boxes with a screwdriver handle or similar light tool. Take care not to strike the system with a heavy tool as this may damage the system.

Check the rubber mountings for splits and ensure they are adequately supporting the system (Fig. A:14).

Exhaust System Replacement

The Fiesta is manufactured with a one-piece exhaust system for production purposes but replacement parts are available in two parts, front and rear. By cutting the original system with a hacksaw, just in front of the silencer, either section can be replaced. A special joining section is available for this purpose - see Fig. A:15.

SEAT BELTS . . . . [14]

Although seat belts are fitted to a car this doesn't necessarily mean that they are working efficiently or, indeed, that they are capable of doing their job when they are actually needed. This is why the condition of the seat belts is now included in the annual MoT test. There are some simple checks to be made on a regular basis to see that they are in working order. They are as follows:
1. Pull each seat belt against its anchorage to see that it is properly secured to the vehicle structure.
2. Examine carefully the condition of the webbing looking for cuts or obvious signs of deterioration.
3. Fasten each seat belt locking mechanism and then try to pull the locked sections apart. Operate the mechanism, whilst pulling on the belt to determine that the mechanism releases when required.
4. Check the condition of the attachment fittings and adjusting fitting on each belt for distortion or fracture.
5. As far as practicable check the condition of the vehicle structure around the seat belt anchorages - this will be best carried out from below the vehicle.
6. If the seat belt is of the retracting type, pull a section of the webbing from the reel unit and then release it to see that the webbing automatically winds back. Bear in mind that some inertia reel belts require some manual assistance before retraction takes place.

BODY CORROSION. . . . . [15]

We all recognise rust when it starts to appear around certain parts of our car's anatomy. Then, before we are aware, it's too late and metal has been replaced by a very poor substitute. The result is costly, can be dangerous and will not win the car any beauty awards!

The only way to beat rust is to prevent it in the first place or at the very least slow it down. To do this, first of all we must realise how rust is formed.

Think of a piece of metal with a bead of water sitting on top. The metal below the water is starved of air and is called anodic. The metal outside this area is known as cathodic. An electrolytic action is formed between these two conditions and it is this process that causes corrosion.

There are acceleration factors involved such as dirt, grit or salt. These can be contained in the water and will increase the conductivity. So basically rust is formed by an electro-chemical reaction. Bear in mind that rain needn't necessarily be the water factor involved in the process - condensation plays its role too.

Obviously it doesn't take much logic to understand how rust can be prevented in the first place. The metal work of the car has to be protected from moisture and air. The protection is partly taken care of by the car manufacturer when the car is put together - paint on the outside and special inhibitors used on the inside. However, the rust protection is only as good as the application of these materials and one spot missed means that rust will accelerate all the more in this particular spot.

The importance of regular washing and touching up paintwork play their part in rust protection. For example, regular hosing down of the underneath of the car can help prevent any build up of mud forming in certain areas. Mud can act like a damp sponge during wet weather so that you have a constant moisture problem even during dry spells. You'll find that common rust problems on particular models usually originate from mud-traps.

You can always go one step further and improve on the manufacturers rust protection by tackling your own rustproofing. This involves applying light viscosity water-displacing material inside all the box sections and/or applying underbody sealant.

There are various kits on the market designed specifically for the keen DIY motorist and even if you don't treat all the box sections it is worthwhile devoting some time to protecting the rust prone areas of your car.

An important part of protection is treating the car with an underbody sealant. Here preparation is of the utmost importance because if the sealant doesn't attach firmly to the car body then the air gap between seal and metal can help accelerate corrosion rather than prevent it.

First of all the car will have to be thoroughly cleaned underneath. A high pressure hose is obviously helpful in removing dirt but better still is to have the car steam cleaned first. Applying an underbody sealant is a dirty job and you should be well prepared with old clothes, gloves and a hat. If you are venturing underneath the car and it has to be jacked up then make certain that it is well supported on axle stands.

After thoroughly cleaning the underside you should go over stubborn dirt or caked mud with a good fine wire brush. The important thing is that the surface to be treated is absolutely clear of any foreign matter. For good application of underbody sealant use a cheap paint brush. It is important that the sealant used will remain flexible and will not chip or flake at a later date. Obviously care will have to be taken not to cover moving parts such as the drive shafts, handbrake linkages, etc. If necessary then mask these areas first.

The first part of this section on corrosion concentrates on the matter of protection, which is fine before corrosion takes place. But what happens if corrosion has already taken a hold?

It can be a costly business when corrosion dictates the vehicle being taken off the road through an MoT failure. As already explained in 'Passing the MoT' page at the beginning of this Repair Manual, an MoT tester will check for damage or corrosion in or on a vehicle that is likely to render it unsafe.

On the Fiesta, the tester will pay special attention to the inner and outer side sills, the floor pan especially around the front strut mounting and the rear suspension attachment points, also the rear part of the inner front wing panel where it joins the front bulkhead.

Also, he'll check the seat belt mounting areas.

Having checked and identified the important areas, the MoT tester will check the extent or level of suspect corrosion. He should do this by pressing hard against the area and testing the amount of 'give' which results. Often he will also tap the component lightly (it should not be necessary to subject the area to heavy blows), listening for differences in sound which will result from unaffected metal compared with corroded metal.

Service Data

SPECIFIED LUBRICANTS

Engine oil . . . . SAE 20W/50 or 20W/40
Transmission . . . . EP gear oil SAE 80
Wheel bearings . . . . High melting point lithium grease
CV joints. . . . . Ford Spec. S-M1C-75-A/SQM-1C-0004-A
Steering rack . . . . Ford Spec. SAM1C-9106-A fluid grease
Brake fluid. ESEA-M6C-1001A

CAPACITIES

Engine oil
   Oil change (inc. filter) . . . . 5.75 pt (3.25 litres)
Gearbox . . . . 5 pt (2.8 litres)
Steering gear. . . . . 0.17 pt (95 cm^3)
Fuel tank. . . . . 7.5 gal (34 litres)
Cooling system (inc. heater) . . . . 9.27 pt (5.27 litres)

CHASSIS

Alternator drive belt tension . . . . 0.5 in (13 mm) on longest run
Front wheel alignment . . . . 0.04 in (1 mm) toe-in to 0.24 in (6 mm) toe-out

TYRE PRESSURES - lb/in^2 (bar)

	Normal		Fully Laden	
	front	rear	front	rear
135SR/12	27 (1.9)	27 (1.9)	31 (2.2)	31 (2.2)
145SR/12	23 (1.6)	26 (1.8)	26 (1.8)	28 (2.0)
155SR/12	23 (1.6)	26 (1.8)	26 (1.8)	28 (2.0)

Tune-Up

INTRODUCTION . . . . [1]

Poor performance, excessive fuel consumption and bad starting can be some of the problems associated with an engine that is badly worn or out of tune. This is why at every major service the engine components should be checked and tuned according to the manufacturer's SERVICE SCHEDULE (see page 9). We have deliberately not covered the engine tune-up in the previous ROUTINE MAINTENANCE so that if your car is in between services and is misbehaving then you can tackle the engine separately. It is possible that there is only one component or part that is at fault and consequently you do not wish to tune the complete engine. However, it is only by gradual elimination that usually the culprit component(s) can be traced. If your car will not start at all then we have included a comprehensive trouble-tracing chart at the end of this section.

The following checks and adjustments have been compiled in a logical sequence and, if checking and tuning the engine, we would advise that you follow the order set out. However, if you just wish to tackle the sparking plugs or, perhaps, the contact breaker points then simply refer to that particular heading. This way just one component can be tackled or, if desired, all of them.

COMPRESSION CHECK. . . . . [2]

Valuable time can be wasted trying to tune an engine which is badly worn. This is particularly applicable in the case of an engine which has covered considerably mileage. It is therefore always worthwhile checking the cylinder compression pressures first to determine the general state of the unit.

A compression tester will be required for this operation, and one of these can be purchased quite cheaply from most motor accessory shops, or even hired.

The compression pressures are given in the Tune-Up Data at the end of this chapter, but it should be noted that the engine must be at normal operating temperature to get reliable readings.

1. Run the engine up to normal operating temperature.

2. Switch off the ignition and remove the spark plugs.
   When disconnecting the leads, grasp the moulded cap and pull it off the plug. Do not pull on the lead itself otherwise the lead core may be damaged.

3. Screw or push the connector of the compression tester into the No. 1 plug hole (Fig. B:1) and, with the throttle held in the wide open position, crank the engine over with the starter. If the compression tester has to be held in position by hand hold it firmly ensuring that there is no leakage of compression.

4. As the engine turns, the gauge reading will increase in steps until a maximum pressure is reached. Note this reading carefully. The number of compression strokes, indicated by the 'pulses' on the gauge, required to reach the maximum pressure should also be noted.

5. Repeat this procedure for the other cylinders, noting the reading obtained and the number of 'pulses'.

6. Compare the readings with the specified figures given in Tune-Up Data. If all the readings are high and within about 10% of each other this indicates that the engine is in good order, provided that the readings are close to the specified figures.

7. If one or more readings are low, the test should be repeated after injecting a small quantity of engine oil into the cylinder through the plug hole to form a seal between the piston and the cylinder walls, if a marked increase in pressure is then obtained, this shows that the leakage is mainly via the piston rings.

8. If no increase in compression is indicated, the fault must be due to leakage past the valves or gaskets. However, it should be noted that if a cylinder has a badly scored bore, the oil seal will fail to seal the leak and no improvement in compression will be obtained.

9. In any case, low readings will necessitate further investigation to determine the cause, and remedial action taken to correct it.

VALVE CLEARANCES . . . . [3]

Checking/Adjustment (Fig. B:2)

Ideally the valve clearances should be checked with

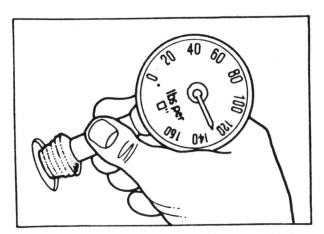

Fig. B:1 Checking cylinder compressions with a
compression tester in spark plug hole

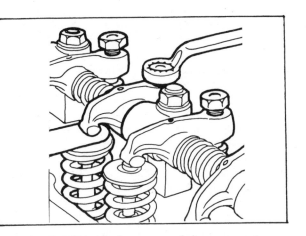

Fig. B:2 Using feeler gauge and ring spanner to
adjust valve rocker clearances

1

2

3

*1. NORMAL – Core nose will be
lightly coated with grey-brown deposits. Replace after 10,000 miles.*

*2. HEAVY DEPOSITS – Condition
could be due to worn valve guides.
Plug can be used again after servicing.*

*3. CARBON FOULING – Caused by
rich mixture through faulty carburettor, choke or a clogged air cleaner.*

4   **5**   **6**

*4. OIL FOULING – Caused by worn
valve guides, bores or piston rings.
Hotter plug may cure.*

*5. OVERHEATING – Reasons could
be over-advanced ignition timing, a
worn distributor or weak fuel mixture.*

*6. PRE-IGNITION – This problem is
caused through serious overheating.
This could result in engine damage.*

**Fig. B:3 Typical spark plug electrode conditions
and their causes**

the engine cold. Remove the air cleaner assembly. Disconnect the HT leads from the spark plugs, unclip them from the rocker cover and place them to one side.

Disconnect the engine breather hose, then remove the four retaining screws and lift off the rocker cover and gasket. It is good practice to renew the gasket each time the cover is removed.

It will facilitate turning over the engine if the spark plugs are removed at this point (see Tune-Up).

Crank the engine until the notch on the crankshaft pulley is aligned with TDC mark on the timing scale on the front cover. It will facilitate matters if the notch on the pulley is suitably marked with white paint to make it more easily seen. Throughout the adjustment procedure the engine must only be cranked in its normal direction of rotation (clockwise).

By turning the crankshaft to and fro a little and, at the same time, observing the rocker assembly, it can be determined whether the valves for No. 1 and No. 4 cylinder are rocking. The two rocker arms will be moving in opposite directions, the exhaust just closing and the inlet just opening if the valves of No. 4 cylinder are rocking, the valve clearances at No. 1 cylinder should be checked.

The setting is correct when the appropriate thickness of feeler gauge is a neat sliding fit between the end of the valve stem and the pad on the rocker arm.

The valve arrangement, from the front, is: Ex - In - Ex - In - Ex - In - Ex - In.

If adjustment is necessary, rotate the adjusting nut on the push rod end of the rocker arm until the correct gap is obtained (Fig. B:2). The adjuster bolts are self-locking and only a suitable size of ring spanner or socket in good condition should be used on them.

When adjustment at No. 1 (or No. 4) cylinder is complete, turn the crankshaft through half a turn and check the clearances at No. 2 or No. 3 cylinder, which ever is appropriate, in the same manner. Continue turning the crankshaft half a turn at a time and checking the appropriate valve clearances until all four cylinder have been done. The sequence is as follows:

Cylinder No. 4 rocking - Adjust cylinder No. 1
Cylinder No. 3 rocking - Adjust cylinder No. 2
Cylinder No. 1 rocking - Adjust cylinder No. 4
Cylinder No. 2 rocking - Adjust cylinder No. 3

When adjustment is completed, refit the rocker cover with a new gasket and tighten the screws evenly. Refit the spark plugs and leads and reconnect the breather hose.

SPARKING PLUGS . . . . [4]

The spark plugs should be removed and examined periodically. Brush or blow any dirt away from around the plug hole before removing the plug.

When disconnecting the leads, from the spark plugs, grasp the moulded cap of the lead, then twist and pull the cap off the plug. Do NOT pull on the lead, otherwise the connection inside the cap may become separated.

Inspect the condition of the insulator tip and the electrodes. Typical examples of spark plug condition are shown in Fig. B:3, and should be interpreted as follows.

Normal (Fig. B:3.1)

Ideally the plugs should look like the condition shown in this photograph. The colour of the electrodes should appear greyish-brown or tan-coloured. White to yellow deposits usually mean that the car has been used for long periods at high, constant speeds. Provided that the sparking plugs have not covered a large mileage they can be cleaned, re-set and refitted.

Heavy Deposits (Fig. B:3.2)

The sparking plug in this condition will probably look worse than it is. Heavy deposits could mean worn valve guides. When deposits have been cleaned off the sparking plug should be okay to use again providing it is not worn.

Carbon Fouled (Fig. B:3.3)

This is identified by dry, fluffy deposits which result from incomplete combustion. Too rich an air/fuel mixture or faulty action of the automatic choke can caused incomplete burning. The mixture being too rich can often be traced to a dirty or blocked air cleaner.

Defective contact breaker points or high tension cables can reduce voltage supplied to the sparking plug and cause misfiring. If fouling is evident on only one or two cylinders, sticking valves may be the problem. Excessive idling, slow speeds or stop/start driving can also keep plug temperatures so low that normal combustion deposits are not burned off.

Oil Fouled (Fig. B:3.4)

This is identified by black wet sludge deposits and is traceable to oil entering the combustion chamber either past the pistons and bores or through the valve guides. Hotter sparking plugs may cure the problem temporarily, but in severe cases an engine overhaul is called for.

Overheated (Fig. B:3.5)

Sparking plugs are usually identified by a white or blistered insulator nose and badly eroded electrodes. The engine overheating or improper ignition timing could be responsible for this problem. If only a couple of sparking plugs are affected the cause may be uneven distribution of the coolant. Abnormal fast driving for sustained periods can also cause high temperatures in the combustion chambers and, in these circumstances, colder sparking plugs should be used.

Sparking plugs which are in good condition and with low mileage can be cleaned, preferably with sand-blast cleaner. Clean the electrode surface and file them flat with a points file.

Check the electrode gap with a gap setting gauge or feeler gauge (Fig. B:4). The gap should be to the setting specified in the Tune-Up Data at the end of this chapter. If necessary, adjust the gap by bending the outer electrode - never attempt to bend the inner electrode otherwise the central insulator may be cracked or broken. When fitting

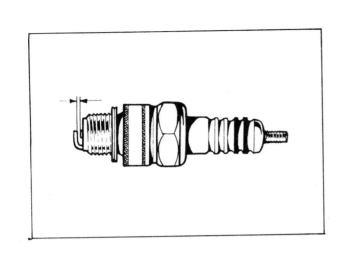

Fig. B:4 Checking the spark plug gap, adjust by bending outer electrode

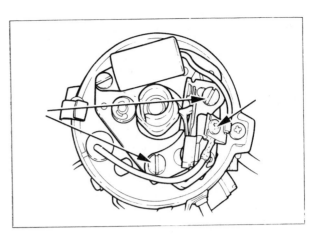

Fig. B:5 Removing the contact breaker points - Motorcraft type

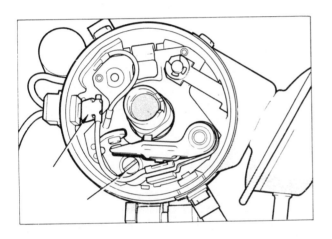

Fig. B:6 Removing the contact breaker points - Bosch type

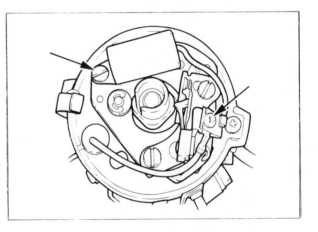

Fig. B:7 The condenser and lead fixing points on Motorcraft distributors

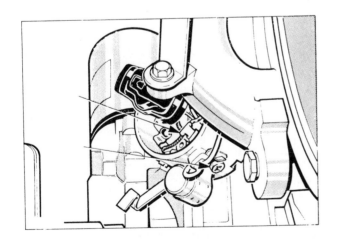

Fig. B:8 The condenser and lead fixings on Bosch type distributors

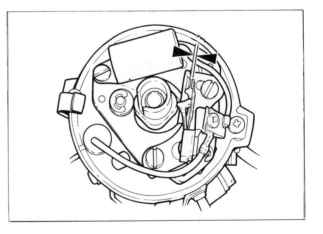

Fig. B:9 Checking the contact breaker gap on Motorcraft distributors

new sparking plugs, the electrode gaps should be checked before installing them. Ensure that the replacement plugs are of the correct grade for the model.

DISTRIBUTOR. . . . . [5]

Contact Replacement (Figs. B:5 and B:6)

As the contact set is a relatively inexpensive item, it is recommended that it be replaced if there is any doubt as to the condition of the contacts. It is not practical to dress the contact points with a file due to the construction of the contact set.
1. Disconnect the battery.
2. Disconnect the HT leads, unclip the distributor cap and position it clear of the distributor.
3. Pull the rotor arm off the central spindle.
4. Turn the crankshaft using a socket and handle in the normal direction of rotation until the heel of the moving contact is on the peak of a cam lobe (Figs. B:5 and B:6).
5. Remove the screw securing the LT and condenser leads to the contact set.
6. Remove the screws securing the contact set to the base plate and lift out the contact set, taking care not to allow the securing screws to fall down inside the distributor.
7. Wipe the spindle cam clean and apply a light smear of high melting point grease around the contact surface of the cam.
8. Position the new contact set on the breaker plate and secure it with the two locking screws. Tighten the screws only lightly at this stage.
9. Reconnect the LT and condenser leads.
10. Adjust the points gap as described below, refit the rotor arm and then the distributor cap.
11. Reconnect the battery and check the ignition timing as described later in this chapter.

Contact Adjustment (Figs. B:9 and B:10)

The contact points can be set either by measuring the gap with feeler gauges, or by measuring the dwell angle with a dwell meter. Where possible, and especially in the case of used points where metal transfer has taken place, the use of a dwell meter is recommended as this is a more accurate method of checking the setting.

Ensure that the points are in good condition and the contact faces abut squarely. Any misalignment of the contact surfaces will cause premature wear, overheating and pitting. If necessary align the points to make full face contact by bending the fixed contact bracket with thin nose pliers. Do NOT bend the breaker arm.

To check the contact points with feeler gauges, turn the crankshaft in the normal direction of rotation until the distributor contacts are fully open, i.e. until the heel of the moving contact is resting on the highest point of the cam lobe. Check the contact gap by inserting a feeler gauge of suitable thickness between the contact points. The gauge should be a neat sliding fit in the gap. The gap setting for the two types of distributor used is given in the

Tune-Up Data at the end of this chapter.
NOTE: When measuring used contact points where a pip has formed on the face of one contact, the gap measurement should be made outside the formation to achieve a correct reading.

If the gap varies appreciably from the specified setting, slacken the two locking screws on the contact breaker bracket and, using a screwdriver inserted into the V notch at the points end of the bracket and the adjacent slot in the breaker plate, adjust the position of the breaker bracket until the correct gap is obtained. Turn the screwdriver clockwise to increase the gap, or anti-clockwise to decrease it. When the gap is correct, tighten the two locking screws and recheck the gap on each cam lobe.

Dwell Angle

1. To check the dwell angle connect a dwell meter to the engine in accordance with the makers' instructions and start the engine.
2. Record the dwell angle at idle and at 2,000 rpm. The dwell angle should be 48° to 52°.
3. If adjustment is necessary, stop the engine, unclip the distributor cap and remove the rotor arm. With the ignition switched on turn the engine over on the starter motor and adjust the contact breaker points.
4. Recheck the dwell angle at idle and 2000 rpm. To crank the engine over, either the ignition switch may be reused or a remote switch connected between a live terminal and the starter solenoid power pick up connection. The angle should be 50° with a tolerance limit of 2° either side. If the reading is outside these limits, adjustment should be carried out as described above for setting the contact gap using a feeler gauge. If the dwell angle is greater than the upper limit the points gap is too small and requires opening up, and if below the lower limit the gap should be decreased.

Condenser

The condenser is connected across the contact breaker point on the Motorcraft distributor and mounted on the outside of the body on the Bosch distributor. Its purpose is to increase the current peak in the primary windings of the ignition coil when the points are open. A further function of the condenser is to minimise erosion and oxidation of the points contact surfaces.

As the condenser is a relatively inexpensive item it should be replaced if in any way suspect. Excessive wear or burning of the points are indications that the condenser is defective.

To remove the condenser (Figs. B:7 and B:8), disconnect the battery and remove the distributor cap. On the Motorcraft distributor remove the screw securing the condenser lead and disconnect the lead. Then remove the condenser retaining screw and remove the condenser. On the Bosch distributor slacken the distributor clamp bolt and rotate its body through 120° in a clockwise direction to make the condenser accessible. Disconnect the condenser leads from the inside of the distributor and the coil and then release the condenser retaining screw. Remove the condenser. Replacement is a reversal of the removal

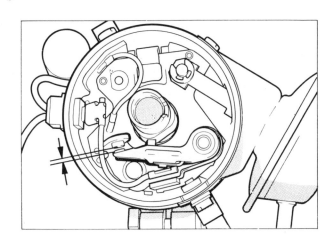

Fig. B:10 Checking the contact breaker gap
on Bosch type distributors

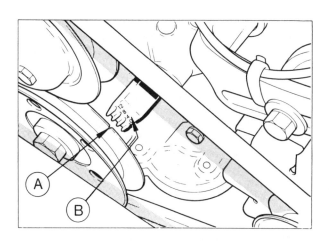

Fig. B:11 Ignition timing marks, notch on
pulley (A) and timing markings (B)

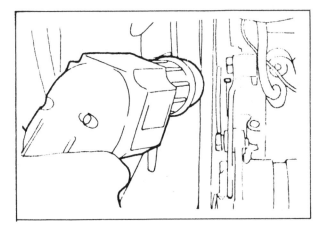

Fig. B:12 Using a strobe light to check the
dynamic ignition timing

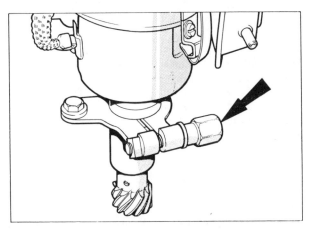

Fig. B:13 The location of the distributor
clamp bolt (arrowed)

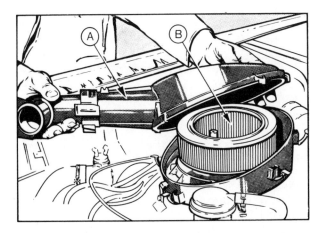

Fig. B:14 Unclip the air cleaner cover (A)
and withdraw filter element (B)

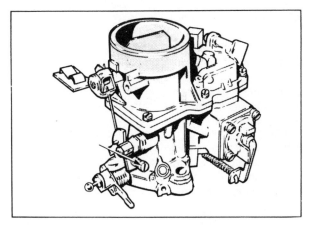

Fig. B:15 The location of the idling speed
throttle stop screw (arrowed)

procedure, noting that the ignition timing should be adjusted in the case of the Bosch unit.

Distributor Cap, HT Leads

Thoroughly clean the distributor cap, inside and out with a clean cloth, paying particular attention to the spaces between the metal electrodes. Check that the electrodes are not excessively eroded and that there are no signs of tracking. Ensure that the small carbon brush in the centre of the cap is undamaged.

Similarly, clean the rotor arm and check for damage or excessive erosion of the electrode. Also check that the rotor is a neat fit on the distributor spindle without excessive play.

Clean the outside surface of the coil tower and check for signs of damage or tracking.

Wipe all grease and dirt from the HT leads and check the leads for signs of cracking, chafing, etc. Ensure that all connections at the spark plugs, ignition coil and distributor cap are secure and the moisture seals at each end of the HT leads are firmly in place.

IGNITION TIMING . . . . [6]

The contact breaker points gap must be correctly set before attempting to check or adjust the ignition timing. Conversely, the ignition setting should be checked after cleaning, adjusting or replacing the contact set.

Static Timing Check

Remove the distributor cap and connect a 12 volt test lamp between the distributor low tension terminal and a good earthing point. Rotate the crankshaft in its normal direction of rotation until the rotor arm is pointing approximately midway between the No. 3 and No. 1 plug lead segments in the distributor cap. The rotor arm rotation is anti-clockwise viewed from above.

With the ignition switched on, rotate the crankshaft slowly until the test lamp just lights up. If the ignition setting is correct the notch on the crankshaft pulley will be aligned with the appropriate mark on the timing scale (Fig. B:11). This should be 10° BTDC for all variants except the 1297 cc 2V engine which should be 6° BTDC. If the timing is incorrect it should be adjusted as described below.

Turn the crankshaft until the notch on the crankshaft pulley is aligned with the correct mark on the timing scale. Slacken the distributor clamp bolt (Fig. B:13) and rotate the distributor body anti-clockwise past the point where the test lamp goes out, then carefully rotate it back clockwise until the lamp just lights up. Tighten the clamp bolt without disturbing the body setting. Re-check the setting as described above.

Dynamic Strobe Light Check (Fig. B:12)

If possible, the ignition timing should be checked dynamically with a stroboscopic timing light to ensure optimum engine performance. In this case the equipment manufacturer's instructions should be followed.

With the distributor vacuum pipe disconnected and the engine running at normal idle speed, the ignition timing marks should be aligned to the same setting as that given for the static check above. It will facilitate observation of the timing mark if the notch on the crankshaft pulley and the appropriate mark on the timing scale are highlighted with chalk or white paint prior to carrying out the check.

If adjustment is required slacken the distributor clamp bolt and rotate the distributor body clockwise to advance the setting or anti-clockwise to retard it.

Checking Distributor Advance Mechanism

The operation of the distributor governor weights may be checked using the stroboscopic light by opening and closing the throttle. As the throttle is gradually opened the notch on the crankshaft pulley should move smoothly away from the timing mark against the direction of engine rotation, and as the throttle is closed the notch will move back in the direction of rotation. Any tendency to erratic operation shown by the notch suddenly jumping away from the timing mark indicates that the governor weights are binding or the springs are weak.

The operation of the vacuum unit can be checked simply by sucking on the vacuum pipe with the mouth and observing the action of the contact breaker plate inside the distributor, The plate should move clockwise slightly under the action of the vacuum unit and return immediately to its original position when the vacuum is released.

AIR CLEANER. . . . . [7]

Filter Element Replacement (Fig. B:14)

1.   Disconnect the battery.
2.   Remove the central screw securing the air cleaner top to the lower section.
3.   Release the five retaining clips and lift off the air cleaner top.
4.   Lift out the paper element and replace it with a new one.
5.   Refit the top and reconnect the battery.

Air Cleaner Assembly - Removal

1.   Disconnect the battery.
2.   Remove the three securing bolts and lift off the air cleaner assembly.

Installation

Installation is a reversal of the removal procedure.

CARBURETTOR . . . . [8]

Adjustment (Fig. B:15)

With the increased severity of emission regulations the use of an EGA (Exhaust Gas Analyser) is essential when adjusting the carburettor. Since the average owner/driver will not possess this kind of equipment, such adjustments should be entrusted to an authorised Ford agent.

However, the slow running speed may be adjusted as necessary. Before doing so, though, all the other items relevant to good engine performance should be checked to ensure that they are in good condition (e.g. contact breaker points, ignition timing, spark plugs, valve clearances, etc). The air cleaner element should also be checked to make sure it is clean and in good condition, and the throttle operation checked for free and unrestricted movement. Also, make sure that no air leaks exist at the carburettor flange or throttle spindle.

Run the engine until normal operating temperature is achieved and then connect a tachometer to the engine in accordance with the makers' instructions - or use the vehicle's tachometer if fitted. Set the idle speed as specified in Tune-Up Data, using the throttle adjusting screw on the carburettor. See Fig. B:15 for reference to the carburettor idling screw.

Tune-up Data

ENGINE

Compression pressure at starter speed
   1.0 LC. . . . . 137-166 lbf/in^2 (9.5-11.5 bar)
   All others. . . . . 159-188 lbf/in^2 (11-13 bar)
Firing order . . . . 1 - 2 - 4 - 3
Valve rocker clearance (engine cold)
1.1 LC/1.0 HC/1.1 HC
   Inlet . . . . 0.009 in (0.22 mm)
   Exhaust. . . . . 0.023 in (0.59 mm)
1.3 2V
   Inlet . . . . 0.010 in (0.25 mm)
   Exhaust. . . . . 0.022 in (0.55 mm)

IGNITION

Spark plug
   Type 957cc/1117 cc . . . . Motorcraft AGRF 22
   Gap . . . . 0.030 in (0.75 mm)
   Type 1.3 . . . . Motorcraft AGR 12
   Gap . . . . 0.024 in (0.6 mm)
Distributor points gap
   Motorcraft . . . . 0.025 in (0.64 mm)
   Bosch . . . . 0.016-0.020 in (0.4-0.5 mm)
Dwell angle . . . . 48°-52°
Rotor rotation (viewed from above) . . . . Anti-clockwise
Static ignition timing
   1297 cc 2V . . . . 6° BTDC
   All others. . . . . 10° BTDC
Timing marks . . . . Notch on pulley, scale on front cover

CARBURETTOR

Idle speed
   1.1 HC . . . . 750-850 rpm
   All others. . . . . 775-825 rpm
Fuel octane requirement
   LC engines. . . . . 90 minimum (2-star, UK)
   HC engines. . . . . 97 minimum (4-star, UK)

NON-START
Trouble Shooter

FAULT	CAUSE	CURE
Starter will not turn engine (headlights dim)	1. Battery low 2. Faulty battery 3. Corroded battery cables or loose connections 4. Starter jammed 5. Seized engine	1. Charge battery and check charging system. 2. Fit new battery. 3. Clean battery connections or replace battery leads. Tighten battery and starter-motor connections. 4. Free starter. 5. Remove spark-plugs to confirm.
Starter will not turn engine (headlights bright)	1. Faulty starter solenoid 2. Faulty starter engagement (starter-motor whine) 3. Faulty starter 4. Faulty ignition switch	1. Replace solenoid. 2. Clean or replace starter bendix. 3. Repair or replace starter motor. 4. Fit new switch.
Engine turns slowly but will not start	1. Battery low 2. Faulty battery 3. Corroded battery leads or loose connections 4. Faulty starter	1. Charge battery and check charging system. 2. Replace battery. 3. Clean battery connections or replace battery leads. Tighten connections. 4. Repair or replace starter motor.
Engine turns but will not fire	1. Ignition fault 2. No spark at plug lead 3. Spark at plug lead 4. Fuel reaching carburettor 5. No fuel to carburettor 6. Car with mechanical pump	1. Check for spark at plug lead. 2. Check coil output to confirm high or low-tension fault. If spark from coil, check HT leads, distributor cap and rotor arm, particularly for cracks, tracking or dampness. If no spark from coil, check ignition-coil connections and contact-breaker points for short circuits or disconnection. 3. Remove air cleaner from carburettor and check choke operation. Loosen petrol-pipe union at carburettor. Turn engine by starter and check if petrol is being delivered. 4. Look into carburettor mouth. Operate throttle and observe whether damp or dry. If dry, clean jets and needle valve. If damp, remove spark-plugs, dry, clean and check gaps. 5. Remove petrol-tank cap and check for fuel. 6. Remove pump-top cover, clean pump filter and make sure the cover, when re-fitted, is airtight. Check flexible pipe to pump for air leaks.
Engine backfires	1. Ignition timing faulty 2. Damp distributor cap and leads	1. Check and reset ignition timing. 2. Dry thoroughly and check firing order.

Engine

OVERHAUL PROCEDURES . . . . [1]

The Fiesta has a transverse mounted but conventional push-rod OHV engine which is one of the easiest for DIY work. The 957 and 1117 cc engines are based on a shortened version of the original 105E Anglia engine with a three bearing crankshaft, whereas the later 1.3 litre engine (introduced August 1977) is an adaption of the Escort Sport engine with five main bearings, although the overhaul procedure detailed, is the same for both types.

With plenty of working room in the engine compartment, it is possible to carry out most repair and overhaul jobs with the engine in-situ. The oil pump, alternator, timing chain, crankshaft, front and rear oil seals plus the remainder of the normal repair components are all easy to get at. The engine sump pan can be removed without much difficulty to replace the crankshaft big-end bearings and for piston removal. The engine will only need to come out to replace the crankshaft, main bearings, camshaft or for any major work on the block such as a rebore.

No unusual special tools are needed to repair or overhaul the engine, a comprehensive Metric socket and spanner set, valve spring compressor tool, piston ring clamp, feeler gauges and possibly a two-legged puller will be sufficient.

CYLINDER HEAD . . . . [2]

Removal

1. Disconnect the battery.
2. Drain the cooling system by disconnecting the radiator bottom hose from the radiator outlet and the top hose from the water outlet hosing on the cylinder head. Collect the coolant in a suitable clean container for use later if required.
3. Remove the air cleaner assembly.
4. Disconnect the heater hoses from the side water pipe.
5. Disconnect the wire from the temperature sender unit at the cylinder head.
6. Disconnect the choke cable from the carburettor by releasing the retaining clip. Disconnect the throttle cable

from the carburettor and remove it from the inlet manifold complete with its bracket which is retained by two bolts (Fig. C:1).
7. Disconnect the fuel supply pipe, distributor vacuum pipe at the carburettor.
8. Disconnect the crankcase ventilation hose and brake servo vacuum hose (where applicable) at the inlet manifold.
9. Disconnect the HT leads from the spark plugs and the ignition coil. Remove the distributor cap and the distributor rotor arm.
10. Disconnect the exhaust pipe from the exhaust manifold.
11. Pull the oil filler cap and breather hoses from the rocker cover and remove the rocker cover.
12. Undo the rocker shaft retaining bolts, releasing them evenly and lift off the rocker assembly (Fig. C:2).
13. Lift out the pushrods. Keep them in their correct order to ensure that they are replaced correctly on assembly.
14. Remove the spark plugs.
15. Release the cylinder head bolts evenly, in the reverse order of that shown in Fig. C:3 and lift off the cylinder complete with inlet and exhaust manifolds. It may be found necessary to tap round the joint between head and cylinder block to break the gasket seal. Do this with a mallet, but on no account try to lever the head off by inserting a screwdriver or similar flat bladed instrument between the mating faces.

Dismantling

1. Undo the bolts and remove the inlet manifold complete with the carburettor and the exhaust manifold from the cylinder head.
2. Support the head upside down on wood blocks and remove all carbon deposits from the combustion chambers, valve heads and valve ports with a suitable scraper and wire brush. Take great care not to damage the machined face of the cylinder head.
3. Similarly clean all deposits from the cylinder block face and piston crowns, but ensure that carbon particles are not allowed to enter oil or waterways in the cylinder

block. These can be covered with pieces of cloth or masking tape.

4. At each valve in turn: Compress the valve spring using a suitable compressor (Fig. C:4) and extract the two split tapered collets from around the valve stem. Release the compressor and remove the spring retainer and valve spring. Remove the oil seal fitted to the valve stem (Fig. C:6) and withdraw the valve. Discard the oil seal. Mate each valve to its spring components and place to one side in removal order.

5. To dismantle the rocker shaft assembly (Fig. C:5), remove the split pin from one end of the rocker shaft and detach the flat washer, crimped spring washer and second flat washer which bear against the end rocker arm. The rocker arms, rocker shaft support pillars and springs can now be removed from the shaft. If necessary tap jammed rocker supports with a plastic hammer to free them. The plugs can be removed from each end of the rocker shaft to facilitate cleaning by piercing a hole in the plug and levering the plug out of the end of the shaft.

Cylinder Head Inspection

Clean all old gasket material, etc., from the machined faces, using emery cloth if necessary. Remove all dirt, grease, etc., with solvent.

Blow out all oil and water passages, particularly the oil transfer passage with compressed air. Probe all bolt holes to ensure they are clear. If necessary, the holes can be cleaned out with a suitable size of tap.

Inspect the head for cracks and all machined surfaces for burrs, scratches, or nicks. Remove any burrs with an oil stone.

Check the cylinder head gasket surface for flatness using a straight edge. If it is found to be distorted, the surface must be planed or ground true, or the head exchanged.

Check the sparking plug holes for stripped or damaged threads. If present, it may be possible to rectify such damage with a suitable size of tap.

Check the core plugs for leakage and replace as necessary.

Valve Inspection

Inspect the valve head for signs of burning, erosion, cracking or warpage. Inspect the valve face and edges for pits, grooves, scores, or other damage.

Inspect the end of the valve stem for grooves or scores. Minor damage may be removed by grinding but do not remove more than 0.010 in (0.25 mm) from the end of the stem. Chamfer the end of the stem as necessary afterwards.

Inspect the valve stem for a bent condition and for a wear ridge. If it is found to be bent or excessively worn, then the valve should be discarded. Replacement valves are available with standard and oversize stems. The appropriate size should be selected dependent on the condition of the valve guide.

Discard valves which are severely damaged.

Valve Guides

After some length of operation an oval wear pattern is produced on the valve spring end of the valve guide bore, at right-angles to the crankshaft axis. Check the valve stem-to-guide clearance of each valve in turn in its respective guide, as shown in Fig. C:7.

If the clearance is excessive, repeat the measurement using a new valve. If excessive guide bore wear is indicated, the guide should either be reamed oversize, and a valve with a suitably oversize stem fitted or a new guide fitted. Both of these operations should be left to a local auto machinist with the correct tools and equipment.

Valve Seats

Inspect the seating surface for pitting or burning. Check the valve seat run-out using an accurate gauge, if available. If the run-out is excessive, or if any other of the above faults are present, the seating surface must be recut to the specified angle. This job is best left to a local auto machinist who will have the necessary equipment for the job.

Only sufficient metal to clean up the pits and grooves, or to correct the valve seat run-out should be removed. If the seat damage is severe then new seat inserts will have to be fitted.

NOTE: Recutting of the valve seats can only be successful if the valve guide bore is not worn.

Where inserts have not been installed previously, it will be necessary to machine an appropriate recess in the cylinder head. If for any reason an existing insert has become loose or damaged, an oversize insert can be fitted.

The necessary machining of the cylinder head and installation of the inserts should be entrusted to a Specialist Machine Shop. After fitting inserts, the valve seats must be cut to the specified angle.

Valve Springs

Inspect the valve springs, spring retainer caps and collets for wear or damage, and discard any visually damaged parts. Check the springs for squareness, using a steel square on a flat surface. Revolve the spring slowly and observe the clearance between the top coil and the square. If the out of square is excessive, discard the spring.

Replace the springs as a matter of course if the car has completed a high mileage.

When fitting new valve springs it is recommended that they be replaced in sets. Ensure that the replacement springs are of the correct rating.

Pushrods

Clean the rods in solvent. Check the ends of the rods for nicks, grooves, roughness or excessive wear. Check each rod for straightness. Replace as necessary. Do NOT attempt to straighten a bent pushrod.

NOTE: The push rods can be checked visually for straightness while installed in the engine by rotating them with the valve closed.

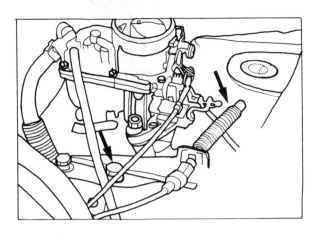

Fig. C:1 Details of the carburettor throttle cable and support bracket fixings

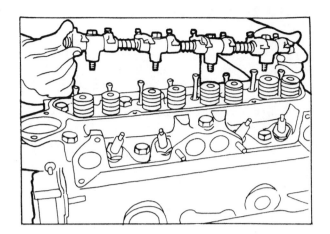

Fig. C:2 Undo rocker pedestal bolts and lift off rocker shaft assembly

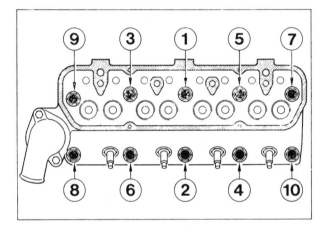

Fig. C:3 Tighten the cylinder head bolts in the order shown

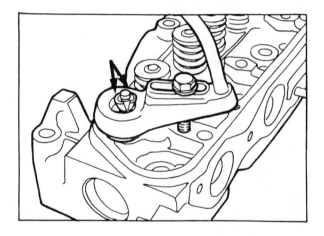

Fig. C:4 Compressing the valve spring to release collets (arrowed)

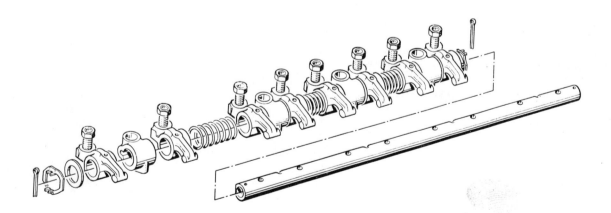

Fig. C:5 An exploded view of the rocker shaft components

Rocker Shaft Assembly

Inspect the shaft and rocker arm bores for nicks, scratches, scores or scuffs. Inspect the pad at the valve end of each rocker arm for indication of scuffing or abnormal wear. If the pad is grooved, replace the arm. Do NOT attempt to true the surface by grinding.

Check the clearance between each rocker arm and the shaft by measuring the inside diameter of the arm bore and the outside diameter of the shaft. If the clearance is excessive, the shaft and/or rocker arm should be replaced.

Check that all oil passages are clear. Replace any damaged adjusting screws.

Cylinder Head Reassembly

Reassemble the cylinder head in the reverse order of dismantling, with special attention to the following points:

a) Lap in each valve in turn using coarse, followed by fine, grinding paste until a gas-tight seal is obtained at the seat. This will be indicated by a continuous matt-grey ring around the valve face and seat. When this has been achieved, clean all traces of paste from the cylinder head and valves - this is most important.

b) Lubricate the valve guides and valves with SAE 90 Hypoid Oil before installing the valves.

c) The valve stem seal must always be renewed. Cover the collet grooves in the end of the valve stem with adhesive foil or tape to avoid damaging the seal during installation (Fig. C:6). Lubricate the seal with oil to make fitting easier. Remove the foil once the seal is in position.

d) Ensure that the valve stem is not damaged by the spring retainer when compressing the valve spring, and that the split tapered collets engage correctly in the valve stem and spring retainer when the spring is released.

e) If the rocker assembly was dismantled, reassemble it in reverse order. If the end plugs were removed, install new plugs in each end of the shaft. The shaft must be positioned so that the oil feed holes in the shaft for rocker lubrication point downwards to the cylinder head. The bolt holes in the rocker shaft support pillars must be located on the same side as the adjusting screws in the rocker arms. The rocker arms are 'handed' and must be fitted on the shaft with the rocker pads inclined towards the support pillars. Install the split pins at the ends of the shaft with their heads upwards, and bend over their legs to secure.

f) When refitting the inlet manifold assembly, apply sealing compound to both sides of the manifold gasket at the central waterway.

Cylinder Head Installation

Installation is a reversal of the removal procedure, with special attention to the following points:

1. Make sure all matings faces, especially those of the cylinder head and block are perfectly clean and free from old gasket material.

2. If the cylinder head was removed to change the cylinder head gasket only, then check the flatness of the cylin-

der head and block before reassembly.

3. Use new gaskets throughout.

4. The use of two tapered guide studs, made up and screwed into the cylinder head bolt holes at diagonally opposite corners (Fig. C:8) will facilitate correct alignment of the cylinder head and gasket during installation. Once the head is installed, the studs can then be unscrewed and replaced by cylinder head bolts.

5. Do not use sealing compound of any type on the cylinder head gasket.

6. The cylinder head bolts are of different lengths, two being shorter than the others according to the varying thickness of the cylinder head casting. Make sure the bolts are fitted in their correct respective positions.

7. Tighten the cylinder head bolts evenly in the sequence shown in Fig. C:3, and in the progressive stages given in the TIGHTENING TORQUES at the end of this manual.

8. Make sure that the pushrods are installed in their original positions. Dip the ends of the rods in clean engine oil prior to installing them.

9. Make sure the rocker arm adjusting screws locate correctly in the cupped ends of their respective pushrods. If any work has been carried out on the valves (e.g. recutting the valve seats) release the rocker arm adjusting screws slightly before installing the rocker shaft assembly. Tighten the shaft retaining bolts evenly to their specified torque.

10. Check the valve clearances as described previously and adjust them if necessary.

11. When installation is complete refill the cooling system, then start the engine and check for oil, water or exhaust system leaks.

11. When installation is complete refill the cooling system, then start the engine and check for oil, water or exhaust system leaks.

12. After the engine has been warmed up, wait for 15 to 20 minutes and retighten the cylinder head bolts to their specified torque.

13. Finally, with the engine at normal operating temperature, check the ignition timing and idle speed. Also take the car to an authorised Ford agent and have him check the mixture setting.

TIMING COVER OIL SEAL . . . . [3]

Replacement

1. Disconnect the battery.

2. Slacken the alternator mounting and pivot bolts and push the alternator towards the engine. Remove the drive belt.

3. Jack up the vehicle and support it on stands. Refer to the jacking information contained in the ROUTINE MAINTENANCE chapter.

4. Place the gear lever in 1st gear and with an assistant applying the brake pedal, undo and remove the centre bolt from the end of the crankshaft. Withdraw the crankshaft pulley, using levers or a suitable puller (Fig. C:9).

5. Withdraw the oil seal from the front cover either

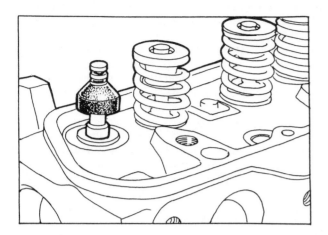

Fig. C:6 When reassembling cylinder head, always fit new valve stem oil seals

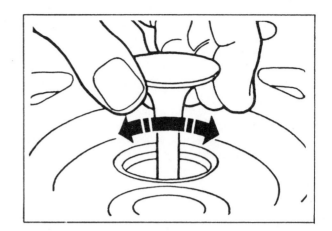

Fig. C:7 Check for valve stem or guide wear by rocking valve as shown

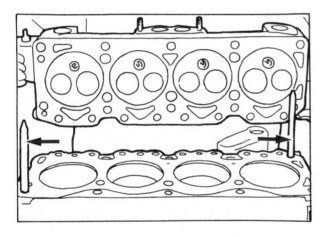

Fig. C:8 Using 'guide' studs (arrowed) when installing cylinder head and gasket

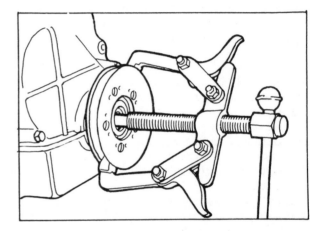

Fig. C:9 Using puller tool to remove crankshaft pulley if it will not lever off

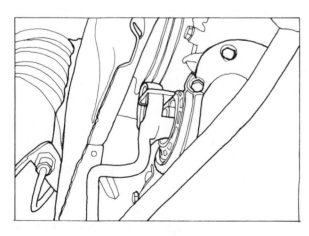

Fig. C:10 Use screwdriver or special tool shown to remove timing cover oil seal

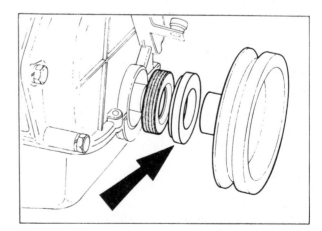

Fig. C:11 Use 'spacer' arrowed and crank pulley to press seal into timing cover

using a special tool (Fig. C:10) or using a screwdriver to gently lever the seal from its bore. However, if the latter method is employed, great care should be taken not to damage the seal bore in any way.

6. Ensure that the bore in the front cover is clean and free from old sealer, etc.

7. Lubricate sealing lips of the new seal and the timing cover bore.

8. Press the new seal into the cover bore, this can be done by inserting a spacer ring between the seal and the pulley and drifting on the pulley to drive the seal home (Fig. C:11). Alternatively, it is possible to fit the seal by gently tapping it into place, using a large socket as a drift. Whichever fitting method is used, it is important the seal lips are not damaged and that the seal is fitted square in its housing.

9. Refit the crankshaft pulley, making sure that the pulley sleeve is well lubricated to prevent damage to the oil seal lips, then refit the pulley bolt.

10. Tighten the pulley bolt to the correct torque using the same method as used to undo it.

11. Lower the car to the ground and refit the alternator drive belt. Check the engine oil level and top-up if necessary. Reconnect the battery.

SUMP PAN . . . . [4]

Removal

1. Disconnect the battery.
2. Disconnect the exhaust pipe from the exhaust manifold and suspend the pipe from the body with a stout piece of wire.
3. Jack up the car, supporting it on stands. Refer to the jacking information contained in the ROUTINE MAINTENANCE chapter. Support the weight of the engine with an engine hoist and chains or wire cables.
4. Remove the sump plug and drain the engine oil into a suitable container. Replace the sump plug.
5. Remove the three clutch cover plate/engine mounting nuts and unscrew the outer stabiliser bar rubber insulator nut.
6. Unscrew the two engine mount bolts from each mount and remove the engine mounts.
7. Remove the sump retaining bolts. It may also be necessary to remove the starter motor depending on the type fitted (see ENGINE ELECTRICS chapter). Carefully use a screwdriver to prise the sump from the crankcase. Leave a tray beneath the engine to catch any oil drips.

Installation

1. Make sure the sump and crankcase mating faces are clean and free from all traces of old gasket material. If necessary, straighten any bent portions of the sump mounting flange.
2. Stick a new sump gasket to the cylinder block with grease. Make sure the gasket is correctly seated (Fig. C: 12).
3. Refit the sump pan, tightening the bolts in three

stages to the correct torque. Refer to Fig. C:13. Stage 1 is in alphabetical sequence, Stage 2 in numerical sequence, and Stage 3 in alphabetical sequence.

4. Refit the starter motor (if removed) and reconnect the clutch cover plate to the engine mounting using three new self-locking bolts. Leave these finger tight at this stage and refit the engine mounting bolts. Now tighten the clutch cover plate and engine mounting bolts to the specified torque.

NOTE: It is essential that new self locking bolts are used for the clutch cover plate and that they are tightened to the correct torque. Overtightening will result in the threads in the gearbox housing becoming stripped.

5. Tighten the stabiliser bar rubber insulator nut.
6. Remove the engine hoist and then lower the vehicle to the ground.
7. Reconnect the exhaust pipe to the manifold.
8. Refill the engine with the correct amount and grade of oil. Reconnect the battery and run the engine to check for oil leaks around the sump joint flange.

ENGINE REMOVAL & INSTALLATION . . . [5]

Removal

1. Disconnect the battery.
2. Drain the coolant into a suitable container, disconnect the radiator lower hose from the outlet neck and the upper hose from the thermostat housing on the cylinder head. Remove the heater hoses from the side water pipe and inlet manifold connector.
3. Remove the air cleaner bolts, lift up the air cleaner and disconnect the engine breather hose from underneath. Place the air cleaner aside.
4. Disconnect the throttle cable from the carburettor and remove the cable complete with its manifold mounting bracket which is secured by two bolts.
5. Prise the choke cable retaining clip from position on the carburettor and remove the choke cable.
6. Disconnect the fuel pipe from the fuel pump, servo vacuum hose from the inlet manifold, alternator leads, leads from the temperature sender unit, oil pressure switch, ignition, the engine earth strap, fan temperature probe wiring (if fitted) and the speedometer cable from its position on the transmission.
7. Depress the exposed portion of the clutch inner cable with the thumb and unhook the cable from the clutch release lever (Fig. C:14). Remove the outer cable from its mounting bracket.
8. Disconnect the exhaust pipe from the exhaust manifold, supporting the pipe temporarily by suspending it from the body with a piece of stout wire. Beneath the car, disconnect the rear exhaust pipe mounting and then remove the complete exhaust system.
9. Jack up both ends of the car and support on stands so that it sits level and high enough to clear the engine, which is removed from underneath. Refer to the jacking information contained in the ROUTINE MAINTENANCE chapter.
10. Slacken the gear selector rod clamp bolt and pull the

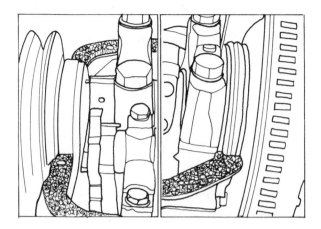

Fig. C:12 When fitting sump gasket, make sure
ends are fitted as shown

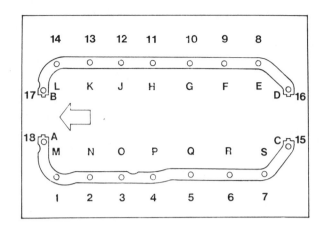

Fig. C:13 Tighten the sump pan bolts in the
sequence shown

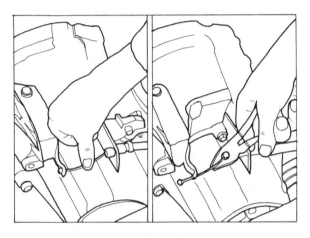

Fig. C:14 Tension clutch cable, then unhook it
from release arm

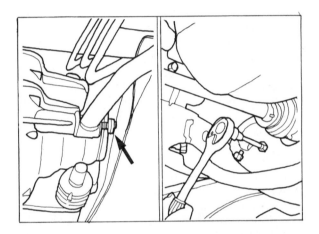

Fig. C:15 Slacken stabiliser rod nuts, then remove
Allen screw from transmission

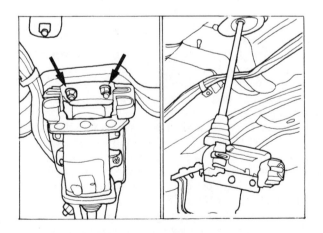

Fig. C:16 Remove transmission then suspend
selector rod and stabiliser rod

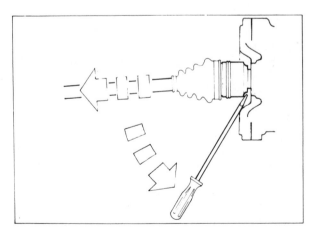

Fig. C:17 Using screwdriver to lever nearside drive
shaft from transmission

rod from the selector shaft at the gearbox. Unhook the spring between the selector rod and lower chassis member.

11. Slacken both stabiliser rubber insulator and engine mounting locknuts turning them away from the transmission housing and engine mount respectively. Slacken the stud locknut and then unscrew the stud with an Allen key so that it is free of the gearbox housing (Fig. C:15).

12. Remove the two bolts holding the gear selector housing to the floorpan and rotate the selector rod and stabiliser through 180°, suspending it from the floorpan with wire (Fig. C:16).

13. Remove the castellated nuts and split pins from the track rod end ballpins and then separate the ball joints from the steering arms with a suitable separating tool. Do NOT hammer on the ballpin to release them.

14. Release the lower suspension arm inner pivot bolts, tapping them out with a suitable drift. Then release the clamp bolts at the outer ends of the arm and withdraw the arms complete with the ball joint. Allow to hang on the end of the tie bar.

15. Disconnect the driveshafts from the transmission (Fig. C:17) as detailed in the CLUTCH & GEARBOX chapter under transmission removal.

16. Secure the differential pinions with a plastic plug or a spare drive joint (Fig. C:18). This is essential to prevent the pinions becoming displaced when the second drive shaft is removed.

17. Disconnect the right hand lower suspension arm in the same manner as the left hand arm. Then disconnect the right hand tie bar bracket from the body. Then remove the tie bar complete with bracket and lower suspension arm.

18. Using a suitable drift, such as a large screwdriver, drive out the right hand drive shaft, pushing the wheel outwards at the same time (Fig. C:19).

19. Disconnect the leads from the starter motor.

20. Refer to Fig. C:20, and place a trolley jack beneath the engine with blocks of wood between the jack cradle and the engine as shown in the illustration. Take the weight of the engine on the jack.

21. Unscrew the front upper engine mounting rubber insulators (Fig. C:21).

22. Remove the two bolts securing the rear engine mounting on each side (Fig. C:22).

23. Lower the engine/gearbox assembly from the car and roll it out on the jack. Have an assistant steady the assembly to prevent it falling off.

Installation

Installation of the engine/gearbox assembly is basically a reversal of the removal procedure, but with special attention paid to the following points:

1. When reconnecting the front upper engine mount, care should be taken to make sure that the rubber insulator is fitted parallel to the engine front face and is not distorted due to tightening.

2. New circlips should be fitted to the driveshaft CV joints and the shafts should be driven into place with a suitable tool acting on the CV joint weld as shown in Fig. C:23. The joint must be driven in until it snaps into place.

If the CV joints do not have a weld bead, remove the cup and drive home by tapping the edge with a rubber or plastic mallet.

NOTE: Refit and adjust the intermediate driveshaft bracket as detailed in the FRONT SUSPENSION/STEERING chapter.

3. When screwing in the stabiliser stud with the Allen key do so until it abuts the gearshift housing. Then tighten the rubber insulator locknut. Next tighten the inner nut against the engine mounting and finally tighten the outer nut against the engine mounting (Fig. C:24).

4. Reconnect the gear selector rod to the selector shaft and refer to the CLUTCH & MANUAL GEARBOX chapter for details on adjusting the linkage.

5. Remember to top up the transmission oil before lowering the vehicle to the ground.

6. When fitting the throttle cable, adjust it so that with the throttle fully open clearance between the throttle stop and pedal lever will not exceed 0.015 in (0.35 mm).

7. Adjust the choke cable as described under FUEL.

8. Refer to TIGHTENING TORQUES at the end of the Manual for the relevant tightening information for all nuts and bolts.

9. Remember to top up the cooling system with the appropriate anti-freeze solution and the engine with the appropriate grade and amount of oil.

10. Replace the air cleaner assembly.

11. Check the ignition timing as described in the TUNE-UP chapter and check the idling speed.

ENGINE OVERHAUL . . . . [6]

Dismantling

1. Remove the clamp securing the side water hose to the water pump. Remove the bolt holding it to the cylinder block and remove the pipe.

2. Drain the oil from the sump (if necessary) into a suitable container and replace the sump plug. Remove the dipstick and unscrew the oil filter. Be prepared for slight oil leakage from the pump when the filter is removed.

3. Disconnect the HT leads from the spark plugs and remove the spark plugs.

4. Disconnect the crankcase ventilation hose from the inlet manifold and the cylinder block and remove the hoses together with the oil filler cap.

5. Disconnect the fuel supply pipe and the distributor vacuum pipe at the carburettor.

6. Detach the water outlet housing from the front of the cylinder head (Fig. C:25) and lift out the thermostat, noting its position for subsequent assembly.

7. Remove the rocker cover and gasket.

8. Release the rocker shaft retaining nuts evenly and lift off the rocker assembly.

9. Lift out the pushrods. Keep them in their correct order to ensure they are not interchanged during reassembly.

10. Release the cylinder head bolts evenly in the reverse order to that shown in Fig. C:3. Lift off the cylinder head assembly complete with inlet and exhaust manifolds. Re-

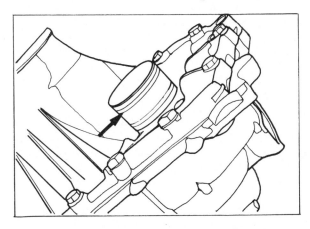

Fig. C:18 Use a plastic cup or similar plug to prevent displacement of the pinion gears

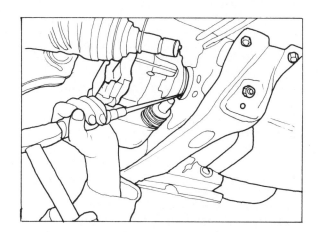

Fig. C:19 Knock out offside drive shaft from
transmission as shown

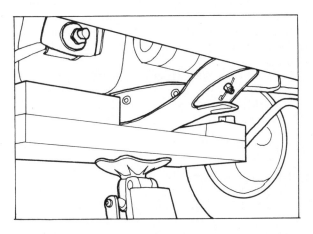

Fig. C:20 Method of supporting engine/trans -
mission assembly from below

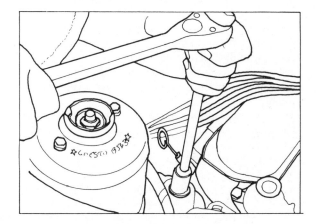

Fig. C:21 Undoing the engine upper mounting
rubber insulators

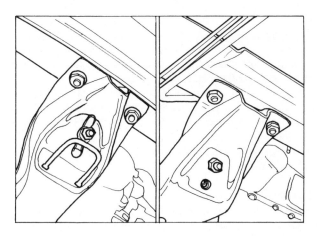

Fig. C:22 Undo engine rear mounting bolts, two
bolts on each side

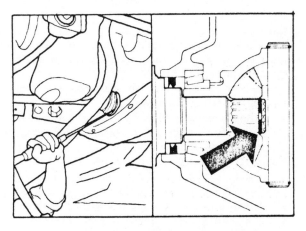

Fig. C:23 Remove plastic plugs then fit drive
shaft so that circlip (arrowed) engages

move and discard the head gasket.

11. Slacken the alternator mounting and pivot bolts and the water pump pulley bolt, remove the drive belt. Remove the alternator complete with its mounting bracket. Remove the water pump pulley.

12. Remove the bolts securing the distributor clamp plate to the cylinder block and carefully withdraw the distributor.

13. Remove the two retaining bolts and detach the fuel pump together with its insulating spacer from the cylinder block (Fig. C:26).

14. Remove the three bolts securing the water pump to the front face of the cylinder block and detach the pump together with its gasket.

15. Remove the three bolts securing the oil pump to the cylinder block and detach the pump together with its gasket (Fig. C:27).

16. Unscrew the oil pressure switch from the side of the cylinder block adjacent to the pump mounting flange.

17. With the engine supported clear of the ground and upright, to prevent sludge and swarf getting into the engine, remove the sump retaining bolts and detach the sump from the bottom of the crankcase. Prise the sump flange from the crankcase with a screwdriver, but take care not to damage the mating surfaces.

18. Place a large tray under the engine to catch any remaining oil, water, etc., and invert the cylinder block assembly.

19. Use a screwdriver in the ring gear teeth to prevent the flywheel/crankshaft turning, then undo and remove the centre bolt from the front end of the crankshaft. Withdraw the pulley from the crankshaft, using levers or a suitable puller.

20. Remove the bolts securing the timing cover to the front of the cylinder block and detach the cover. Remove the oil slinger from the crankshaft, noting which way the dished side is facing for future reference (Fig. C:28).

21. Unbolt the oil pick-up pipe from the crankcase and remove it by moving it to and from until it is free.

22. Unbolt the timing chain tensioner assembly (Fig. C:29) from the lower face of the cylinder block. Withdraw the tensioner arm from the pin on the front main bearing cap.

23. Release the lock plate tabs, remove the two retaining bolts and detach the camshaft sprocket complete with timing chain (Fig. C:30).

24. Release the lock plate tabs and remove the two bolts securing the camshaft thrust plate.

25. With the cylinder block positioned upside down turn the camshaft through one complete revolution to bring all the followers into the TDC position, then withdraw the camshaft from the cylinder block (Fig. C:31).

26. Extract the cam followers from their bores in the cylinder block, keeping them in their original installed order.

27. If required, withdraw the timing chain sprocket from the front end of the crankshaft using a suitable puller (Fig. C:32). Extract the Woodruff key from the slot in the crankshaft.

28. Check that all bearing caps, both main and big end, are suitably marked so that they can be installed in their original locations (Fig. C:33).

29. For each piston and con-rod in turn: Turn the crankshaft as necessary to bring the con-rod to the bottom of its travel.

30. Unscrew the big-end bolts two or three turns and tap them to release the bearing cap.

Completely remove the big end bolts and detach the bearing cap from the con-rod.

31. Push the piston and con-rod assembly up out of the cylinder bore, using the handle end of a hammer. If this is difficult due to the rings contacting a wear ridge at the top of the bore try inserting two or three feeler gauges down past the rings to ease them past the wear ridge as the piston is withdrawn. Withdraw the assembly from the top of the cylinder block.

32. Remove the bearing shells from the cap and con-rod. Identify the shells if they are to be re-used. Refit each cap to its respective con-rod, this is important.

33. Remove the piston rings from the piston. Raise one end of the ring out of its groove and insert a 0.020 in (0.5 mm) feeler blade between the ring and piston. Rotate the feeler around the piston while applying upward pressure to the raised portion of the ring until the ring rests on the land above the ring grooves. The ring can then be eased off the piston.

NOTE: The rings must always be removed and refitted over the piston crown - NEVER over the piston skirt.

34. The removal of the piston from its con-rod requires a suitable press and heating of the con-rod small end on reassembly. This job is best entrusted to a local auto machinist with the proper equipment.

Suitably identify the various components of the assembly so that they may be refitted, if necessary, in their original positions.

35. Slacken the clutch pressure plate bolts evenly and remove the pressure plate together with the clutch disc from the flywheel.

36. Remove the flywheel mounting bolts and remove the flywheel. It will be necessary to jam the crankshaft with a lump of wood to prevent the crankshaft turning.

37. Detach the crankshaft rear oil seal carrier from the rear face of the cylinder block (Fig. C:34).

38. Release the main bearing retaining bolts and detach the caps. When removing the centre main bearing cap, note the position of the two thrust half washers and mark them accordingly (Fig. C:35).

39. Carefully lift the crankshaft out of the crankcase.

40. Remove the main bearing shells from the crankcase and the bearings caps. Identify the shells if they are to be re-used.

41. Remove the oil seals from the timing cover and rear oil seal carrier.

Inspection

NOTE: The components of the cylinder head assembly have already been dealt with under the heading CYLINDER HEAD previously.

Cylinder Block

Thoroughly clean the dismantled block. Remove all

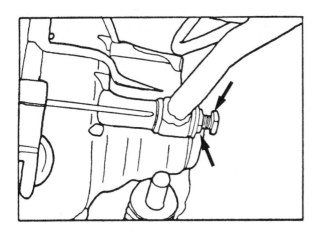

Fig. C:24 Tightening stabiliser bar to engine mounting nuts

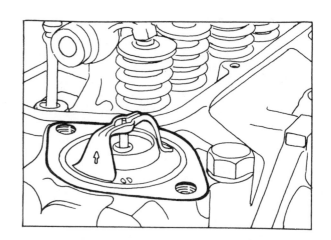

Fig. C:25 Note position of thermostat before removing it from cylinder head

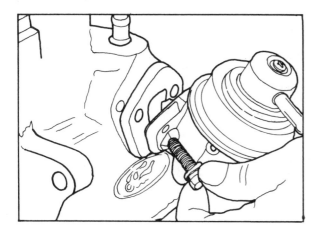

Fig. C:26 Undo two bolts and remove fuel pump from engine block

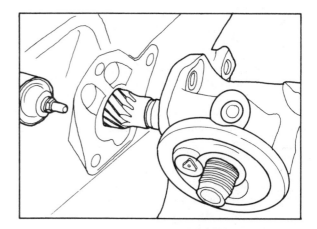

Fig. C:27 Undo three bolts and withdraw oil pump and drive gear from engine

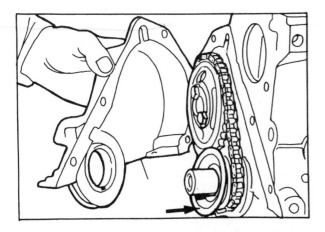

Fig. C:28 Detach timing cover from engine. Note position of oil slinger ring (arrowed)

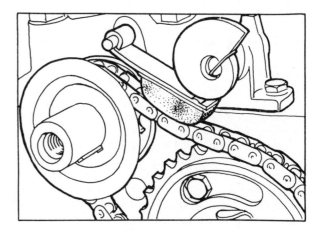

Fig. C:29 Unbolt and detach timing chain tensioner assembly

old gasket material from the surfaces. Clean and blow out all passages, bolt holes, etc.

Check all machined surfaces for burrs, nicks, scratches and scores. Remove minor imperfections with an oil stone.

Check the cylinder head gasket mating surface for flatness and have the block face corrected by planing if necessary.

Replace any core plugs which show signs of leakage.

Cylinder Bores

Inspect the cylinder walls for scoring, scuffing, roughness or other signs of wear.

If the bores look in reasonable condition, check them for wear, using an accurate internal micrometer. Measure the diameter of each bore at the top, middle and bottom, with the gauge placed first at right angles, then parallel to the centre line of the engine. The difference between the measurements at the same level will give the out of round or ovality of the bore, and the difference between either measurements at the top of the bore and the corresponding measurement at the bottom of the bore will give the bore taper (Fig. C:36). This is best done by a local auto machinist who will have the necessary equipment for the job.

It may be possible to remove minor imperfections by honing, but cylinders which are deeply scored or excessively worn must be rebored to the next oversize.

Cylinders which are already over bored to the maximum, or which cannot be rebored within the maximum specified limit may be restored by fitting dry liners. If liners have not previously been fitted, the cylinder block must be suitably machined to accept the liners.

Needless to say, both the boring the lining operations must be entrusted to a specialist engineering firm who will have the necessary skill and equipment required to carry out work of this nature.

NOTE: All main bearing caps must be in position during the reboring operation to avoid distortion of the main bearing bores. The main bearing caps should therefore be fitted when delivering the block for machining.

After any reboring, honing or deglazing operation, the cylinder bores should be washed with soap or detergent and water, then rinsed thoroughly with clean water and wiped dry with a clean lint free cloth. Finally, smear the bores with engine oil to prevent corrosion.

Pistons

Remove all carbon and oil deposits from the piston surfaces. Clean any gum or varnish from the piston skirt, piston pin and rings with solvent. Do NOT use a caustic cleaning solution or wire brush to clean the pistons.

Clean all carbon deposits from the ring grooves using a piece of piston ring as a scraper, or preferably a proper ring groove cleaner tool if available. Take great care not to damage the side of the groove, otherwise excessive sideplay will result with consequent loss of gas tightness and excessive fuel consumption. Ensure that the oil drain holes in the oil control ring groove are clear.

Inspect each piston for fractures at the ring lands, skirt and pin bosses, and for roughness, scoring or scuffing on the skirt.

Inspect the piston grooves for high steps at the inner portion of the lower lands caused by wear. Spongy, eroded areas near the edge of the piston crown are usually caused by detonation or pre-ignition. Replace any piston which shows signs of wear, wavy or stepped ring lands, or fractures or damage from detonation or pre-ignition.

When fitting oversize pistons, each cylinder bore must be machined to give the correct fit for the individual piston.

Piston Rings

Renew piston rings which are worn or damaged. Rings should not be transferred from one piston to another, regardless of mileage. It is recommended that new rings be fitted as a matter of course when overhauling the engine.

Where new rings are being installed in a used cylinder, the glaze must first be removed from the cylinder walls with a glaze breaker tool. (Except in the case where Cords piston rings are used).

Check the end gap of each piston ring in its respective cylinder bore, using a feeler gauge. Use the inverted piston to position the ring squarely in the bore. With worn bores, the ring should be located just below the wear ridge at the top of the bore (Fig. C:37). If the gap is too small, then it can be enlarged to the specified figure by careful filing. If the gap is greater than the specified limit, try another ring set. Check that the ring to groove clearance is within the figure specified in Technical Data (Fig. C:38). If the gap is too great, then either a new piston is needed or the grooves will have to be machined to accept ring 'inserts'.

Piston Pins

Inspect each piston pin for wear, etching or fracture. The piston pins are selected to give the correct interference fit in the piston pin bore and clearance fit in the connecting rod small end bush, and should not be interchanged.

Replacement pistons are supplied complete with the piston pin to ensure the correct interference fit. The piston pin bores and piston pin diameters are graded with corresponding paint marks and they must match one another. The paint marks can be found on the piston crown and edge of the pin.

Connecting Rods

Check that each connecting rod and cap is marked with its respective cylinder number. If the connecting rods and caps are unmarked, they should be suitably stamped, unless they are being discarded.

Clean the rods and caps with petrol or other suitable solvent, and dry thoroughly with compressed air. Blow out the oil passages with compressed air.

Inspect the rods for signs of fracture and the big end bearing bores for out of round or taper. Renew any rod

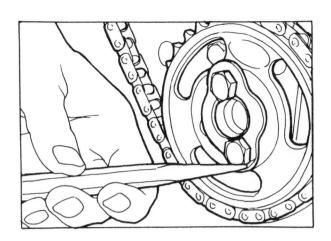

Fig. C:30 Unlock tabs then undo bolts to detach camshaft sprocket and chain

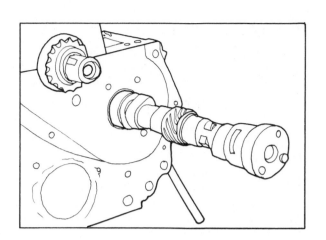
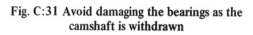

Fig. C:31 Avoid damaging the bearings as the camshaft is withdrawn

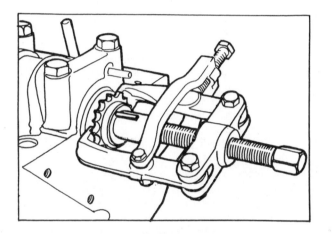

Fig. C:32 Use levers or puller tool to remove sprocket from crankshaft

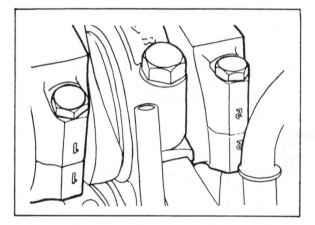

Fig. C:33 Check that markings on connecting rod and caps match before removing

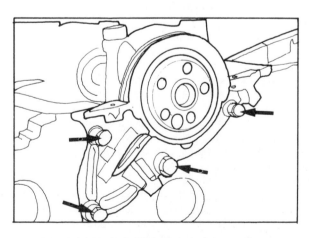

Fig. C:34 Undo bolts and detach rear oil seal carrier from engine

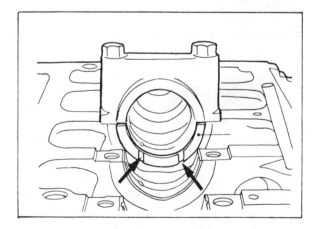

Fig. C:35 Note position of thrust washer slots when removing crankshaft

which is unsatisfactory.

Abnormal wear of the big end bearings can be caused by either a bent rod, a worn or damaged crankpin or a tapered big end bore. A shiny surface on the pin boss side of the piston, above the pin on one side and below it on the other usually indicates that the rod is bent or the piston pin hole is not in proper relation to the piston skirt and ring grooves. A proper checking jig will be required to check for these conditions and this work should be entrusted to a specialist machine shop.

Check the inside diameter of the bronze bush in the connecting rod small end. Replace the bush or complete rod if the bore is worn or damaged. Inspect the condition of the connecting rod big end cap bolts and replace if defective.

Crankshaft

Wash the crankshaft with petrol or other suitable solvent and dry thoroughly. Take great care to avoid damaging the machined surfaces. Blow out the oil passages with compressed air. In some cases it may be necessary to probe the passages with a piece of wire to ensure they are clear.

Inspect each bearing journal for scratches, scores, grooves or cracks. Inspect the oil seal contact surface at the crankshaft rear journal for nicks, scratches, sharp edges or burrs which may damage the oil seal or cause premature seal wear. Remove any minor imperfections with an oil stone or emery cloth.

Measure the diameter of each journal in at least four places to determine out of round, taper or undersize. If the taper or out of round is excessive, or if any of the journal surfaces are severely marked the crankshaft should be reground or replaced. If any of the journals will not clean up within the minimum specified regrind diameter, the crankshaft must be replaced.

The main bearing journals may be either standard diameter or 0.010 in (0.25 mm) undersize, even in new engines. Standard journals are not marked but undersize journals are indicated by a green paint mark on the first balance weight on the crankshaft.

The big end journals may also be either standard size or 0.010 in (0.25 mm) undersize. In the case of undersize, the web next to the journal is marked with a green paint spot. Standard journals are unmarked.

Main/Big-End Bearings

Clean the bearing shells thoroughly with petrol or other suitable solvent and dry thoroughly with compressed air. Do NOT scrape gum or varnish deposits from the shells.

Inspect the bearing surface of each shell carefully. Bearings which have worn, scored, chipped or pitted surfaces should be replaced. If the bearing base is visible the bearing is worn and should be replaced, also the respective journal checked for ovality.

Check the clearance of bearings which appear to be satisfactory, as described below.

The main bearing parent bore in the cylinder block

may be either standard diameter or 0.015 in (0.38 mm) oversize. Where an oversize exists the main bearing caps are marked with white paint spots.

Bearing Clearances

NOTE: The procedure given below is for checking the main bearing clearances, but the big-end clearances are checked in a similar manner.

1. Ensure that the crankshaft surface bearing shells and bearing caps are perfectly clean and free from oil and dirt.
2. Fit the upper halves of the bearing shells into their locations in the crankcase, ensuring that the tag on each shell correctly engages the corresponding notch in the housing.
3. Carefully lower the crankshaft into place in the crankcase.
4. Fit the lower half of the shell into the cap of the bearing being measured, again ensuring that the shell is correctly located.
5. Place a piece of Plastigage across the full width of the crankshaft journal, and about 0.25 in (6 mm) off centre (Fig. C:39).
6. Install the main bearing cap and tighten the cap bolts to their normal specified torque.
NOTE: None of the remaining bearing caps must be fitted during this procedure. Each bearing must be measured separately.
7. Release the bolts and remove the bearing cap.
NOTE: The crankshaft must not be moved while the Plastigage is in position.
8. Measure the width of the compressed plastic filament using the scale provided on the Plastigage pack (Fig. C: 40). The widest point will give the minimum clearance and the narrowest point the maximum clearance. The difference between the two readings will therefore give the taper on the journal.
9. To check the journal for out of round, clean all traces of Plastigage from the journal and bearing insert, rotate the crankshaft a quarter of a turn and repeat the measuring procedure. The difference between the two readings will indicate the out of round of the journal.
NOTE: When the measurement is completed, all Plastigage material must be cleaned off the bearing insert and crankshaft journal.

Camshaft

Clean the camshaft thoroughly with petrol or other suitable solvent, then wipe it dry. Inspect the cam lobes and journals for scoring or signs of abnormal wear.

Lobe wear characteristics may result in slight pitting in the general area of the lobe toe, but this is not detrimental to the operation of the camshaft, and the camshaft need not therefore be replaced until the lobe lift loss exceeds 0.005 in (0.127 mm).

Check the teeth of the distributor drive skew gear for wear or damage. If damaged, the camshaft must be replaced. If this the case, then the skew gears on the oil pump and distributor should also be checked.

The camshaft runs in three steel-backed, white metal

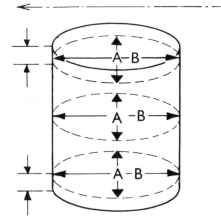

Fig. C:36 Measure cylinder bores for wear at points indicated

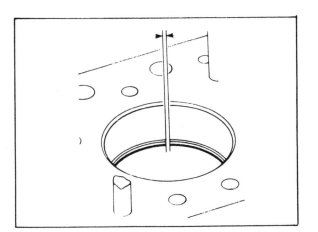

Fig. C:37 Place new ring square in bore below wear ridge and measure ring gap

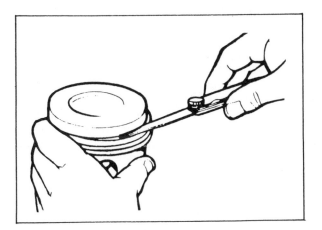

Fig. C:38 Measuring the piston ring to groove clearance

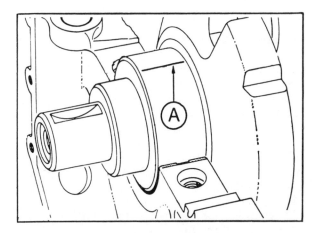

Fig. C:39 Place Plastigage strip at point (A) on crankshaft journal

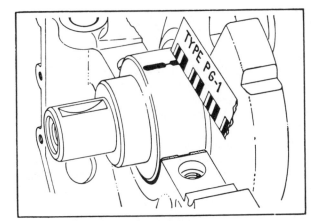

Fig. C:40 Measuring Plastigage to check the bearing clearance

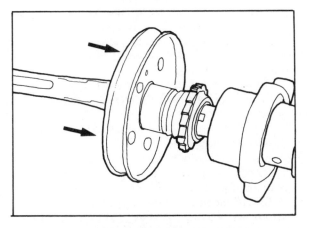

Fig. C:41 Using pulley and centre bolt to press sprocket onto crankshaft nose

bushes. If one or more of the bushes are worn or damaged, all three bushes should be replaced, otherwise camshaft alignment may be affected. It is recommended that bush replacement be entrusted to an authorised Ford agent as special service tools are required to ensure correct alignment during installation.

Check the cam followers for wear or scoring. Followers which are only slightly worn on their lower faces may be used again with the original camshaft, but replacement is preferable. New cam followers must ALWAYS be used when fitting a new camshaft.

Timing Gears/Chain

Inspect the timing chain for wear or looseness at the link pins. Inspect both the timing sprockets for cracks and worn or damaged teeth.

Inspect the rubber pad on the tensioner arm. In use, the chain links wear two grooves in the pad so that the chain runs directly on the roller. Do NOT dress the surface of the pad in an attempt to remove the grooves. If necessary, the tension pad arm should be replaced.

Engine Reassembly

1. Clean the housings of the crankshaft rear oil seal carrier and the timing cover, inspecting them for nicks, etc. Lubricate both seals and fit them to their appropriate housings using a hammer and hardwood block or a suitable size socket or tubular drift. Drive the seals in squarely up to their stops.
2. If removed, refit the Woodruff key in the nose of the crankshaft and press on the crankshaft sprocket, securing it by means of the pulley centre bolt and washer (Fig. C: 41).
3. Lubricate the camshaft journals, lobes and bearings thoroughly. Insert the camshaft into the cylinder block from the front, taking great care to avoid damaging the bearing bushes. Fit the camshaft thrust plate and secure to the block face using a new lockplate. Secure the two bolts after tightening them to their correct torque with the lockplate tabs.
4. Lubricate the cam followers and insert them into their respective bores in the cylinder block.
5. Install the selected main bearing shells dry in the cylinder block and main bearing caps. Ensure that the locating tag on each shell correctly engages the corresponding notch in the housing.
6. Install the two half thrust washers on each side of the centre main bearing. With the oil groove facing away from the centre bearing Fig. C:35.
7. Coat the crankshaft journals and bearing shells liberally with clean engine oil.
8. Carefully position the crankshaft in the cylinder block, and fit the main bearing caps in their respective locations. Tighten the cap bolts to their specified torque.
NOTE: *All the main bearing caps must be fitted with the cast arrows pointing forwards. The caps are marked for correct positioning: F for front, C for centre and R for rear.*
9. Using a dial indicator gauge located with the stylus against the crankshaft flange, as shown in Fig. C:42, check the crankshaft endfloat. Push the crankshaft towards the rear of the engine by levering on the crankshaft web with a screwdriver, and note the reading on the indicator dial. If the endfloat exceeds the specified limit, the thrust washers must be replaced with ones of suitable oversize to bring the figure within specification.

If a dial gauge is not available, the endfloat can be measured using feeler gauges between the face of the thrust washer and the crankshaft web.
10. Turn the crankshaft until the timing mark on the sprocket is pointing towards the camshaft centre. Temporarily fit the camshaft sprocket and turn the camshaft until the timing mark on the sprocket is adjacent to and in line with the crankshaft timing mark (Fig. C:43). Remove the camshaft sprocket and fit the timing chain to the sprocket. Locate the chain around the crankshaft sprocket and refit the sprocket on the camshaft flange. Fit the sprocket retaining bolts with a new locking plate. Tighten the bolts to their specified torque and secure by bending up the lockplate tabs. Check that the timing marks are still correctly aligned.
11. Locate the chain tensioner arm on the pivot pin at the front main bearing cap. Preload the spring of the tensioner assembly and secure the tensioner in place with the two retaining bolts. Release the chain tensioner spring.
12. Fit the oil slinger on the front of the crankshaft the correct way round (Fig. C:28). Lubricate the lip of the seal in the front cover, slide the crankshaft pulley sleeve through the cover oil seal and fit the front cover. Use the pulley sleeve to centralise the cover before tightening the front cover bolts and the crankshaft centre bolt to their specified torques.
13. Slide the rear oil seal carrier over the crankshaft, the seal lips being lightly lubricated to avoid damage. Tighten the carrier retaining bolts evenly to their specified torque.
14. Make sure that the mating faces of the flywheel and crankshaft flange are perfectly clean and free from burrs, then locate the flywheel squarely on the crankshaft flange, and tap into place. Apply oil resistant sealer to the threads of the retaining bolts, then fit and tighten the bolts to their specified torque.
NOTE: *Only re-use flywheel retaining bolts if they are in good condition.*
15. Make sure the friction surfaces of the flywheel and clutch pressure plate are perfectly clean and free from oil or grease. Place the clutch disc on the flywheel, the flat side of the disc facing the flywheel. Align the driven plate with a mandrel or home-made centralising tool and attach the clutch pressure plate. Tighten the pressure plate retaining bolts evenly to the specified torque. Remove the centralising tool.
16. As detailed earlier, assembling the pistons to the conrods requires the use of special jigs and heating of the conrod small end. This is a job that should be entrusted to an authorised Ford agent. On receipt of these assemblies, make sure the arrows on the piston crown and conrod splash bore point in the same direction Fig. C:44.
17. For each piston and connecting rod in turn:

Fit the piston rings to the piston from the crown side, the oil control ring first, followed by the lower and then

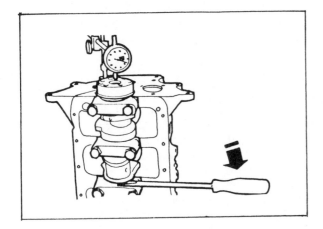

Fig. C:42 Measuring crankshaft end-float using clock gauge or feeler gauges

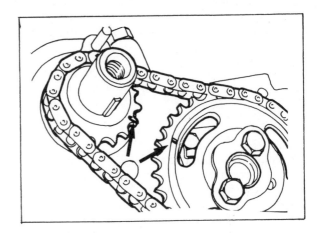

Fig. C:43 Align sprocket marks (arrowed) when refitting sprockets and chain

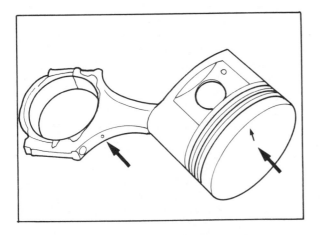

Fig. C:44 The correct relationship of piston marks and conrod oil hole

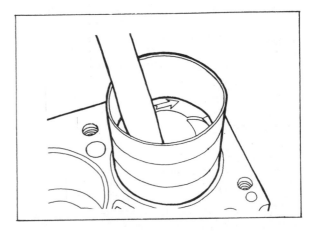

Fig. C:45 Inserting the pistons in the bores using a piston ring compressor tool

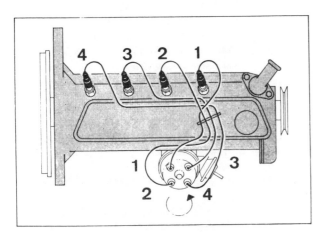

Fig. C:46 Reconnect the distributor cap and plug leads in the order shown

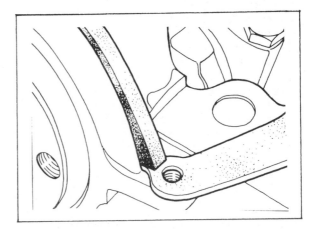

Fig. C:47 Overlap end seal on sump gasket as shown when refitting sump pan

the upper compression rings. The oil control ring may be fitted either way round, but the compression rings must be fitted with the TOP marking facing the piston crown. Note that when fitting new rings to partly worn bores, the top compression ring should have a step in it (ridge dodger) and should be fitted with the ridge facing upwards. Position the piston rings with their gaps staggered. The oil control ring gaps should be to the rear, the lower compression ring gap at 90° to the oil ring gap and the upper compression ring gap at 180° to the oil ring gap.

Lubricate the cylinder bore liberally with clean engine oil.

18. Install the piston assembly in its correct respective bore with the arrow marking on the piston crown pointing towards the front of the engine.

19. Compress the piston rings, using a proper ring compressor tool (Fig. C:45) and push the piston into the cylinder bore with the handle end of a hammer until the piston crown is slightly below the top of the cylinder. Do NOT attempt to fit the pistons by hand, otherwise breakage of the rings may result.

20. Fit the bearing shells, dry, in the con-rod and big end caps. Ensure that the locating tag on each shell correctly engages the corresponding notch in the bearing housing.

21. Coat the crankshaft journal and bearing shells liberally with clean engine oil, then pull the con-rod assembly down firmly on to the crankshaft journal and fit the cap to the rod. Ensure that the cap is correctly located on the two dowel pins, and tighten the cap bolts to their specified torque.

NOTE: The identification numbers on the con-rod and cap must be on the same side of the assembly. Apply suitable metal jointing compound to the oil pickup pipe and press it into position. Tighten the retaining bolt.

22. Fit new rubber sump sealing strips in the grooves in the lower faces of the front cover and rear oil seal carrier with the chamfered edge of the seal into the groove. Apply sealing compound to the mating surfaces at the joints between the front cover and rear oil seal carrier and crankcase. Position a new sump gasket on the cylinder block flange, smearing it with grease before fitting to help locate it in position. The ends of the sump gasket should be located under the ends of the sealing strips (Fig. C:47).

23. Fit the sump and install the retaining bolts. Tighten the bolts evenly in three stages to the torque figures specified in TIGHTENING TORQUES. Refer to Fig. C:13. Stage 1 is in alphabetical sequence, Stage 2 in numerical sequence and Stage 3 in alphabetical sequence.

24. Fit a new sealing ring in the sump drain plug and tighten the plug to its specified torque. Screw the oil pressure switch into the side of the cylinder block to its specified torque.

25. Refit the oil pump using a new gasket and tighten the pump retaining bolts to the specified torque. When a new or overhauled pump is being fitted it should be filled with engine oil and turned by hand through a complete rotation prior to installation.

26. Wet the rubber seal on the oil filter cannister with engine oil and screw the filter on to the threaded adaptor by hand until the gasket just contacts the pump flange. Then further tighten ¾ of a turn.

NOTE: Overtightening of the oil filter may result in leak-age from the sealing ring.

27. Fit the fuel pump to the cylinder block using a new gasket. Make sure that the pump operating arm lies on the camshaft eccentric not underneath it. Secure with the two retaining bolts.

28. Locate the water pump together with a new gasket on the front face of the engine and secure it in position with the three retaining bolts.

29. Turn the crankshaft to bring No. 1 cylinder to TDC. Position the distributor on the engine with the vacuum unit pointing to the rear and approximately 35° out from the engine. Turn the rotor arm until the electrode is immediately over the end of the condenser cannister. Insert the distributor into the engine and secure the clamp plate in the block with the retaining bolt.

30. Refit the alternator and mounting bracket to the engine. Fit the water pump pulley, then fit the drive belt and adjust the tension so that a total deflection of 0.5 in (13 mm) is possible at a point midway along the longest run of the belt. Tighten the alternator mounting bolts. Fully tighten the water pump pulley bolts.

31. Refit the cylinder head assembly, using a new head gasket. The use of two tapered guide studs, made up and screwed into the cylinder head bolt holes at diagonally opposite corners of the block will facilitate correct alignment of the head and gasket during installation. Once the head is installed, the studs can then be unscrewed and replaced by cylinder head bolts.

32. Tighten the cylinder head bolts finger tight initially. It should be noted that the head bolts are different lengths, two being shorter than the others, according to the varying height of the cylinder head. Ensure that the bolts are fitted in their correct respective positions. Tighten the head bolts evenly, in the sequence shown in Fig. C: 3 and in the progressive stages given in TIGHTENING TORQUES.

33. Dip the ends of the push-rods in engine oil and install them in their original positions. Position the rocker shaft assembly on the cylinder head, ensuring that the arm adjusting screws locate correctly in the cupped ends of their respective pushrods. Tighten the shaft retaining bolts evenly to their specified torque.

34. Adjust the valve clearances as described previously in the TUNE-UP chapter.

35. Refit the rocker cover with a new gasket. Fit the breather hose to the inlet manifold and the cylinder block and then fit the oil filler cap to the rocker cover.

36. Install the thermostat in its location in the cylinder head. Ensure that the thermostat is correctly located in the housing, otherwise overheating of the engine will result. Position a new gasket on the housing flange, fit the water outlet housing over the thermostat and secure with the two retaining bolts.

37. Fit the sparking plugs and torque them to their specified setting. Refit the distributor cap and reconnect the HT leads to the spark plugs (Fig. C:46).

38. Reconnect the fuel supply pipe and the distributor vacuum pipe at the carburettor.

39. Insert the dipstick and attach the side water pipe to the water pump connection and to the side of the cylinder block.

Technical Data

GENERAL

Type. . . . . Four cylinder, inline, ohv, crossflow
Valve control . . . . By pushrods and rocker arms
Camshaft position . . . . .In crankcase on right side
Bore
    1.0 and 1.1. . . . . 2.91 in (73.96 mm)
    1.3 . . . . .3.188 in (80.98 mm)

	1.0 LC	1.0 HC
Stroke	2.19 in (55.7 mm)	2.19 in (55.7 mm)
Swept volume	957 cc	957 cc
Compression ratio	8.3:1	9.1:1
Compression pressure (starter speed)	137-166 lb/in^2 (9.5-11.5 bar)	159-188 lb/in^2 (11-13 bar)
Idle speed	775-825 rpm	775-825 rpm
Max. continuous speed	5800 rpm	6300 rpm
Engine output (DIN)	40 hp (29 Kw) at 5500 rpm	45 hp (33 Kw) at 6000 rpm
Torque (DIN)	47.2 lbf. ft at 2700 rpm	47.9 lbf. ft at 3000 rpm

	1.1 HC	1.3 HC 2V
Stroke	2.56 in (64.98 mm)	2.478 in (62.99 mm)
Swept volume	1117 cc	1297 cc
Compression ratio	9.1:1	9.0:1
Compression pressure (starter speed)	159-188 lbf/in^2 (11-13 bar)	142-170 lbf/in^2 (10-12 bar)
Idle speed	750-850 rpm	775-825 rpm
Max. continuous speed	6300 rpm	5800 rpm
Engine output (DIN)	53 hp (39 Kw) at 5700 rpm	70 hp (51 Kw) at 5500 rpm
Torque (DIN)	59 lb ft at 3000 rpm	67 lb ft at 4000 rpm

PISTONS

Piston to bore clearance . . . . 0.0018-0.0020 in (0.045-0.050 mm)
Piston ring end gap - Top and centre . . . . 0.0098-0.0177 in (0.25-0.45 mm)

CRANKSHAFT

Crankshaft endfloat. . . . . 0.003-0.011 in (0.079-0.279 mm)
Main bearing journal dia.
    Standard . . . . .2.2433-2.2441 in (56.980-57.000 mm)
    0.254 in u/size . . . . .2.2333-2.2341 in (56.726-56.746 mm)
    0.508 in u/size . . . . .2.2233-2.2241 in (56.472-56.492 mm)
    0.762 in u/size . . . . .2.2133-2.2141 in (56.218-56.238 mm)
Crankpin dia.
    Standard . . . . 1.6925-1.6933 in (42.99-43.01 mm)
    0.254 in u/size . . . . 1.6827-1.6835 in (42.74-42.76 mm)
    0.508 in u/size . . . . 1.6728-1.6736 in (42.49-42.51 mm)
    0.762 in u/size . . . . 1.6630-1.6638 in (42.24-42.26 mm)
Thrust washer thickness
    Standard . . . . 0.1102-0.1122 in (2.80-2.85 mm)
    Oversize. . . . . .0.1177-0.1197 in (2.99-3.04 mm)

VALVE TIMING

	1.0 LC/1.0 HC/1.1 HC	1.3 2V
Inlet valve		
Opens	21° BTDC	27° BTDC
Closes	55° ABDC	65° ABDC
Exhaust valve		
Opens	70° BBDC	65° BBDC
Closes	22° ATDC	27° ATDC

CYLINDER HEAD

Valve seat angle . . . . 44°30' to 45°
Valve guide inside diameter . . . . 0.311-0.312 in (7.907-7.937 mm)

VALVES

Inlet
    Stem to guide clearance . . . . 0.021-0.070 mm
    Valve stem dia.
        Standard . . . . 0.3098-0.3105 in (7.868-7.866 mm)
        0.076 mm o/size . . . . 0.3128-0.3135 in (7.944-7.962 mm)
        0.38 mm o/size . . . . 0.3248-0.3255 in (8.249-8.257 mm)
Length . . . . .105.45-106.45 mm
Exhaust
    Stem to guide clearance . . . . 0.043-0.092 mm
    Valve stem dia.
        Standard . . . . 0.3089-0.3096 in (7.846-7.864 mm)
        0.076 mm o/size . . . . 0.3119-0.3126 in (7.922-7.940 mm)
        0.38 mm o/size . . . . 0.3239-0.3246 in (8.227-8.245 mm)
Length . . . . .105.15-106.15 mm

VALVE CLEARANCES

	1.0 LC/1.0 HC/1.1 HC
Inlet	0.009 in (0.22 mm)
Exhaust	0.023 in (0.59 mm)

	1.3 HC
Inlet	0.010 in (0.25 mm)
Exhaust	0.022 in (0.55 mm)

LUBRICATION SYSTEM

Sump initial fill capacity . . . . 6.25 pt (3.55 litres)
Sump refill capacity (incl. filter) . . . . 5.75 pt (3.25 litres)
Oil filter capacity . . . . .0.9 pt (0.5 litre)
Min. oil pressure at 80°C and 750 rpm . . . . 8.7 lbf/in^2 (0.6 bar)
Min. oil pressure at 80°C and 2000 rpm . . . . 21.75 lbf/in^2 (1.5 bar)
Relief valve opening pressure . . . . 35-40 lbf/in^2 (2.42-2.75 bar)

ENGINE
Trouble Shooter

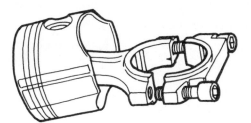

FAULT	CAUSE	CURE
Noisy tappet (with correct clearance)	1. Wear in rocker pad face and/or rocker sleeve and shaft 2. Worn cam follower	1. Reface pad surface, replace rockers or shaft 2. Fit new followers
Lack of compression	1. Faulty valve seat, excessive wear in stem or guide. 2. Faulty head gasket. 3. Worn pistons, rings and bores.	1. Recut seat and valve, fit new guide and valve. 2. Fit new gasket or reface head. 3. Either fit new rings, pistons and rings and rebore. If engine badly worn then recon. engine.
Smoke from exhaust. Lack of power	1. As above. 2. Blocked crankcase breather.	1. As above. 2. Check breathing apparatus as above.
Piston slap	1. As above (except blocked breather).	1. As above
Big-end knock	1. Wear between big-end shell and crankcase. Wrong torque on bolts.	1. Depending on wear, fit new shells, regrind crankshaft and check torque.
Mains rumble	1. Wear between main bearing shells and crankshaft.	1. As above.
Cam follower tap	1. Camshaft worn or follower dished.	1. Examine and replace followers or camshaft. Or both.
Knocking when clutch depressed. Movement at crank pulley	1. Excessive crankshaft end-float. Wear between crank and thrust washer.	1. Fit new thrust washers and recheck clearance.
Clattering from front of engine	1. Worn or slack timing chain, worn chain tensioner.	1. Fit new chain and tensioner. Adjust chain where necessary.
Small-end or gudgeon pin knock	1. Excessive wear between gudgeon pin and con-rod.	1. Fit new bush to con-rod.
Lack of oil pressure	1. Excessive wear in crankshaft journals. 2. Faulty oil pump. 3. Blocked oil pick-up strainer. 4. Faulty pressure-relief valve. 5. Blocked oil filter. 6. Lack of Oil.	1. Overhaul engine. 2. Fit new pump. 3. Clean pick-up. 4. Fit new relief valve. 5. Fit new filter. 6. Install fresh oil.
Oil leaks	1. Sump gaskets or packings. 2. Front and rear crankshaft oil seal. 3. Rocker or camshaft gasket. 4. Oil filter.	1. Fit new gaskets. 2. Fit new seals. 3. Fit new gasket. 4. Check filter seal.
Lack of power (engine in good condition)	1. Faulty ignition timing. Faulty sparking plugs, points or condenser. Wrong valve clearance.	1. Tune engine.

Engine Electrics

ALTERNATOR .... [1]

Removal

1. Disconnect the battery.
2. Disconnect the cable multi-plug or plugs, depending on the alternator type, from the back of the alternator.
3. Slacken the alternator mounting and pivot bolts and push it towards the engine (Fig. D:2).
4. Lift the drive belt over the pulleys and remove it.
5. Finally, remove the alternator mounting bolts and detach the unit from the engine.

Installation

Installation of the alternator is a reversal of the removal procedure, noting that the drive belt should be adjusted to give a deflection of 0.5 in (13 mm) at the middle of its longest run under normal thumb pressure (Fig. D:3). The tension is obtained by moving the alternator away from the engine until the tension is correct and then fully tightening the mounting bolts. If it is necessary to apply leverage to the alternator in order to obtain the correct belt tension, do so only with a wooden lever (such as a hammer handle) bearing against the drive end bracket.

Replacing Brushes - Bosch Type

1. Disconnect the battery.
2. Remove the two screws attaching the regulator to the back of the alternator (Fig. D:4) and lift away the regulator.
3. Unsolder the brush wiring connections and remove the brushes and springs (Fig. D:5).
4. Fit the new brushes and springs into the brush box and resolder the wiring connections.
5. Refit the regulator to the alternator and reconnect the battery.

Replacing Brushes - Lucas Type

1. Disconnect the battery.
2. Pull off the wiring multi-plug from the back of the alternator.
3. Remove the two screws attaching the alternator rear cover in place and remove the cover.
4. Undo the brush retaining screws (Fig. D:6) and remove the brush assemblies from the brush box (Fig. D:7).
5. Fit the new brushes in the reverse manner.

Replacing Brushes - Femsa Type

1. Disconnect the battery.
2. Undo the four nuts attaching the rear cover to the alternator and remove the cover.
3. Pull off the brush box wiring, noting the connections, remove the retaining screw and withdraw the brush box (Fig. D:8 and D:9).
4. Lift the brushes from the brush box.
5. Refit the new brushes in the reverse manner.

Checking Brush Condition

1. With the brushes in the free position, measure the amount by which they protrude beyond the brush box moulding. If the amount protruding is worn to, or approaching, the wear limit specified in Technical Data, then the brush assemblies should be renewed.
2. Check the brushes for freedom of movement in their holders. Clean a seized brush with a petrol moistened cloth, or by lightly polishing the brush sides on a smooth file if necessary until the brush slides freely.
3. Inspect the surface of the slip rings on the end of the rotor. If there is any evidence of roughness or burning this can be cleaned off with very fine glass paper. On no account should emery cloth or similar abrasive be used.
4. Clean off any dirt or oil which may have collected around the apertures in the end cover and the slip ring end bracket.
5. Check the brushes are correctly positioned in their holders before refitting the brush box.

Regulator Replacement

The regulator on the Bosch alternator is screwed to the outside of the rear cover, so removal is a simple matter.

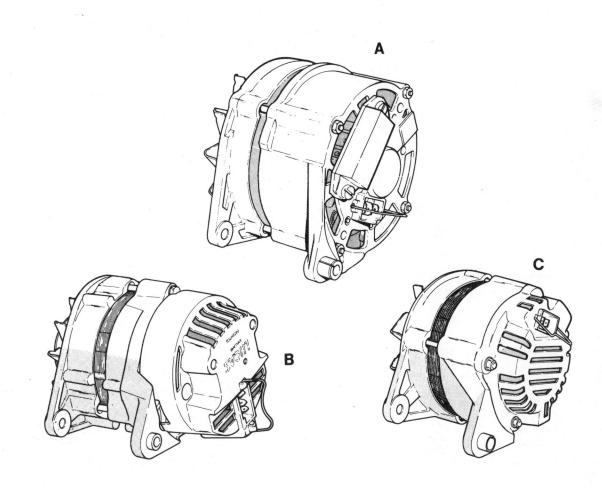

Fig. D:1 Alternator types, Bosch type (A) Lucas type (B) and Femsa type (C)

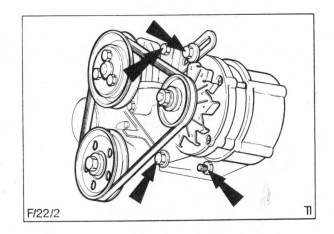

F/22/2

Fig. D:2 Slacken mounting bolts (arrowed) to adjust alternator belt tension

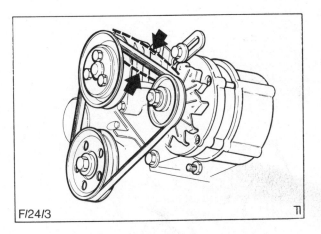

F/24/3

Fig. D:3 Check tension at point (arrowed) on longest belt run between pulleys

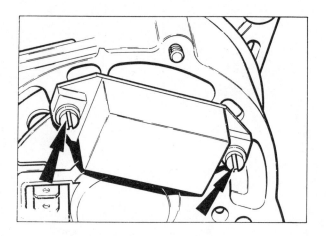

Fig. D:4 Regulator retaining screws on Bosch type alternator

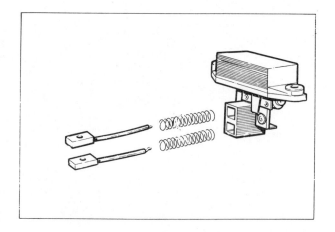

Fig. D:5 Details of the brush and brush box - Bosch type

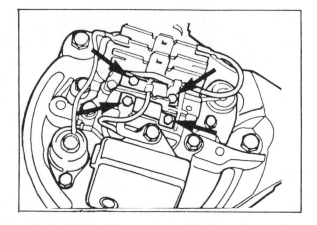

Fig. D:6 Undo four screws to remove brushes on Lucas alternators

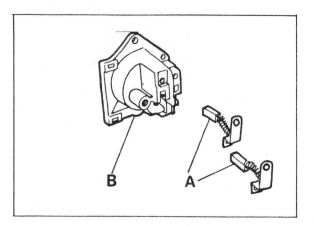

Fig. D:7 An exploded view of the Lucas brushes (A) and brush box (B)

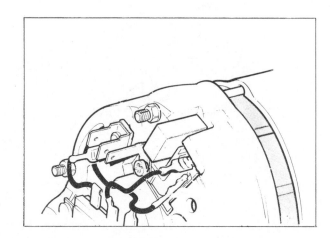

Fig. D:8 Details of the brush box installation - Femsa type

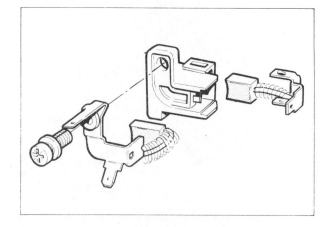

Fig. D:9 An exploded view of the brush box arrangement - Femsa type

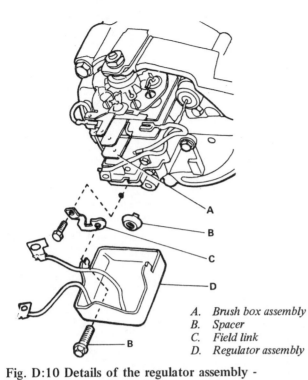

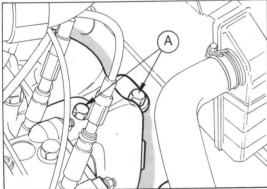

A. Brush box assembly
B. Spacer
C. Field link
D. Regulator assembly

Fig. D:10 Details of the regulator assembly -
Lucas type

Fig. D:11 Regulator retaining screws on Femsa
type alternators

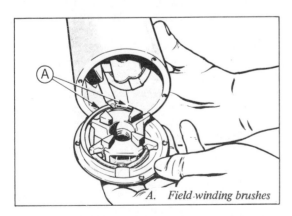

Fig. D:12 To remove starter motor, first undo
exhaust pipe clamp bolts (A)

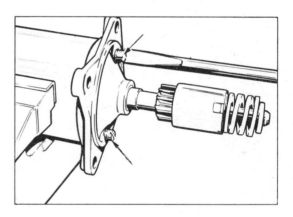

Fig. D:13 Removing the endplate retaining
screws from starter motor (arrowed)

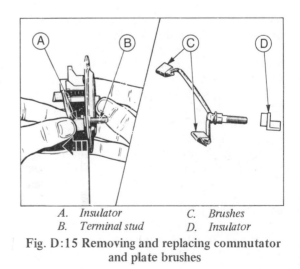

A. Field winding brushes

Fig. D:14 Withdrawing commutator end plate
to expose brushes

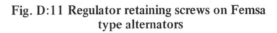

A. Insulator   C. Brushes
B. Terminal stud   D. Insulator

Fig. D:15 Removing and replacing commutator
and plate brushes

The battery should be disconnected and the retaining screws removed, followed by the regulator unit.

The Lucas and Femsa alternators require the removal of the multi-plugs and rear covers before access can be gained on their regulators (Figs. D:10 and D:11). In each case the wiring should be disconnected and the retaining screws removed in order to lift out the regulators. Replacement is a reversal of the removal procedure.

Drive Pulley Removal/Installation

1. Disconnect the battery.
2. Slacken the alternator mounting and pivot bolts and push the alternator towards the engine to allow removal of the drive belt.
3. Undo the pulley retaining nut and pull the pulley off the shaft.

Installation

This is a reversal of the removal procedure, noting that the drive belt should be adjusted to give a deflection of 0.5 in (13 mm) in the centre of its run between the water pump and alternator pulleys. This tension can be achieved by pulling the alternator away from the engine and finally tightening the bolts when the tension is correct. If it is necessary to apply leverage to the alternator, do so only with a wooden lever (such as a hammer handle) bearing against the drive end bracket.

Alternator Overhaul

In most instances of wear or damage to the alternator, other than the brushes or the regulator unit, it will probably be more economical and convenient to replace the complete unit under an exchange scheme rather than attempt to obtain replacement parts and repair it.

STARTER MOTOR (INERTIA TYPE) .... [2]

Removal

1. Disconnect the battery.
2. Jack up the front of the vehicle, referring to the jacking information contained in the ROUTINE MAINTENANCE chapter at the front of the book.
3. Disconnect the main feed cable from the starter motor.
4. Remove the two bolts securing the exhaust downpipe to the exhaust manifold (Fig. D:12) and carefully lower the exhaust pipe until it provides sufficient clearance to remove the starter motor.
5. Remove the three bolts attaching the starter motor to the clutch housing and detach the starter motor (Fig. D:17).

Installation

Installation is a reversal of the removal procedure, noting that care should be taken to ensure the exhaust

pipe is correctly joined to the manifold to prevent exhaust gases escaping, and the starter motor should be tested for correct operation.

Brush Replacement

1. Remove the starter motor as described previously and mount it in a vice fitted with 'soft' jaws.
2. Undo the two screws attaching the commutator drive end plate to the yoke (Fig. D:13) and withdraw armature assembly. Remove the plastic cover from the end of the armature shaft and then the four screws holding the commutator end plate to the starter motor. Remove the end plate (Fig. D:14). Take care not to damage the commutator end plate gasket during removal.
3. Inspect the brushes for wear (Fig. D:15). Brushes which are worn to, or approaching, the minimum length of 0.32 in (8 mm) must be renewed as a set.
4. Inspect the contact face on the end of the commutator for oil contamination - if present, the brushes must be renewed. If the commutator surface is blackened or dirty, clean it with a petrol moistened cloth. If there is evidence of burning, this can be cleaned off with very fine glass paper. On NO account should emery cloth or similar abrasive be used for this purpose.
5. To replace the brushes on the commutator end plate, remove the nut, washer and insulator from the main terminal stud. Push the stud and second insulator through the end plate, remove the two brushes from the brush box and remove the stud and brushes. The new brushes should be replaced in the reverse manner.
6. To renew the brushes on the field windings, cut the existing leads about 0.25 in (6 mm) from the field winding conductor (Fig. D:16). Clean the ends of the original leads still attached to the field coils and solder the new brush leads to them. Make sure the long and short leads are fitted in the same positions as originally.
7. Fit the brushes into their respective holders and check for freedom of movement. Sticking brushes can usually be freed by cleaning them and their holders with a petrol moistened cloth, or by lightly polishing the brush sides with a smooth file.
8. Check the brush spring pressures with the brushes fitted in their respective holders. Press the top of the brush with a push type spring gauge until the top of the brush protrudes about 0.125 in (3.0 mm) above the brush box moulding. A reading of approximately 28 oz (800 gm) should be obtained. If the spring pressures are appreciably incorrect, the end brush box assembly should be renewed.
9. Making sure the brushes are secure in their respective channels, align the commutator end plate on the yoke and secure it with the four mounting screws.
10. Refit the plastic end cap and replace the starter motor.
11. Reconnect the exhaust system and battery.

Drive Pinion Gear

If difficulty is experienced with the starter motor pinion not meshing correctly with the ring gear, it may be that the drive assembly requires cleaning. The pinion bar-

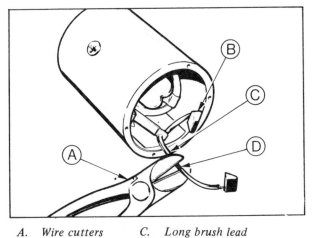

A. Wire cutters C. Long brush lead
B. Short brush lead D. Cut 6 mm from conductor

Fig. D:16 Cutting off old field winding brush leads to solder on new ones

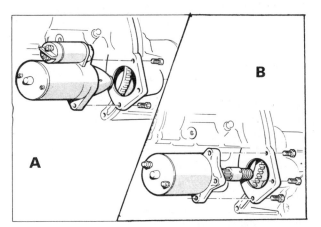

A. Pre-engaged type B. Inertia type

Fig. D:17 Details of starter motor mounting arrangement

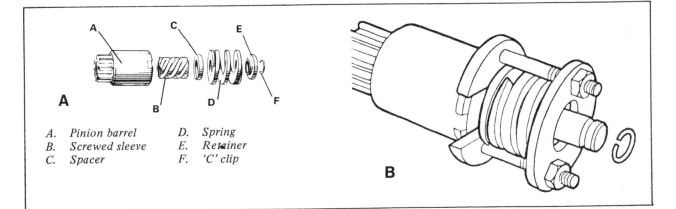

A. Pinion barrel D. Spring
B. Screwed sleeve E. Retainer
C. Spacer F. 'C' clip

Fig. D:18 Details of pinion assembly (A) and retaining clip removal (B)

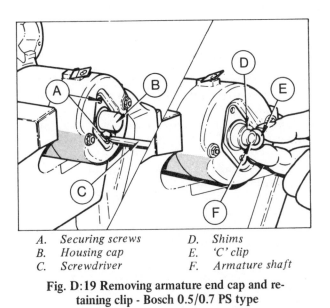

A. Securing screws D. Shims
B. Housing cap E. 'C' clip
C. Screwdriver F. Armature shaft

Fig. D:19 Removing armature end cap and retaining clip - Bosch 0.5/0.7 PS type

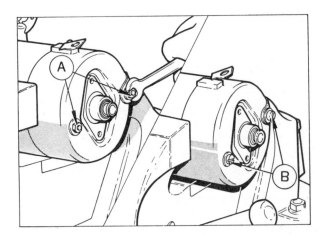

Fig. D:20 Undo end cap nuts (A) or screws (B) to expose brushes - Bosch type

rel assembly should move freely on the screwed sleeve. If there is dirt or other foreign matter on the sleeve, it should be washed off with petrol or paraffin. If required, the drive assembly can be lubricated with a silicone based aerosol lubricant, but on NO account must grease be used as this would attract dirt.

1. To remove the pinion assembly, proceed as follows (Fig. D:18): Compress the drive spring sufficiently to expose the C-clip which can be sprung from its position on the armature shaft.
2. Remove the main drive pinion assembly from the armature shaft. It may be necessary to depress it and turn it slightly to disengage it from the shaft splines.
3. The pinion and barrel is serviced as a complete assembly with the screwed sleeve and no attempt should be made to dismantle the assembly.
4. Fit the new pinion assembly on the armature shaft, with the pinion teeth towards the starter motor. Assemble the thrust washer, drive spring and spring seat on the shaft, compress the drive spring and fit the jump ring. Ensure that the ring is correctly seated.

STARTER MOTOR (PRE-ENGAGED TYPE) [3]

Removal

1. Disconnect the battery.
2. Jack up the front of the car, referring to the jacking information contained in the ROUTINE MAINTENANCE chapter at the front of the book.
3. Disconnect the main feed cable and two smaller wires from the starter motor solenoid.
4. Remove the two bolts holding the exhaust pipe to the exhaust manifold and lower the exhaust pipe to provide sufficient clearance to allow removal of the starter motor.
5. Remove the two bolts attaching the starter motor to the clutch housing (Fig. D:17) and detach the starter motor.

Installation

Installation is a reversal of the removal procedure, noting that care should be taken to ensure the exhaust pipe is correctly joined to the manifold to prevent exhaust gases escaping, and the starter motor should be tested for correct operation.

Brush Replacement - Bosch Type

1. If still connected, detach the starter motor connecting strap from the terminal on the solenoid switch, then remove the starter motor as described previously and clamp it in a vice fitted with 'soft' jaws.
2. Remove the nut and washer holding the field winding cable to the solenoid and remove the cable.
3. Remove the two screws holding the commutator end housing cap in place and remove the cap and rubber seal (Fig. D:19).
4. Wipe the grease from the end of the armature shaft and then remove the C-clip and shims from the armature end.

5. Remove the two nuts and washers or screws securing the commutator end housing and lift off the housing (Fig. D:20).
6. Remove the brushes (Fig. D:21) from the brush plate assembly by carefully prising the retaining/tensioning springs clear and sliding the brushes from their locations.
7. Inspect the brushes for wear and renew if necessary. Brushes worn to or approaching the wear limit of 0.39 in (10 mm) should be renewed as a set.
8. To replace the brushes, cut the old brush leads at a point mid way between their base and brush and solder the new brush leads to them.
9. Fit the four brushes in their respective holders and retain them with the brush springs.
10. Fit the commutator end housing in position (Fig. D:22), sliding the rubber insulator into the commutator housing cutout. Secure the housing in place with the nuts and washers or screws, depending on which are used.
11. Fit sufficient shims to the end of the armature shaft to prevent any endfloat when the C-clip is sprung into place and then fit the clip.
12. Install the bearing cap seal, smear a small quantity of lithium based grease on the end of the armature shaft and refit the bearing cap, securing it with the two screws.
13. Reconnect the field winding cable to the solenoid terminal.
14. Refit the starter motor to the car, reconnect the exhaust pipe to the manifold and then reconnect the battery.
15. Check the operation of the starter motor.

Brush Replacement - Femsa Type

1. Remove the starter motor as described previously.
2. Mount the starter motor in a vice fitted with 'soft' jaws.
3. Slacken the brush cover securing screw and slide the brush cover and rubber seal from the body of the motor (Fig. D:23).
4. Carefully lever the brush springs from the tops of the brushes and support them clear of the brushes with a piece of rod. See Fig. D:24.
5. Remove the screws securing the brush leads to the field winding and remove the brushes from their holders.
6. Check for sticking brushes and if necessary clean them and their holders with a petrol moistened cloth. Also, a file can be used to smooth their sides. Emery should NOT be used.
7. Brushes worn to or approaching their wear limit of approximately 0.47 in (12 mm) should be renewed as a set.
8. Refit the brushes by sliding them into their holders and securing the leads with the cross head screws.
9. Release the brush springs and allow them to rest on top of the brushes.
10. Refit the brush cover and rubber seal, making sure that the latter is correctly fitted to prevent ingress of dirt and water.
11. Refit the starter motor, reconnect the exhaust pipe and reconnect the battery.
12. Check the operation of the starter motor.

Engine Electrics

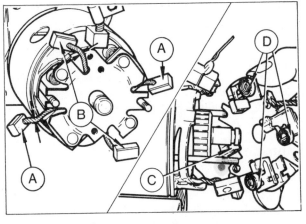

A. Field brushes
B. Terminal brushes
C. Brush plate
D. Brush retaining springs

Fig. D:21 Details of the brush gear arrangement - Bosch type

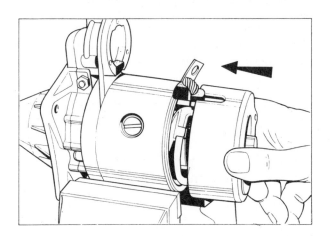

Fig. D:22 Refitting commutator end housing, fit rubber insulator into housing slot

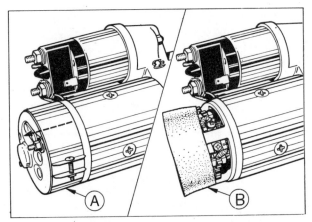

Fig. D:23 Removing brush cover (A) and rubber seal (B) on Femsa type starter

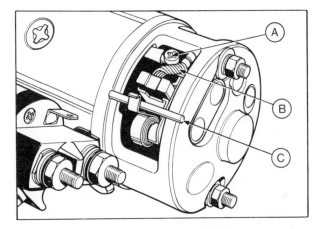

A. Brush lead to field screw
B. Brush lead
C. Spring retaining rod

Fig. D:24 Method of keeping brush springs clear when removing brushes

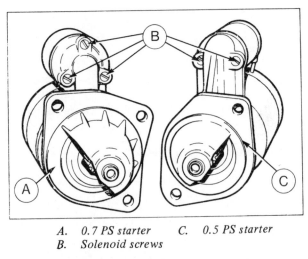

A. 0.7 PS starter
B. Solenoid screws
C. 0.5 PS starter

Fig. D:25 Solenoid securing screws - Bosch type pre-engaged starters

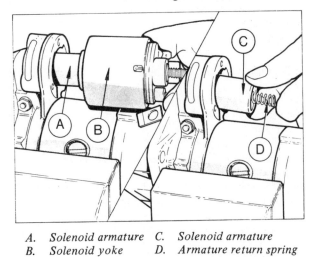

A. Solenoid armature
B. Solenoid yoke
C. Solenoid armature
D. Armature return spring

Fig. D:26 Removing the solenoid assembly on 0.7 PS type starters

Starter Solenoid Removal - Bosch Type

1. Remove the starter motor as described previously.
2. Clamp the starter in a vice fitted with 'soft' jaws.
3. Disconnect the field winding cable from the solenoid terminal.
4. On the 0.7PS model, remove the three screws securing the solenoid to the drive end housing. Guide the solenoid yoke away from the drive end housing and solenoid armature. Unhook the solenoid armature from the actuating lever. On the 0.5PS model, remove the two solenoid mounting screws and lift it clear, unhooking the solenoid from the actuating arm (Fig. D:25, 26 and 27).

Installation

Installation is a reversal of the removal procedure, noting that the solenoid armature hook should be smeared with lithium based grease before locating it over the actuating arm in the drive end housing.

Starter Solenoid Removal - Femsa Type

1. Disconnect the battery.
2. Disconnect the wiring from the solenoid, noting the connections (Fig. D:28).
3. Unscrew the retaining screws and remove the solenoid.

Installation

Installation is a reversal of the removal procedure.

Starter Motor Overhaul

In most instances of wear or damage to the starter motor, it will probably be more economical and convenient to replace the complete unit under an exchange scheme rather than attempt to obtain replacement parts and repair it.

DISTRIBUTOR. [4]

Removal

1. Disconnect the battery.
2. Disconnect the spark plug leads and unclip the distributor cap, moving it clear of the distributor.
3. Turn the engine over manually so that number 1 cylinder is at TDC (Fig. D:30). This is indicated by the rotor arm being in a position where it would be touching the number 1 contact in the distributor cap and the mark on the crankshaft pulley being aligned with the correct timing mark.
4. Remove the single bolt located at the base of the distributor and then remove the assembly. Mark the position of the rotor arm relative to the distributor body with a scribed mark (Fig. D:31). This will aid repositioning.

Installation

1. Making sure the engine is set with number 1 cylinder

at TDC and that the rotor is aligned with the mark on the distributor body, insert the distributor and tighten the clamp bolt (Fig. D:32).
2. Reconnect the battery.
3. Check and adjust the contact gap or dwell angle as necessary (Figs. D:33 and D:34).
4. Make sure the distributor cap is clean and refit it. Reconnect the HT leads.
5. Check and adjust the timing as described in the TUNE-UP chapter.

Distributor Overhaul

In most cases of wear or damage to the components of the distributor, especially after considerable mileage, it will probably be more economical and convenient to exchange the complete distributor assembly for a new or reconditioned unit.

IGNITION TIMING . . . . [5]

The contact breaker points gap must be correctly set before attempting to check or adjust the ignition timing. Conversely, the ignition setting should be checked after cleaning, adjusting or replacing the contact set.

Static Timing Check

Remove the distributor cap and connect a 12 volt test lamp between the distributor low tension terminal and a good earthing point. Rotate the crankshaft in its normal direction of rotation until the rotor arm is pointing approximately midway between the No. 3 and No. 1 plug lead segments in the distributor cap. The rotor arm rotation is anti-clockwise viewed from above.

With the ignition switched on, rotate the crankshaft slowly until the test lamp just lights up. If the ignition setting is correct the notch on the crankshaft pulley will be aligned with the appropriate mark on the timing scale (see TUNE-UP chapter). This should be 10° BTDC for all models except the 1297 cc 2V engine which should be 6° BTDC. If the timing is incorrect it should be adjusted as described below.

Turn the crankshaft until the notch on the crankshaft pulley is aligned with the correct mark on the timing scale. Slacken the distributor clamp bolt and rotate the distributor body anti-clockwise past the point where the test lamp goes out, then carefully rotate it back clockwise until the lamp just lights up. Tighten the clamp bolt without disturbing the body setting. Re-check the setting as described above.

Dynamic Strobe Light Check

If possible, the ignition timing should be checked dynamically with a stroboscopic timing light to ensure optimum engine performance. In this case the equipment manufacturer's instructions should be followed.

With the distributor vacuum pipe disconnected and the engine running at normal idle speed, the ignition timing marks should be aligned to the same setting as that given for the static check above. It will facilitate observat-

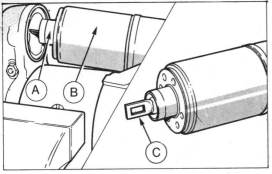

A. *Solenoid armature* C. *Actuating arm hook*
B. *Solenoid yoke*

Fig. D:27 Removing the solenoid assembly on
0.5 PS type starters

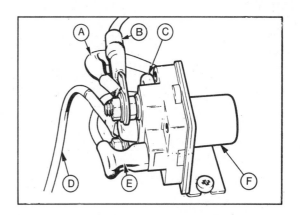

A. *Battery cable* C. *Ignition wire* E. *Ballast resistor wire*
B. *Loom cable* D. *Starter cable* F. *Solenoid*

Fig. D:28 Details of the solenoid in inertia type
starter motors

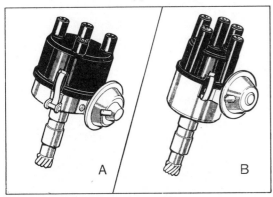

Fig. D:29 Distributor identification, Motorcraft
type (A) and Bosch type (B) with red cap

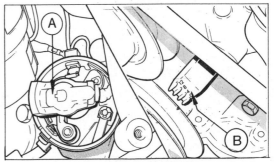

Fig. D:30 Setting up timing marks and distributor prior to removal

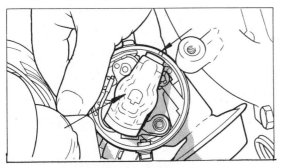

Fig. D:31 Mark rotor position on body flange
after removal

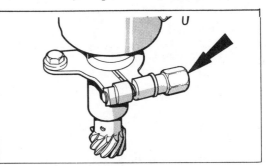

Fig. D:32 Details of distributor clamp plate
and bolt (arrowed)

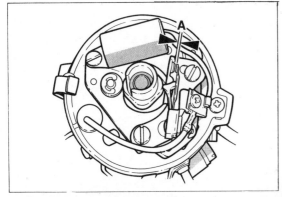

Fig. D:33 Check/adjust contact gap, contact
heel on peak of cam-Motorcraft type

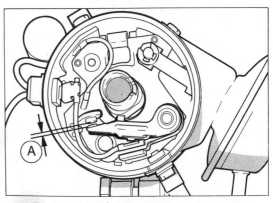

Fig. D:34 Check/adjust contact gap, contact
heel on peak of cam - Bosch type

ion of the timing mark if the notch on the crankshaft pulley and the appropriate mark on the timing scale are highlighted with chalk or white paint prior to carrying out the check.

If adjustment is required slacken the distributor clamp bolt and rotate the distributor body clockwise to advance the setting or anti-clockwise to retard it.

Technical Data

ALTERNATOR

Bosch G1-28A/K1-45A
Earth polarity . . . . Negative
Output at 13.5 v and 6000 rpm
    G1-28A . . . . 28 amps
    K1-45A . . . . 45 amps
Brush length (protrusion) . . . . .0.197 in (5 mm)
Regulating voltage @ 4000 rpm . . . . 13.7 - 14.5 v
Lucas 15ACR/17ACR/18ACR
Earth polarity . . . . Negative
Output at 13.5 v and 6000 rpm
    15ACR . . . . 28 amps
    17ACR . . . . 35 amps
    18ACR . . . . 45 amps
Brush length (protrusion) . . . . .0.197 in (5 mm)
Regulating voltage @ 4000 rpm . . . . 14.2 - 14.6 v
Femsa ALT-12N/ALS-12N
Earth polarity . . . . Negative
Output at 13.5 v and 6000 rpm
    ALT-12N . . . . 32 amps
    ALS-12N . . . . 45 amps
Brush length (protrusion) . . . . 0.28 in (7 mm)
Regulating voltage @ 4000 rpm . . . . 13.7 - 14.5 v
Drive belt tension . . . . 0.5 in (13 mm) total free movement

STARTER MOTOR

Lucas M35J Inertia
    Minimum brush length . . . . 0.32 in (8 mm)
    Brush spring tension. . . . . 6.16 lb.f (2.8 kg.f)
Bosch 0.5PS/0.7PS
    Minimum brush length . . . . .0.39 in (10 mm)
    Brush spring tension. . . . . 2.0 - 2.7 lb.f (0.9 - 1.3 kg.f)
Femsa MOA12-10
    Minimum brush length . . . . .0.47 in (12 mm)
    Brush spring tension. . . . . 1.54 - 3.08 lb.f (0.7 - 1.4 kg.f)

DISTRIBUTOR

Make. . . . . Motorcraft or Bosch
Contact breaker gap
    Motorcraft . . . . 0.025 in (0.64 mm)
    Bosch . . . . .0.016 - 0.020 in (0.4 - 0.5 mm)
Dwell angle . . . . .48-52°
Rotor rotation (viewed from above) . . . . .Anti-clockwise
Firing order . . . . 1 - 2 - 4 - 3
Location of number 1 cylinder. . . . . .At pulley end of engine

IGNITION TIMING

Static setting
    1297 cc 2V . . . . 6° BTDC
    All others. . . . . 10° BTDC

Cooling

DRAINING & REFILLING . . . . [1]

Draining

1. Set the heater controls to 'HOT'.
2. If the car has been run recently, take great care when removing the radiator cap since considerable pressure can build up in the cooling system causing steam and scalding hot water to be ejected on removal of the cap. To prevent accidental injury, muffle the cap with a heavy cloth and turn it slowly anti-clockwise to the first stop. This will allow any pressure to escape whilst the cap is still firmly held to the radiator filler neck. When satisfied that all pressure has been released, depress the cap and turn it further anti-clockwise until it is possible to lift it clear.
3. Place a suitable container below the bottom radiator hose to catch the coolant when it drains out. If the system contains an anti-freeze mixture which is to be reused, make sure the container is clean.
4. Release the clip securing the bottom radiator hose to the radiator and pull the hose free, allowing the coolant to drain away (Fig. E:2).
NOTE: If the cooling system is to be left drained for any period of time, it is advisable to leave a reminder on the vehicle to prevent it being run in this condition.

Flushing Cooling System

It is recommended that the cooling system be flushed every two years. This involves back-flushing both the radiator and cylinder block with a high pressure water hose. The procedure for this is as follows:
1. Remove the radiator as described later in this chapter.
2. Refit the radiator cap, turn the radiator upside down, position the hose in the bottom hose neck and back-flush the unit until all sludge and deposits have been removed. Flush any accumulations of dirt, leaves etc. from the outside fins of the radiator.
3. Remove the thermostat housing and thermostat as described later in this chapter.
4. Insert the high pressure hose in thermostat location and back-flush the cylinder block until all sludge and deposits have been removed (Fig. E:3).
5. Refit the thermostat and its housing, using a new gasket.

6. Refit the radiator and reconnect the radiator hoses.
7. Refill the cooling system.

Refilling

1. Make sure all hose connections are tight and that the heater controls are set to 'HOT'.
2. Refill the system with coolant, making sure it is a solution of water and anti-freeze or water and a corrosion inhibitor. On no account refill with plain water only. The anti-freeze or corrosion inhibitor should be diluted in accordance with the makers' instructions and poured into the system slowly through the radiator filler neck. Pouring it in slowly will allow any air into the system to escape. Top up the system to the base of the filler neck and replace the radiator cap.
3. Run the engine for a short while to allow the coolant to circulate and to ensure that all air is expelled from the system.
4. Stop the engine and recheck the level in the radiator. If necessary, top up to the base of the filler neck. Replace the radiator cap.
5. Check the level of coolant in the expansion tank. If below the 'MIN' mark. top up to the 'MAX' mark with water/anti-freeze or water/corrosion inhibitor solution.
NOTE: Take care when removing both radiator and expansion tank caps after running the engine, muffling them with a heavy rag and allowing the pressure in the system to escape before finally removing either cap.

Topping-Up

The coolant in the system should only be topped up with a water/anti-freeze or water/corrosion inhibitor solution to match that in the system. Topping up with plain water will further dilute the solution and will reduce the effects of either.

When checking the coolant level make sure the engine is cold.

Anti-freeze/Corrosion Inhibitor

Where protection against freezing is required, the system should be filled with a solution of 55% water and 45% anti-freeze and always topped up with a solution of similar strength. The quantity of anti-freeze to be added when filling the system, can be calculated from the cooling system capacity specified in the Technical Data section at the end of this chapter.

When refilling the system with a fresh water/anti-freeze mixture, it may be mixed in one of two ways: either by mixing the exact quantity of coolant for the system in a large container and then pouring it into the system, or by partially filling the system with plain water, pouring in the exact amount of anti-freeze and then finally topping up with water. In the latter case, the engine should be run for a while to thoroughly mix the water/anti-freeze solution. The anti-freeze contains a corrosion inhibitor so its strength should be maintained throughout the year. Its specific gravity should be checked periodically. It should be 1.065 for a 45% solution.

An 'all season' type anti-freeze should be used and changed every two years. If it is necessary to drain the system for any reason during that period, catch the water/anti-freeze solution in a clean container so that it may be reused.

Where the climate is warm enough to prevent the likelihood of the coolant in the system freezing, it is only necessary to add a corrosion inhibitor to the coolant. Unless otherwise stated on the container, the solution should be 97½% water to 2½% inhibitor meeting Ford Spec. SS-M97B-9100A. It should be maintained at this strength at all times.

FAN ASSEMBLY . . . . [2]

Removal

1. Disconnect the battery.
2. Disconnect the wiring from the fan motor and then from the securing clip on the fan shroud.
3. Release the four bolts securing the fan/shroud assembly to the radiator and lift it away.
4. Mark the fan blade unit and motor shaft with alignment marks and remove the retaining clip and washer, allowing the fan blade unit to be removed (Fig. E:4).
5. Release the three nuts and washers securing the fan motor to the shroud and lift away the motor.

Installation

1. Refit the motor to the shroud, making sure that the hole in the body (Bosch) or backplate (Femsa) is at the bottom.
2. Replace the fan blade unit, aligning the marks made previously and using a new retaining clip.
3. Refit the shroud assembly and reconnect the wiring.
4. Reconnect the battery and test the operation of the fan. On the 957 cc variants the fan operates continuously when the ignition is switched on. On the larger models the fan is operated by a thermal switch and is only switched on when the water temperature has risen to a certain level. For this reason it will be necessary to run the engine until warm to check the fan operation.
NOTE: Care should be taken when working in the vicinity of cars equipped with a thermal switch controlled fan motor. The ignition should be switched off since a rise in temperature could cause the fan to operate suddenly.

RADIATOR . . . . [3]

Removal

1. Disconnect the battery.
2. Drain the radiator as described previously.
3. Disconnect the radiator top hose and pull the expansion tank pipe from the radiator neck.
4. Disconnect the wiring from the fan motor and then from its retaining clip on the fan shroud.
5. Remove the two lower radiator retaining bolts from the front of the car and then the two upper radiator retaining bolts which are accessible from inside the engine compartment (Fig. E:5).
6. Lift out the radiator and fan shroud assembly (Fig. E:6). If required, remove the latter by releasing its four retaining bolts.

Installation

Installation is basically a reversal of the removal procedure, noting the following points:
1. Be sure to tighten all hose connections.
2. Refill the system with the required water/anti-freeze or water/corrosion inhibitor solution.
3. Reconnect the battery and run the engine to check for leaks. Top up the coolant level if necessary.

EXPANSION TANK . . . . [4]

Removal

1. Remove the radiator cap and pull off the expansion tank pipe from the radiator filler neck.
2. Remove the two screws from the top of the expansion tank and lift the tank upwards to release its retaining tongue from the body panel (Fig. E:7).

Installation

Installation is a reversal of the removal procedure, noting that the coolant level should be topped up as necessary and the engine run to check for any leaks.

WATER PUMP . . . . [5]

Removal

1. Disconnect the battery.
2. Drain the radiator as described previously.
3. Loosen the three pump pulley retaining bolts (Fig. E:8). This should be done whilst the drive belt is still attached as this will help prevent the pulley from turning whilst pressure is applied to the bolts. If difficulty is experienced, a second ring spanner or socket can be used to hold one bolt head whilst turning another. This will prevent the pulley turning. When two bolts have been loosened, a heavy screwdriver can be placed across them and used to hold the pulley whilst loosening the third bolt.
4. Loosen the three alternator mounting bolts followed

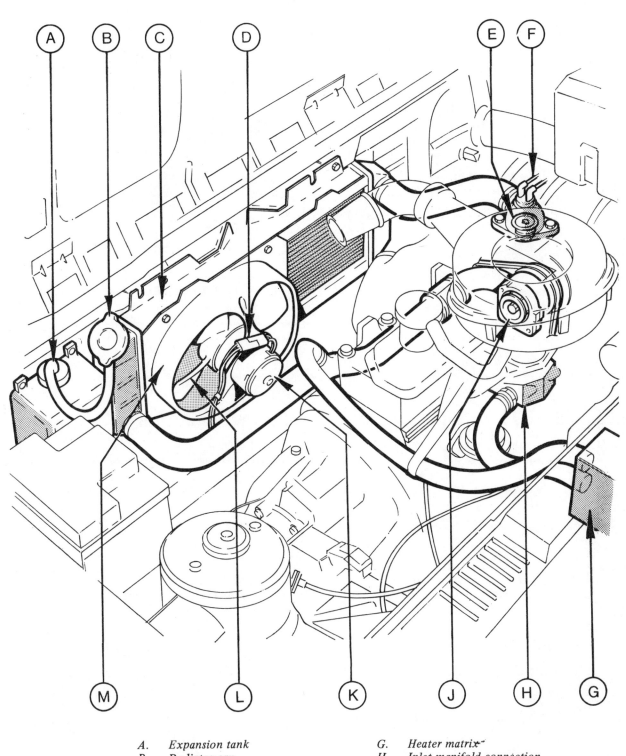

A.	Expansion tank	G.	Heater matrix
B.	Radiator cap	H.	Inlet manifold connection
C.	Radiator	J.	Water pump
D.	Loom connection	K.	Fan motor
E.	Thermostat	L.	Fan
F.	Thermal switch	M.	Radiator fan shroud

Fig. E:1 The Fiesta cooling and heater system components

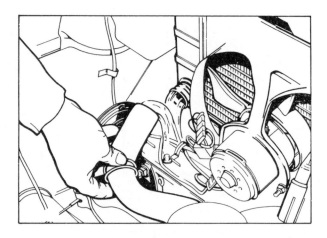

Fig. E:2 Remove the bottom radiator hose to drain or flush the system

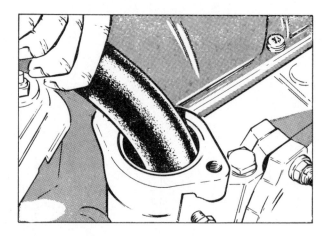

Fig. E:3 Insert a high pressure hose into thermostat housing to back flush engine block

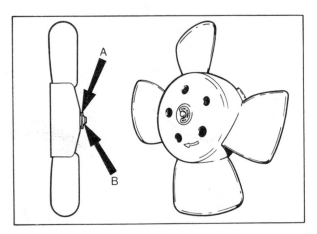

Fig. E:4 Details of the fan to motor attachment, washer (A) and retaining clip (B)

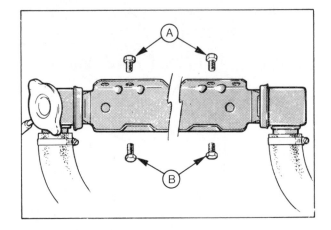

Fig. E:5 The radiator is attached by two upper bolts (A) and two lower bolts (B)

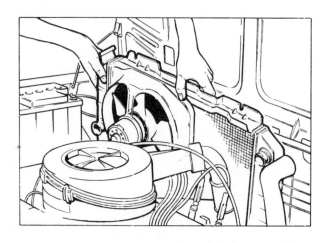

Fig. E:6 Removing the radiator complete with fan and motor from the car

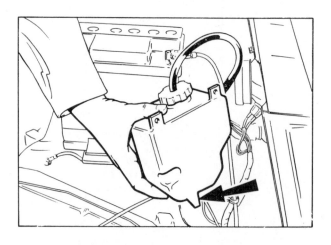

Fig. E:7 Details of the expansion bottle mounting, note locating tongue (arrowed)

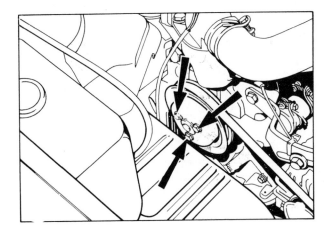

Fig. E:8 Undo the three bolts (arrowed) to detach water pump pulley

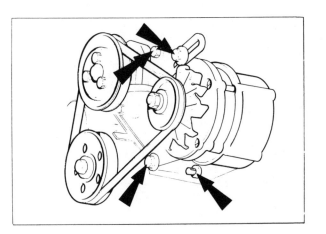

Fig. E:9 Slacken the alternator mounting bolts (arrowed) to remove drive belt

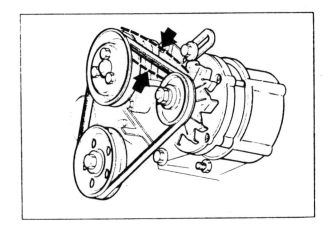

Fig. E:10 Adjust the belt to the correct tension, measuring at points arrowed

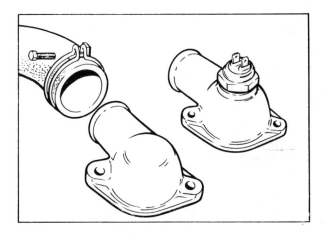

Fig. E:11 Details of the thermostat housing showing thermal switch - if fitted

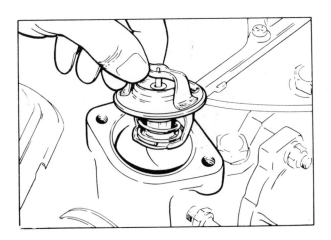

Fig. E:12 Note position of thermostat before removing it from the housing

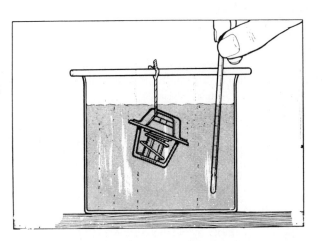

Fig. E:13 Method of testing thermostat operation in hot water

by the bolt securing the adjusting arm to the cylinder block. Swing the alternator towards the block sufficiently to be able to remove the drive belt (Fig. E:9).

5. Loosen the clip securing the radiator hose to the pump and remove the hose.
6. Remove the pump pulley retaining bolts and then lift away the pulley.
7. Finally, remove the three pump retaining bolts and lift away the pump.

Installation

1. Remove all traces of old gasket material from the cylinder block and pump mating surfaces.
2. Push the radiator hose on to the water pump, making sure the retaining clip is already over the hose, and using a new gasket refit the pump to the block.
3. Refit the pulley.
4. Refit the drive belt, adjusting the tension as described below.
5. Finally tighten the water pump pulley retaining bolts to the torque specified in 'Tightening Torques'.
6. Refit the radiator hose and tighten the retaining clips. Refill the cooling system, reconnect the battery and run the engine to check for leaks. Top up the system as necessary.

DRIVE BELT . . . . [6]

Adjustment

1. Slacken the alternator mounting and pivot bolts illustrated in Fig. E:10.
2. Swing the alternator away from the cylinder block to tighten the belt.
3. The belt should be tensioned so that a deflection of 0.5 in (13 mm) is achieved by applying normal fingertip pressure at the mid point of the belt run between the alternator and water pump (Fig. E:10).
4. Tighten the alternator mounting and pivot bolts. Make sure both ends of the adjusting link are tightened.

THERMOSTAT. . . . .[7]

Removal

1. Disconnect the battery and, if a fan motor thermal switch is fitted, remove the wiring from the switch in the thermostat housing (Fig. E:11).

2. Drain the radiator as described previously.
3. Loosen the clip holding the top radiator hose to the thermostat housing and pull the hose from the housing.
4. Remove the two bolts holding the thermostat housing to the cylinder block and lift the housing from the block. It may be necessary to tap round the joint with a mallet or rubber hammer to break the gasket seal.
5. Lift out the thermostat (Fig. E:12).

Thermostat Checking

1. Suspend the thermostat in a suitable container full of water so that it does not touch the sides or bottom (Fig. E:13).
2. Gradually heat the water, checking the temperature frequently with an accurate thermometer. The thermostat should begin to open between $82^{\circ}C$ ($180^{\circ}F$) and $92^{\circ}C$ ($198^{\circ}F$), and be fully open between $99^{\circ}C$ ($210^{\circ}F$) and $102^{\circ}C$ ($216^{\circ}F$).

If the thermostat does not open at the right time, refuses to open fully or does not open at all, replace it with a new unit.

Installation

1. Remove all traces of old gasket material from the block and thermostat housing mating faces.
2. Place the new thermostat in position and refit the housing, using a new gasket. Secure the two retaining bolts and refit the radiator hoses.
3. Refill the cooling system, reconnect the battery and run the engine to check for leaks. Top up the cooling system if necessary.

HOSES . . . . [8]

Checking

The cooling system hoses should be checked periodically - particularly at the beginning of winter - to ensure that they are in good condition and their clips are secure.

Examine each hose carefully for cracks, particularly on the bends, separation of the layers, swelling or excessive softness of the rubber. Also inspect them for damage, especially chafing due to contact with other components.

Replace any hoses which are suspect, making sure the hose spigots are clean. When fitting new hoses that are tight, a little lubrication in the form of soap or petroleum jelly will assist in fitting them over their spigots.

Technical Data

System capacity (inc. heater). . . . . 9.27 pt (5.27 litres)
Radiator cap rating . . . . 13 lb/in^2 (0.91 bar)
Thermostat
 Opening temperature . . . . 85-89°C (185-193°F)*
 Fully open temperature . . . . 99-102°C (210-216°F)*
 *± $3^{\circ}C$ (± $5^{\circ}F$) for used thermostats
Water pump belt tension. . . . . .0.5 in (13 mm) deflection at mid
point on longest run
Anti-freeze spec. gravity . . . . 1.065 for 45% concentration

COOLING
Trouble Shooter

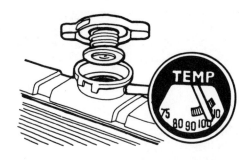

FAULT	CAUSE	CURE
Loss of coolant	1. Damaged radiator 2. Leak at heater connection or plug 3. Damaged cylinder head gasket 4. Cracked cylinder block. 5. Cracked cylinder head. 6. Loose cylinder head bolts	1. Repair or replace radiator. 2. Repair or replace. 3. Replace gasket. Check engine oil and refill as necessary. 4. Replace cylinder block. Check engine oil in crankcase for mixing with water. 5. Replace cylinder head. 6. Tighten cylinder head bolts.
Poor circulation	1. Restriction in system 2. Insufficient coolant 3. Inoperative water pump 4. Slack generator drive belt 5. Inoperative thermostat	1. Check hoses for crimping. Clear the system of rust and sludge. 2. Replenish. 3. Replace water pump. 4. Adjust drive belt 5. Replace thermostat.
Corrosion	1. Excessive impurity in water 2. Infrequent flushing and draining of system	1. Use soft, clean water. 2. Flush thoroughly at least twice a year.
Overheating	1. Inoperative thermostat 2. Radiator fin choked with mud, leaves etc. 3. Incorrect ignition and valve timing 4. Dirty oil and sludge in engine 5. Inoperative water pump 6. Slack generator drive belt 7. Restricted radiator 8. Inaccurate temperature gauge 9. Impurity in water 10. Faulty fan thermo switch	1. Replace thermostat. 2. Clean out air passage. 3. Tune engine. 4. Change engine oil and filter. 5. Replace (or check-electrical). 6. Adjust tension. 7. Flush radiator. 8. Replace temperature gauge. 9. Use soft, clean water. 10. Check/replace switch unit
Overcooling	1. Inoperative thermostat 2. Inaccurate temperature gauge	1. Replace thermostat. 2. Replace temperature gauge.

Fuel System

INTRODUCTION . . . . [1]

Two types of carburettor are used on the Fiesta, both the 957 cc and 1100 cc engines have a Motorcraft single venturi carburettor (IV) with a 'Sonic By-Pass' idling system.

1300 cc engines use a Weber twin venturi carburettor (2V) incorporating an electrically heated by-metal spring automatic choke.

To conform with the exhaust emission regulations in various countries, both types of carburettor are 'tamper-proofed' with a blanking plug over the mixture control screw which is factory set.

Carburettor running adjustment is therefore normally confined to a single throttle stop screw which is used to adjust the engine idle speed. See TUNE-UP.

FUEL PUMP . . . . [2]

Cleaning

1. Disconnect the battery.
2. Remove the retaining screw and lift off the pump cover, removing seal and filter from the pump (Fig. F:1).

3. Blow the cover and filter clean or wash them in clean petrol. Inspect the sealing ring and replace it if perished, worn or damaged in any way.
4. Reassemble the filter to the pump cover and then carefully fit the assembly to the pump, making sure the seal is not damaged in process.
5. Refit the securing screw.
6. Reconnect the battery and run the engine to check for fuel leaks.

Removal

1. Disconnect the battery.
2. Disconnect the fuel supply and delivery pipes from the pump, plugging the ends to prevent loss of fuel and ingress of dirt. If a crimped hose securing clip is fitted these should be cut off and replaced with normal screw type clips.

3. Remove the two pump mounting bolts and lift away the pump (Fig. F:2).

Installation

1. Make sure all traces of old gasket material are removed from the cylinder block and fuel pump mating faces.
2. Using a new gasket, refit the pump to the cylinder block securing it with the two bolts.
3. Reconnect the supply and delivery pipes.
4. Reconnect the battery and run the engine to check for correct operation and for any fuel leaks.

CARBURETTOR - MOTORCRAFT TYPE . . . [3]

Cleaning

The carburettor float chamber should be cleaned out periodically to remove any accumulations of sediment. The fuel pump filter and fuel pipes should also be cleaned out at this time.
1. Disconnect the battery.
2. Remove the air cleaner as described in the TUNE-UP chapter.
3. Making sure the exterior of the carburettor is clean, disconnect the float chamber vent tube and the fuel supply pipe from the carburettor, plugging the end of the latter (Fig. F:3).
4. Undo the seven screws and remove the upper body from the main body of the carburettor (Fig. F:4). Disconnect the choke link (arrowed) and move it clear of the carburettor.
NOTE: Once the upper body is removed, the accelerator pump discharge valve will be exposed in its bore in top face, and care should be taken when operating the throttle linkage, otherwise the ball valve and weight may be ejected and this would cause serious damage if the valve was allowed to enter the engine.
5. Withdraw the float arm pivot pin and remove the float and gasket (Fig. F:5). Extract the needle valve from its housing, unscrew the housing from the upper body and extract the gauze filter screen. Check the condition of the

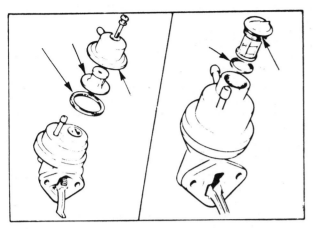

Fig. F:1 Details of the fuel pump filter arrangement depending on model fitted

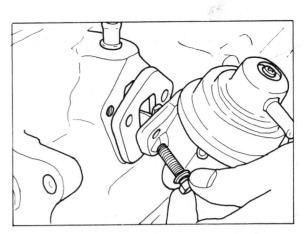

Fig. F·2 Undoing bolts to detach fuel pump from engine

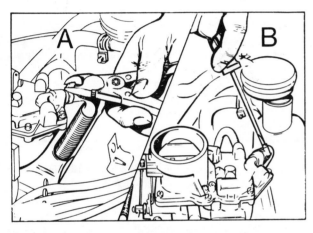

Fig. F:3 Cut off crimped type clamp (A) and replace with screw type (B) Motorcraft carb.

Fig. F:4 Removing upper body on Motorcraft carburettors, note choke link (arrowed)

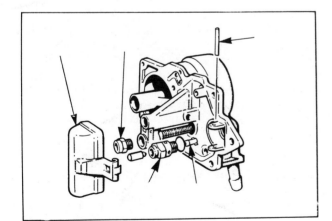

Fig. F:5 Details of the upper body jets, float and needle valve components

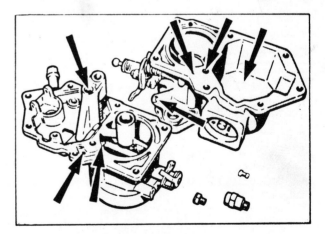

Fig. F:6 The main items to be cleaned with carburettor dismantled. Motorcraft type

needle valve and replace if necessary. Unscrew the main jet.

6. Using a tissue or piece of lint-free cloth, soak out any fuel in the float chamber and then clean out the chamber and jets with an airline (Fig. F:7). When doing this, position a finger over the accelerator pump weight location to ensure that the valve weight and ball are not blown out and lost. Also, make sure that full air pressure is not directed into the bleed location as this will result in damage to the pump diaphragm.

7. Wash the fuel float and gauze filter in clean petrol and flush all traces of sediment from the filter, using clean petrol.

8. Refit the main jet, gauze filter, needle valve housing and needle valve. Locate the gasket on the upper body and refit the float assembly and pivot pin. Check the float level setting as described later in this section.

9. Refit the carburettor top body, reconnecting the choke link, holding the choke mechanism in the fully closed position (Fig. F:8). (This will ensure that the choke cam does not go over centre when the carburettor upper body is fitted).

10. Reconnect the float chamber vent tube and the fuel supply pipe.

11. Refit the air cleaner assembly.

12. Reconnect the battery.

Checking/Adjusting Float Level

1. Remove the upper body of the carburettor as described previously, and detach the gasket from the upper body.

2. Hold the upper body in a vertical position with the float hanging down so that the needle valve is shut. Measure the distance between the upper body face and the base of float (Fig. F:9).

3. If necessary, adjust the level of the float to match the figure given in Technical Data by bending the tab resting against the needle valve.

4. Refit the carburettor upper body and gasket as described previously.

Carburettor - Removal (Fig. F:10)

1. Disconnect the battery.

2. Remove the air cleaner as described in the TUNE-UP chapter.

3. Disconnect the throttle inner cable from the carburettor lever.

4. Disconnect the choke inner and outer cables at the carburettor.

5. Disconnect the vacuum, vent and fuel feed pipes. Some vehicles may be fitted with a crimped clamp securing the fuel supply pipe. This should be cut free and replaced with a normal screw-type clamp (Fig. F:3).

6. Remove the two nuts and washers securing the carburettor and lift it away from the inlet manifold.

Installation

1. Make sure all traces of old gasket material are cleaned from the carburettor and inlet manifold mating surfaces.

2. Using a new gasket, refit the carburettor to the inlet manifold.

3. Reconnect the choke cable and adjust it as described under the appropriate heading in this chapter.

4. Reconnect the throttle link, vacuum, vent and fuel pipes, refit the air cleaner and reconnect the battery.

5. Start the engine and adjust the throttle stop screw to the correct idle speed with the engine at normal operating temperature. See Technical Data.

Choke Plate Pull Down Adjustment

This can be done with the carburettor on the engine, as follows:

1. Remove the air cleaner assembly as detailed in the TUNE-UP chapter.

2. Hold the choke mechanism in the fully closed position by rotating the cam on to its stop (Fig. F:11).

3. Open the choke plate against its spring tension and measure the gap between the lower edge of the choke plate and the side of the intake venturi (Fig. F:11) using the shank of a twist drill.

4. Adjust the gap, if necessary, by bending the tag (arrowed) in Fig. F:11.

5. Refit the air cleaner assembly.

Fast Idle Adjustment

1. Remove the air cleaner as detailed in the TUNE-UP chapter. Connect a RPM meter to the coil LT terminals.

2. Start the engine and run it up to normal operating temperature. With the engine idling, hold the choke plate in the fully open, vertical position with a screwdriver (Fig. F:12) and operate the choke control mechanism as far as it will go without altering the choke plate position. Note that this will be about 1/3 of choke control total travel, and as the choke control is pulled out, the engine speed should increase to the Fast Idle speed.

3. Note the fast idle speed on the RPM meter. If it is outside the figure specified in the Technical Data at the end of this chapter, then it can be adjusted by bending the tag (arrowed 'A') in Fig. F:12.

4. Push the choke control fully in and recheck the basic idle speed, then pull the choke control out as detailed previously and recheck the fast idle speed.

5. Stop engine and disconnect RPM meter, then replace air cleaner assembly.

CARBURETTOR - WEBER TYPE . . . . [4]

Cleaning

The carburettor float chamber should be cleaned out periodically to remove any accumulations of sediment. The fuel pump filter and fuel pipes should also be cleaned out at this time.

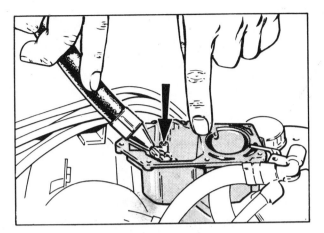

Fig. F:7 Holding ball valve in position when using an air line

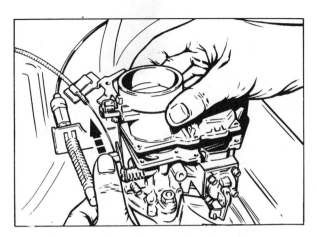

Fig. F:8 Hold choke lever fully closed (arrowed) when refitting upper body

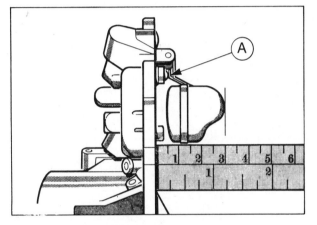

Fig. F:9 Measuring float height (gasket removed) adjust by bending tag (A)

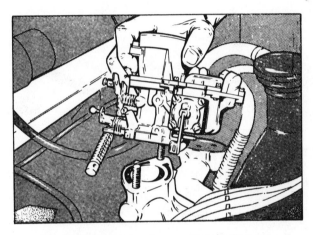

Fig. F:10 Removing the complete carburettor assembly from the inlet manifold

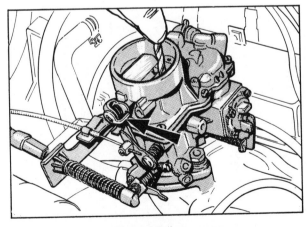

Fig. F:11 Checking/adjusting choke plate pull down. Adjusting tag arrowed

Fig. F:12 Setting the carburettor fast idle, adjust by bending tag (A)

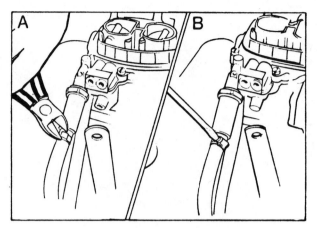

Fig. F:13 Cut off crimped type clamp (A) and
replace with screw type (B) Weber carb.

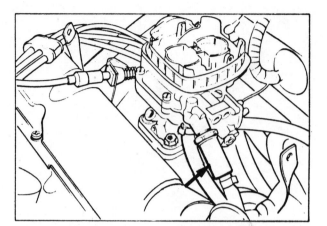

Fig. F:14 The location of the fuel intake filter -
Weber carburettor

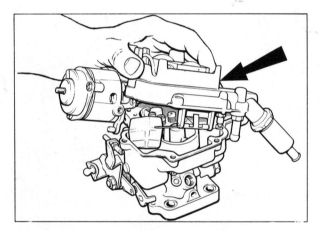

Fig. F:15 Hold choke lever (arrowed) when removing upper body. Weber carb.

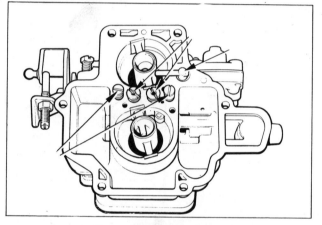

Fig. F:16 The location of the jets to be removed
for cleaning

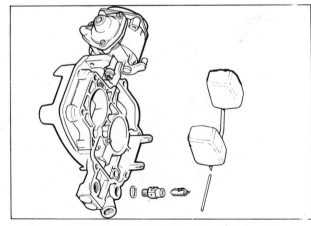

Fig. F:17 Details of the upper body float and
needle valve components

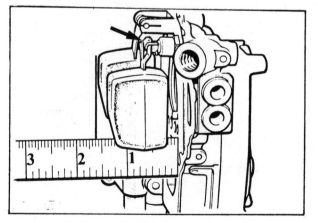

Fig. F:18 Measuring the float height (gasket
fitted) on Weber carburettors

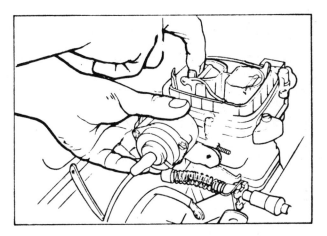

Fig. F:19 Setting the linkage to hold it in the fast idle position - Weber carb.

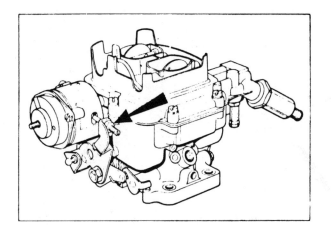

Fig. F:20 The location of the fast idle adjustment screw - Weber carb.

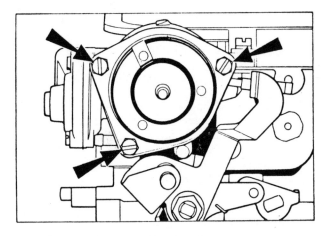

Fig. F:21 Undo and remove screws arrowed to dismantle auto choke housing components

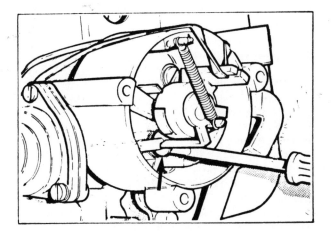

Fig. F:22 Insert thin screwdriver to push vacuum diaphragm rod fully in

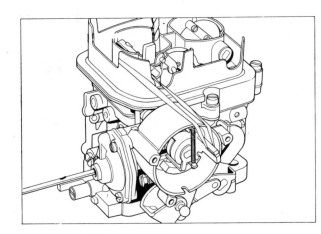

Fig. F:23 Checking/adjusting maximum vacuum choke plate pull down

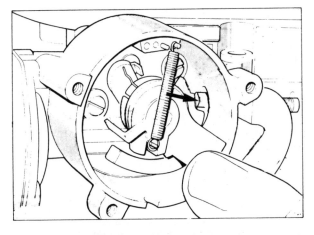

Fig. F:24 Setting the choke mechanism at phase point, with screw on cam centre

1. Disconnect the battery, then remove the air cleaner assembly as detailed in the TUNE-UP chapter.
2. Clean the outside of the carburettor, then detach the fuel supply and return pipes at the carburettor. Note that where the pipe is secured by a crimped type clamp, this should be cut off (Fig. F:13) and replaced with a screw type clamp.
3. Unscrew the fuel supply filter from the side of the carburettor upper body (Fig. F:14) and disconnect the wire to the electric auto-choke.
4. Undo and remove the six screws attaching the carburettor upper body, then, holding the fast idle operating lever clear of the choke housing (arrowed, Fig. F:15), lift the upper body off the main carburettor body.
5. Using a tissue or piece of lint-free cloth, soak out any fuel remaining in the float chamber and blow any sediment from the float chamber with an air line.
6. Note the positions of all jets before removing them. Clean out the air and fuel passages using the air line (Fig. F:16).
7. Clean the jets by blowing through them. Do not use fine wire to clear any obstructions as this will damage the finely calibrated jet drilling.
8. Clean any dirt or sediment from the fuel intake filter and replace it if it is damaged.
9. Refit all jets into their original positions ensuring that the main and idling jets are fitted the correct way round. See Technical Data. Note that the primary jets are located on the left-hand side of the carburettor.
10. Withdraw the pivot pin and detach the float from the upper body (Fig. F:17).
11. Unscrew the float needle valve assembly and check to see if it is sealing properly by blowing through it with the valve in the closed position. If the valve shows signs of leaking - indicated by a 'hiss' of escaping air, check the condition of the valve needle. If there is a distinct wear ridge on the needle end, then it is worn and a new needle valve assembly is needed.
12. Refit the needle valve and float, then check the float height as detailed later in this section.
13. Check that the upper body gasket is in good condition, then refit the upper body in the reverse order of removal. Tighten the screws evenly.
14. Reconnect the fuel pipes and the choke wire, the fuel intake filter; the air cleaner assembly, then reconnect battery. Start the engine and check the carburettor for leaks.

Checking/Adjusting Float Level

1. Disconnect the battery, remove the air cleaner assembly and the carburettor upper body as described previously.
2. Hold the upper body in the vertical position with the float hanging and gasket fitted as shown in Fig. F:18.
3. Measure the distance between the gasket and base of the float. It should be to the distance specified in Technical Data.
4. To adjust the float height, bend the tag (arrowed) in Fig. F:18 until the adjustment is correct.
5. Refit the upper body and ancilliaries in the reverse order of removal.

Fast Idle Adjustment

1. Remove the air cleaner assembly from the carburettor as detailed in the TUNE-UP chapter.
2. Connect a RPM meter to the coil LT terminals, start the engine and run it up to normal operating temperature, then stop the engine.
3. Hold the throttle linkage in the half open position with one hand, close the choke plates fully with the other hand, then release the throttle linkage followed by the choke plates (Fig. F:19).
   The throttle mechanism will now hold the choke assembly in the fast idle position.
NOTE: When the choke plates are released, they should return to the vertical position, if not, then either the engine has not reached normal operating temperature or the auto choke is faulty.
4. Without touching the accelerator pedal or the throttle linkage, start the engine and note the engine speed. If the fast idle speed is not within the limits specified in the Technical Data, then it can be adjusted by slackening the locknut and screwing the fast idle adjuster in or out to obtain the correct speed as shown in Fig. F:20.

Adjusting Automatic Choke

1. Remove the air cleaner assembly as detailed in the TUNE-UP chapter.
2. Disconnect the wire at the auto choke housing, then undo the three screws securing the outer housing (Fig. F:21). Detach the outer housing complete with bi-metal spring assembly and internal heat shield.
3. Check and adjust the maximum vacuum choke plate pull down by attaching an elastic band to the choke plate lever and positioning it so that it holds the choke plates fully closed. Check that the choke plates are fully closed by opening the throttle fully, then releasing it.
4. Using a clean thin screwdriver, push the vacuum diaphragm operating rod up to its fully open stop, and hold it in this position (Fig. F:22).
5. Using a twist drill shank inserted between the lower part of the primary choke plate and the venturi, measure the clearance - see Fig. F:23.
6. If adjustment is needed, remove the plug from the end of the vacuum unit insert a thin screwdriver and turn the adjusting screw in the housing until the specified clearance figure is obtained (Fig. F:23). Replace the vacuum unit plug and remove the elastic band.
7. Check and adjust the choke phasing as follows; hold the throttle partly open and position the fast idle cam so that the adjusting screw locates on the cam centre step (Fig. F:24).
8. Measure the clearance between the lower part of the primary choke plate and the venturi, using a twist drill shank. If the clearance is outside the limit specified in the Technical Data, then it can be adjusted by bending the tag (arrowed) in Fig. F:25.
9. Refit the housing internal heat shield, checking that the peg on the cover locates in the slot cast into the housing Fig. F:26.
10. Reconnect the bi-metal spring to the choke lever,

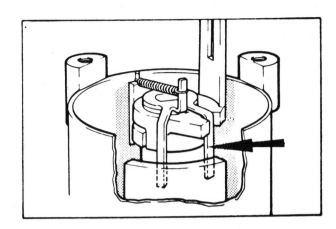

Fig. F:25 Adjusting choke phasing by bending tag arrowed

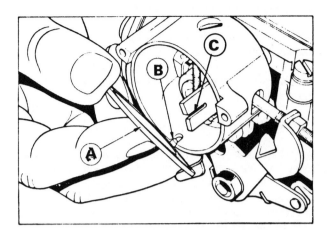

Fig. F:26 Refitting internal heat shield, make sure peg (B) engages with slot (C)

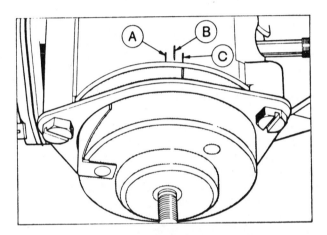

Fig. F:27 Adjusting choke outer housing with alignment marks

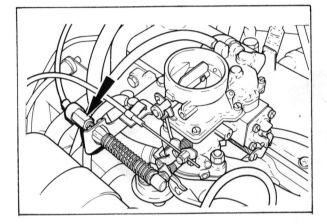

Fig. F:28 Turn adjuster sleeve (arrowed) to adjust throttle cable

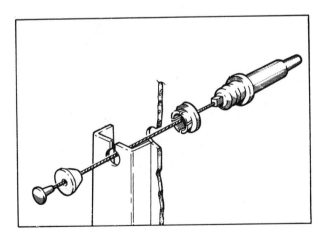

Fig. F:29 Details of the throttle cable attachment at the accelerator pedal lever

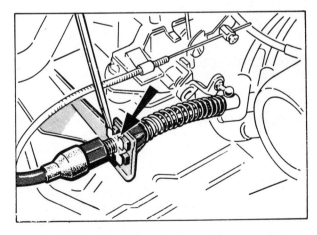

Fig. F:30 Disconnecting the throttle outer cable from the support bracket

then position the outer housing and loosely fit the free retaining screws.

11. Turn the outer housing until the mark is aligned with the appropriate marks on the spring housing - see Fig. F: 27, then tighten the housing securing screws.

12. Reconnect the wire to the choke housing and refit the air cleaner.

Carburettor - Removal

1. Disconnect the battery and remove the air cleaner assembly as detailed in the TUNE-UP chapter. Disconnect he throttle cable at the carburettor linkage.

2. Disconnect the wires at the auto choke housing and the anti-run on valve on the side of the carburettor. Also pull off the distributor vacuum advance pipe.

3. Detach the fuel supply and return pipes from the carburettor. Note that where a pipe is secured by a crimped type clamp, this should be cut off (Fig. F:13) and replaced by a screw type clamp.

4. Undo the four nuts and detach the carburettor from the manifold, complete with gasket.

Installation

Installation is a reversal of the removal procedure, making sure that the manifold gasket is in good condition. If necessary, adjust the engine idling speed afterwards as detailed previously.

THROTTLE CABLE....................[5]

Adjustment

1. Remove the air cleaner as detailed in the TUNE-UP chapter.

2. Depress the accelerator pedal as far as it will go and wedge it in this position with a wood block or something similar.

3. Using a spanner on the outer cable adjuster sleeve (Fig. F:28), turn the sleeve back until the carburettor linkage has just reached the fully open position.

4. Release the accelerator pedal and then depress it fully again to check that a fully open throttle is achieved. If necessary, readjust the setting.

5. Refit the air cleaner assembly in the reverse order of removal.

Cable Replacement

1. From inside the car, remove the fascia lower insulator panel.

2. Disconnect the inner cable from the accelerator pedal by first pulling the cable securing grommet from the pedal shaft and then disconnecting it through the slot in the shaft (Fig. F:29).

3. Disconnect the outer cable from the bulkhead. To do this, the cable securing grommet has to be punched out from inside the car. This will shatter the grommet and it cannot be refitted or replaced.

4. Remove the air cleaner as detailed in the TUNE-UP chapter.

5. Disconnect the inner cable from the carburettor throttle lever using a screwdriver to prise it off.

6. Detach the outer cable from the bracket (Fig. F:30) using a screwdriver or large pair of pliers to depress the clip retaining lugs and then twist out the cable and withdraw it from the car.

7. Feed the new cable assembly through the bulkhead hole and reconnect the inner cable to the accelerator pedal shaft.

8. To clip the outer cable grommet into the bulkhead, first pull the outer cable back to expose the inner cable. Make up a simple tool as shown in Fig. F:31 using a length of 0.5 in (13 mm) dia. steel tube with a slot cut on one side and bent at an angle. Insert the tool into the bulkhead, feeding the inner cable into the slot, then locate the outer cable grommet in position and tap it home with a hammer and tube tool.

9. Slide the outer cable into the grommet, then reconnect the other end to the support bracket and carburettor linkage.

10. Refit the air cleaner assembly and the fascia lower insulator panel in the reverse order of removal.

11. Adjust the throttle cable as detailed in the previous section.

Choke Cable - Adjustment

1. Remove the air cleaner assembly as detailed in the TUNE-UP chapter.

2. Loosen the choke inner cable securing screw at the carburettor (Fig. F:32).

3. From inside the car, pull the choke control knob out from the fascia approximately 0.25 in (6 mm).

4. Making sure that the choke plate is fully open, remove any slack from the inner cable without disturbing the choke control setting and then tighten the clamp screw.

5. Push the choke control fully home and then check its operation.

6. Refit the air cleaner in the reverse order of removal.

Choke Cable Replacement

1. Remove the air cleaner as described in the TUNE-UP chapter.

2. Slacken the inner and outer cable clamp screws at the carburettor and remove the cable from the carburettor (Fig. F:32).

3. Remove the outer cable bulkhead grommet.

4. From inside the car remove the three screws attaching the steering column lower shroud in place and remove the shroud (Fig. F:33).

5. Remove the bolt securing the cable to the steering column (Fig. F:34).

6. Attach a drawcord to the engine end of the cable then pull the cable through the bulkhead into the car to remove it.

7. Detach the cable from the drawcord, and attach it to the end of the new cable to facilitate replacement.

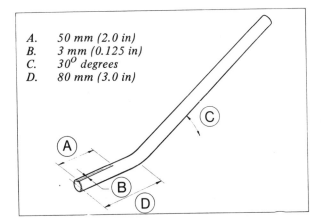

A.   50 mm (2.0 in)
B.   3 mm (0.125 in)
C.   30° degrees
D.   80 mm (3.0 in)

Fig. F:31 Details of the bulkhead grommet replacing tool

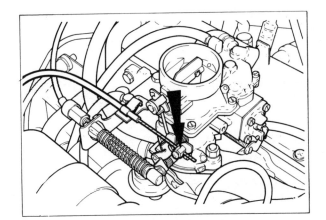

Fig. F:32 Undo clamp screw (arrowed) to adjust/ replace choke cable

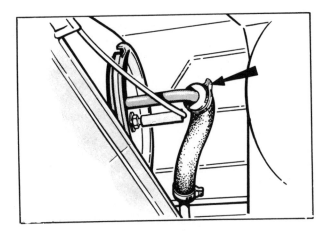

Fig. F:33 Detach steering column lower shroud to expose choke cable upper bracket

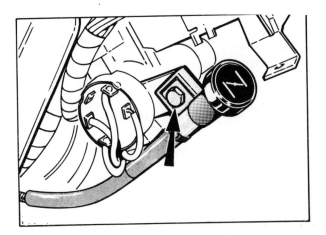

Fig. F:34 Undo bolt (arrowed) to release upper end of choke cable

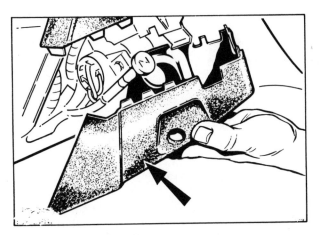

Fig. F:35 The fuel pipe and wiring connections at the sender unit

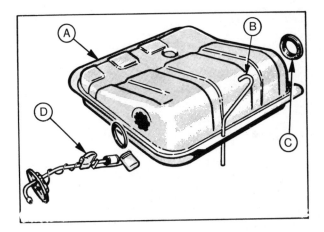

Fig. F:36 Details of the fuel tank and ancilliary components

8. Refit the bulkhead cable grommet and pull the cable into position until the PVC protection sleeve abuts the grommet. Remove the drawcord.

9. Reconnect the cable to the steering column and refit the column lower shroud.

10. Reconnect the cable at the carburettor end and adjust it as described previously.

11. Refit the air cleaner assembly in the reverse order of removal.

FUEL TANK.........................[6]

Removal (Figs. F:35 and F:36)

1. Disconnect the battery.
2. Syphon any fuel in the tank into a closed container.
3. Jack up the rear of the car, chocking the front wheels and fitting axle stands. On no account work beneath the car unless it is securely supported. Make sure the work area is clean.

4. Disconnect the fuel supply pipe from the tank sender unit. If a crimped pipe clip is fitted it should be cut off and replaced with a screw type clip.

5. Disconnect the tank sender unit wiring. To remove the sender unit, refer to GENERAL ELECTRICS chapter.

6. Remove the four bolts holding the tank in place and remove the tank leaving the fuel filler pipe in position.

Installation

Installation is basically a reversal of the removal procedure, noting that the exterior of the filler pipe should be lubricated with clean engine oil and the tank positioned to ensure that the pipe locates fully in the tank. Also make sure the vent pipe is not kinked or trapped under the tank.

Technical Data

CARBURETTOR (MOTORCRAFT)

	957 cc HC	957 cc LC	1117 cc HC
Code number	77BF 9510 KBA/KGA	77BF 9510 KEA/KJA	77BF 9510 KAA/KHA
Throttle barrel dia.	32 mm	32 mm	32 mm
Venturi dia.	23 mm	23 mm	24 mm
Main Jet	110	112	122
Float level setting	1.14 in (29 mm)	1.14 in (29 mm)	1.22 in (31 mm)
Idle speed (all models)			800±50 rpm
Fast idle			
957 cc			1100±100 rpm
1117 cc			1500±100 rpm
Mixture % CO			1.25±0.5

CARBURETTOR - WEBER

1300 cc only
Code number	781F 9510 AB
Throttle barrel dia	32/32 mm
Venturi dia	22/22 mm
Main jet	107/105
Air jet	230/165
Emulsion tube	F22/F30
Idle jet	50/55
Float level setting	1.42 in (36 mm)
Idle speed	800±25 rpm
Fast idle speed	2800 (at high cam)
Mixture % CO	1.5±0.25

FUEL TANK
Capacity .... 7.5 gal (34 litres)

FUEL PUMP
Delivery pressure .... 3.22-5.1 lbf/in^2 (0.22-0.35 bar)

FUEL
Trouble Shooter

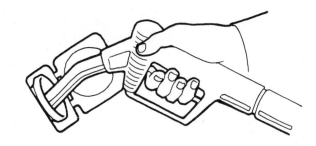

FAULT	CAUSE	CURE
Flooding	1. Improper seating or damaged float needle valve or seat 2. Incorrect float level 3. Fuel pump has excessive pressure	1. Check and replace parts as necessary. 2. Adjust float level. 3. Check fuel pump.
Excessive fuel consumption	1. Engine out of tune 2. Float level too high 3. Loose plug or jet 4. Defective gasket 5. Fuel leaks at pipes or connections 6. Choke valve operates improperly 7. Obstructed air bleed	1. Tune engine. 2. Adjust float level. 3. Tighten plug or jet. 4. Replace gaskets. 5. Trace leak and rectify. 6. Check choke valve. 7. Check and clear.
Stalling	1. Main jet obstructed 2. Incorrect throttle opening 3. Slow-running adjustment incorrect 4. Slow-running fuel jet blocked 5. Incorrect float level	1. Clean main jet. 2. Adjust throttle. 3. Adjust slow-running. 4. Clean jet. 5. Adjust float level.
Poor acceleration	1. Defective accelerator pump (if fitted) 2. Float level too low 3. Incorrect throttle opening 4. Defective accelerator linkage 5. Blocked pump jet	1. Overhaul pump. 2. Adjust float level. 3. Adjust throttle. 4. Adjust accelerator linkage. 5. Clean pump jet.
Spitting	1. Lean mixture 2. Dirty carburettor 3. Clogged fuel pipes 4. Manifold draws secondary air	1. Clean and adjust carburettor. 2. Clean carburettor. 3. Clean or replace pipes. 4. Tighten or replace gasket.
Insufficient fuel supply	1. Clogged carburettor 2. Clogged fuel pipe 3. Dirty fuel 4. Air in fuel system 5. Defective fuel pump 6. Clogged fuel filter	1. Dismantle and clean carburettor. 2. Clean fuel pipe. 3. Clean fuel tank. 4. Check connections and tighten. 5. Repair or replace fuel pump. 6. Clean or replace filter.
Loss of fuel delivery	1. Pump faulty 2. Pump body screws loose 3. Diaphragm cracked 4. Loose fuel pipe connections 5. Defective valves 6. Cracked fuel pipes	1. Replace pump. 2. Tighten body screws. 3. Overhaul fuel pump. 4. Tighten fuel pipe connections. 5. Replace valves. 6. Replace fuel pipes.
Noisy pump	1. Loose pump mounting 2. Worn or defective rocker arm 3. Broken rocker arm spring	1. Tighten mounting bolts. 2. Replace pump 3. Replace spring.

Clutch & Gearbox

CLUTCH CABLE . . . . [1]

Replacement

1. In the engine compartment, take hold of the clutch inner cable between the support bracket and clutch release lever. Push it forwards so that the ball on the end of the cable is clear of the release lever and then slide the cable through the slot in the lever to detach it (Fig. G:2).
2. Inside the car remove the left-hand lower fascia insulating panel by bending the retaining tabs upwards and releasing the retaining screws (Fig. G:3).
3. Pull the clutch pedal to the rear and rotate the toothed clutch cable retaining segment forwards in order to release the cable. Allow the toothed segment to swivel backwards as shown in Fig. G:4 and pull the cable into the engine compartment through the recess between the pedal and automatic cable adjusting device to remove it.
4. Push the new cable through the bulkhead into the passenger compartment and swivel the toothed segment back in order to hook the cable end to it (Fig. G:5).
5. In the engine compartment push the outer cable into the support bracket and hook the inner cable to the clutch release lever.
6. Operate the cable two or three times to settle the cable and operate the automatic adjusting device.
7. Refit the fascia insulating panel.

CLUTCH ASSEMBLY. . . . . [2]

Removal (Fig. G:1)

1. Remove the transmission assembly as described later in this chapter.
2. Release the six clutch retaining bolts working diagonally and releasing them evenly (Fig. G:6).
3. Holding the pressure plate cover with one hand, remove the bolts and then withdraw the pressure plate and clutch disc assembly from the flywheel.

Clutch Disc Inspection

Inspect the friction linings on the disc for wear, burning or contamination by oil or grease. The disc hub should be a free sliding fit on the gearbox input shaft splines without excessive side-play. If the linings are worn down to or near the rivet heads, or if any other of the above conditions are apparent, the disc must be replaced.

If oil or grease is present on the friction faces, the source must be determined and the fault rectified before fitting a new disc. This may be due to a defective gearbox input shaft oil seal or crankshaft rear oil seal.

Pressure Plate Inspection

Inspect the diaphragm fingers for any deep scoring. Inspect the contact surface of the pressure plate for cracks, signs of burning and wear. Place a flat edge across the surface of the pressure plate and check for any distortion. If necessary, replace the plate.

Flywheel Inspection

Inspect the friction surface of the flywheel - blueing or small cracks are of no particular importance, but if any deep scratches, scores, cracks or heat marks are present, the flywheel should be machined down, or preferably replaced.

Clutch Release Lever and Bearing

Both clutch release lever and bearing can be removed after the transmission has been removed. Release the bolt securing the bearing assembly to the lever shaft (Fig. G:7). Slide the shaft out of the gearbox and then remove the bearing. If the bearing shows signs of wear, damage or looseness, replace it.

Clutch Replacement

1. Make sure the friction surfaces of the flywheel and pressure plate are perfectly clean and free from oil or grease.
2. Place the clutch disc on the flywheel, the flat side of the disc facing the flywheel.
3. Align the disc with a centralising tool (mandrel) and refit the clutch pressure plate (Fig. G:8).
4. Tighten the pressure plate bolts evenly to the correct torque, then remove the centralising tool.

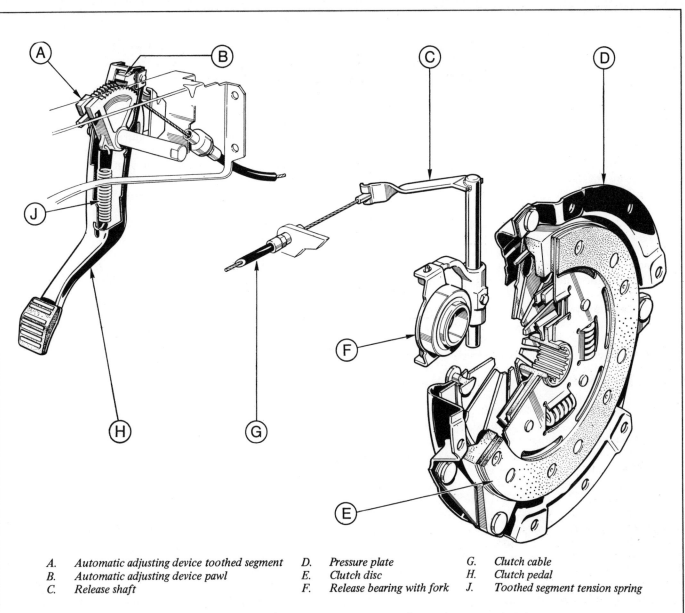

A. Automatic adjusting device toothed segment
B. Automatic adjusting device pawl
C. Release shaft
D. Pressure plate
E. Clutch disc
F. Release bearing with fork
G. Clutch cable
H. Clutch pedal
J. Toothed segment tension spring

Fig. G:1 An exploded view of the clutch and operating system components

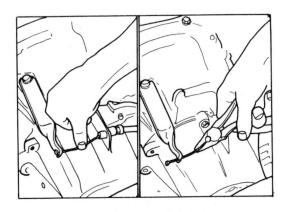

Fig. G:2 Method of detaching clutch operating cable from release arm

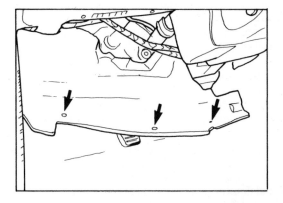

Fig. G:3 Removing the fascia left-hand lower insulating panel

5. Refit the transmission as detailed in the following section.

TRANSMISSION ....[3]

Removal

1. Disconnect the battery.
2. Engage fourth gear and leave the gear lever in that position.
3. Attach an engine hoist, or support bar, (Fig. G:9) to the engine to take its weight.
4. Unscrew the knurled speedometer driven gear retainer and pull the cable clear of the gearbox.
5. Disconnect the clutch cable at the gearbox as described previously.
6. Unscrew the four upper clutch housing flange bolts (Fig. G:10).
7. Jack up the vehicle and support it on stands. On no account work beneath the car unless it is securely supported.
8. Undo the clamping screw and pull the shift rod from the selector shaft gear (Fig. G:11). Unhook the spring between shift rod and selector rail.
9. Remove the shift mechanism stabiliser from the transmission by unscrewing the lock nuts on the stud and unscrewing the stud with an Allen key, leaving it in the engine/transmission support (Fig. G:12).
10. Using a suitable balljoint separator, disconnect the track rod ends from the steering arms (Fig. G:13).
11. Remove the left hand lower suspension arm from the body by undoing the single retaining nut and bolt and disconnecting the ball joint from the spindle carrier by releasing the retaining screw and nut (Fig. G:14).
12. Place a suitable container beneath the transmission to catch any oil that may spill out and disconnect the nearside drive shaft and CV joint from the transmission. Do this by inserting a large screwdriver blade between the transmission housing and CV joint. Strike the screwdriver handle with the ball of the hand, levering the axle shaft out at the same time (Fig. G:15).
13. Suspend the axle shaft from the floor pan to avoid overloading the CV joints (Fig. G:16) and secure the drive pinions of the differential gear from displacement with a plastic cap or suitable plug (Fig. G:17).
14. Remove the offside lower suspension arm in a similar manner to the nearside one.
15. On 957 and 1117 cc models, knock out the offside driveshaft from the transmission (Fig. G:18) and suspend it from the floorpan to prevent straining the CV joint. 1300 models only, undo the six socket headed bolts securing the CV joint to the intermediate shaft and support the shaft to prevent straining the outer CV joint.
16. Undo the two socket headed bolts securing the intermediate shaft bearing housing to the support bracket. Detach the housing from the bracket and withdraw the intermediate shaft from the transmission.
17. Disconnect the cable from the starter motor, release the retaining bolts and remove the starter.
18. Unscrew the lower transmission flange bolts (Fig. G: 19) and the three bolts from the engine mounting and withdraw transmission from under the car.

Installation

1. Before refitting the transmission make sure the splines of the driveshaft and differential gear are lightly greased and that the engine adaptor plate is correctly positioned on the hollow engine guide dowels.
2. Fit the transmission, installing the two flange bolts shown in Fig. G:19. Tighten these lightly by hand.
3. Make sure the holes in the engine adaptor plate coincide with those in the engine mounting and temporarily secure them in place with two drifts (Fig. G:20).
4. Use three NEW self-locking bolts to attach the engine adaptor plate to the engine mounting. Lower the engine and tighten these three bolts and the two flange bolts previously mentioned to the specified torque. It is essential that new bolts are used in the engine mounting and it is very important that the tightening torque figure is adhered to. Overtightening of these bolts could well result in damage to the transmission housing since it is of light metal construction.
5. Refit the starter motor and reconnect the cable.
6. Replace the offside drive shaft making sure a new snap ring is fitted to the CV joint. Use a heavy screwdriver or similar drift placed against the joint weld to drive the joint home. CV joints without a weld should have the rubber gaiter removed and be driven home with a plastic headed hammer acting against the joint front edge. It is essential that the joint snap ring engages with the differential assembly (Fig. G:21). On 1300 cc models, refit the intermediate shaft support bracket and adjust it as detailed in the FRONT SUSPENSION/STEERING chapter.
7. Insert the right hand lower suspension arm ball joint into the spindle carrier and screw in the clamping bolt. Fit the other end of the arm to the body with its retaining bolt and tighten the bolts to the specified torque figure.
8. Repeat the above operations for the left-hand axle shaft, CV joint and lower suspension arm.
9. Refit the stabiliser gear to the transmission by turning the Allen screw as far as the stop in the gearbox housing and locking it with a nut on the rubber coupling of the stabiliser. Bring the inner nut on the stud into contact with the mounting (Fig. G:22) and then tighten the outer nut to the specified torque (Fig. G:23).
10. Making sure that the gearshift shaft is still in the top gear position, slide the selector rod on to the shaft.
11. Pull the selector rod and gear lever downwards until the holes in the end of the gear lever and selector housing are aligned. Lock them in this position with a 0.16 in (4 mm) diameter pin.
12. The next stage requires the fabrication of a wooden block to the shape and dimensions shown in Fig. G:24. Pull the selector rod down and to the right (viewed from the driver's seat) and wedge the spacer between the rod and floorpan as shown in Fig. G:25.
13. Using a suitable mandrel, turn the shaft clockwise to its stop. Push the shaft into the transmission case, hold it there and lock the selector rod clamp bolt. Remove the wooden spacer mandrel and pin.

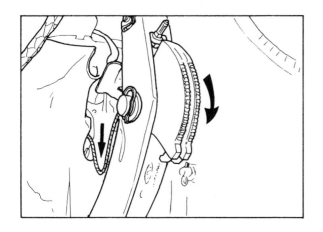

Fig. G:4 Detaching clutch cable, pull toothed
segment forwards to release cable

Fig. G:5 Swivel toothed segment back and connect new cable end to it

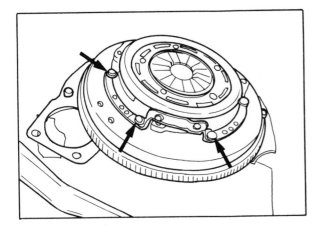

Fig. G:6 Undo the clutch pressure plate bolts
(arrowed) evenly

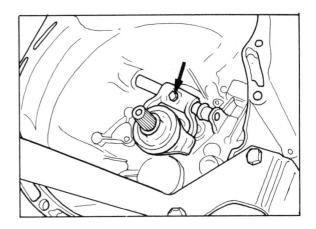

Fig. G:7 Undo bolt (arrowed) and withdraw
shaft to detach release bearing assembly

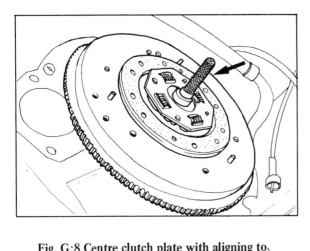

Fig. G:8 Centre clutch plate with aligning to
then refit pressure plate

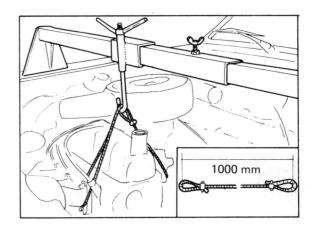

Fig. G:9 Details of engine support bar and wire/
rope sling arrangement

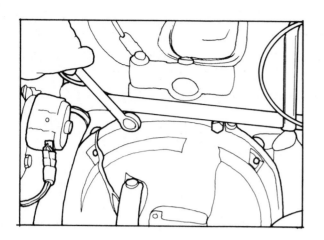

Fig. G:10 Undoing the four clutch housing upper attachment bolts

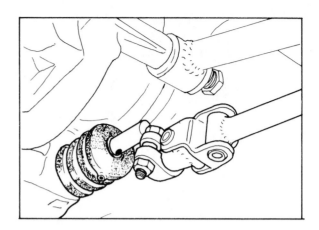

Fig. G:11 Detaching the gear shift rod from the gearbox selector shaft

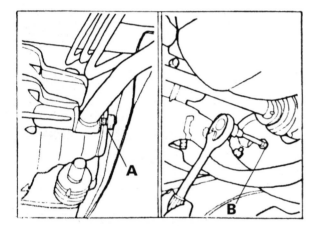

Fig. G:12 Reposition inner nuts (A) then undo Allen screw (B)

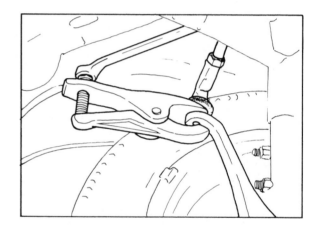

Fig. G:13 Using a ball joints taper breaking tool to detach track rod ends

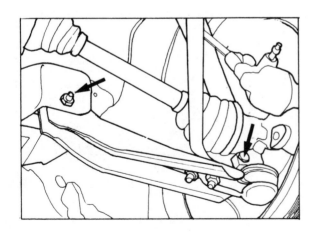

Fig. G:14 Undo bolts (arrowed) to detach track control arm

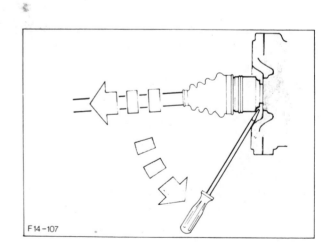

F 14 –107

Fig. G:15 Using a screwdriver to lever out the driveshafts from transmission

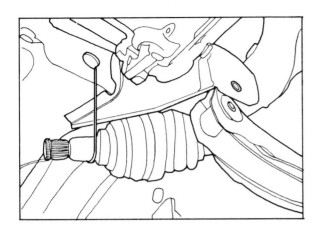

Fig. G:16 Suspend the driveshaft from the floor-pan, clear of the transmission

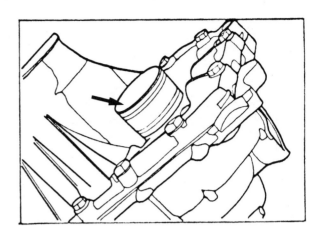

Fig. G:17 With driveshafts removed, keep drive pinions in place with plastic plug

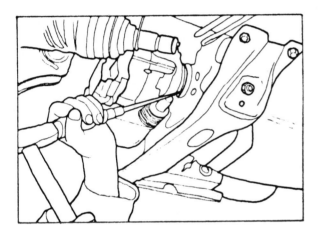

Fig. G:18 Method of knocking out offside drive shaft from transmission

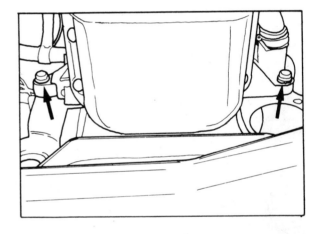

Fig. G:19 The lower clutch housing and engine mounting bolts

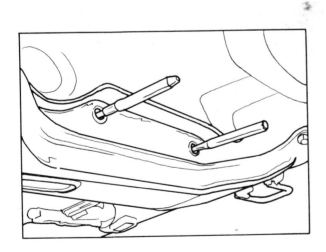

Fig. G:20 Using two drifts to locate the cover plate on engine mounting

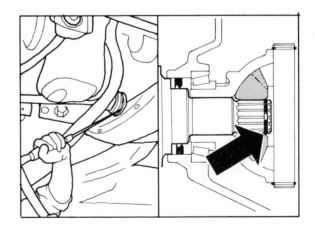

Fig. G:21 Refit each drive shaft, knock in until snap ring engages

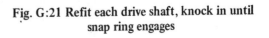

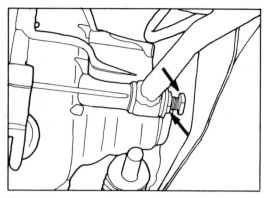

Fig. G:22 Detail of the stabiliser nut and locknut

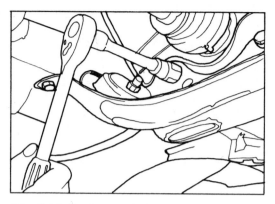

Fig. G:23 Method of tightening the outer nuts of the stabiliser

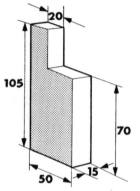

Fig. G:24 Dimensions of wood block used to refit the gearshift selector rod

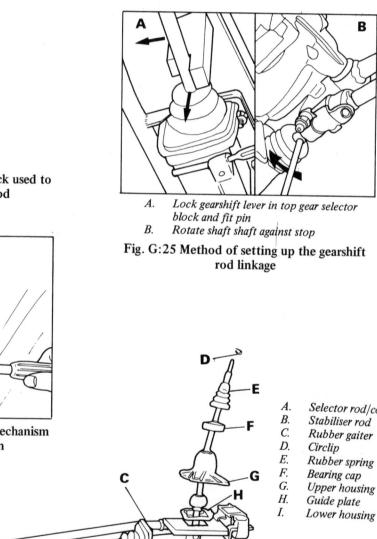

A. Lock gearshift lever in top gear selector block and fit pin
B. Rotate shaft shaft against stop

Fig. G:25 Method of setting up the gearshift rod linkage

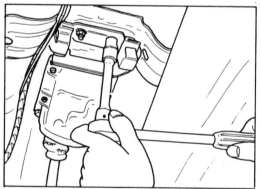

Fig. G:26 Removing the gearshift mechanism from bottom plate on floorpan

A. Selector rod/coupling
B. Stabiliser rod
C. Rubber gaiter
D. Circlip
E. Rubber spring
F. Bearing cap
G. Upper housing
H. Guide plate
I. Lower housing

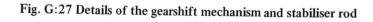

Fig. G:27 Details of the gearshift mechanism and stabiliser rod

14. Check the gearchange operation.

15. Hook the selector rod spring to the chassis member.

16. Top up the transmission oil to the level of the filler hole.

17. Replace the upper clutch housing flange retaining bolts and tighten them to the specified torque.

18. Refit the clutch cable, speedometer cable and reconnect the battery.

19. Remove the engine support bar or hoist, whichever was used.

Speedometer Driven Gear.

Remove the speedometer driven gear from the transmission by pulling out the pinion bearing locking pin. Remove the pinion bearing complete with cable attached. The cable may be unscrewed from the bearing and likewise the pinion. On replacement, fit the pinion and bearing in the transmission securing it with the locking pin, and finally reconnect the drive cable.

GEARSHIFT LINKAGE.................[4]

Removal

1. Select fourth gear, unscrew the gearlever knob and lift off the rubber lever gaiter.

2. Jack up the vehicle and support it on stands. On no account work beneath the vehicle unless it is adequately supported.

3. Unhook the long spring between the gearchange rod and the chassis side rail. Slacken the gearchange rod clamp bolt and remove the rod from the control shaft.

4. Unscrew the two inner nuts on the stabiliser rubber coupling and engine mounting and reposition them as shown in Fig. G:12. Slacken the lock nut and withdraw the bolt from the transmission housing with an Allen key.

5. Remove the two nuts holding the gearshift mechanism to the floor pan (Fig. G:26) and withdraw the assembly complete with the gearlever and selector rod.

Dismantling (Fig. G:27)

1. Clamp the stabiliser in a vice and remove the four nuts and bolts holding the shift mechanism to it. Pull off the rubber gaiter and lift off the lower housing section. Withdraw the selector rod and gaiter through the aperture in the stabiliser base plate.

2. Clamp the base of the gear lever in a vice and drill out the rivet connecting the selector rod to the gear lever. Remove the two plastic bushes and remove the selector rod and guide plate.

3. Turn the gearlever round and reclamp in the vice. Use a screwdriver to prise off the rubber gaiter retaining circlip. Remove the gaiter, half shell and upper housing section from the gear lever.

Assembly

Assembly is a reversal of the dismantling procedure noting the following points:

1. Use a new rivet to connect the gear lever to the selector rod.

2. Lubricate the gear lever guide in the selector housing and guide plate with graphite grease.

3. Pay particular attention to the seating of the guide plate when bolting together the upper and lower housing sections. The upper housing and guide plate must be fitted together so that the two bevelled corners of the housing are facing in the direction of travel.

Installation

1. Insert the gearshift mechanism and loosely tighten the two floorpan mounting nuts.

2. Attach the stabiliser to the transmission. Screw the Allen bolt into the transmission housing as far as its stop and lock it in place with the nut on the stabiliser rubber coupling. Turn the other nut until it makes contact with the engine mounting and then tighten the outer nut to the specified torque.

3. Tighten the gearshift mechanism to floorpan nuts to the specified torque.

4. Refit the selector rod to the gearshift shaft and adjust as described under TRANSMISSION.

5. Refit the gearlever gaiter and knob.

Technical Data

CLUTCH

Type. . . . . .Single dry plate, diaphragm spring
Diameter
    957 cc/1117 cc models. . . . . .6.5 in (165 mm)
    1.3 models . . . . .7.5 in (190 mm)

Actuation . . . . .Self-adjusting cable
Lining material . . . . Ferodo 2124F and 11F324
Lining thickness . . . . 0.12-0.126 in (3.05-3.2 mm)

GEARBOX

Capacity . . . . 5 pt (2.8 litres)
Oil type. . . . . EP Gear Oil SAE 80

CLUTCH
Trouble Shooter

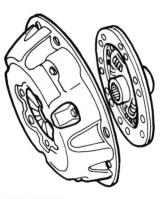

FAULT	CAUSE	CURE
Clutch slips	1. Clutch facing worn. 2. Clutch facing contaminated. 3. Warped clutch cover or pressure plate. 4. Incorrect adjustment (if adjustable).	1. Replace clutch assy. 2. Replace clutch assy. 3. Replace clutch assy. 4. Adjust clutch.
Clutch drags	1. Faulty clutch hydraulics (if hydraulic). 2. Faulty clutch adjustment (if adjustable). 3. Clutch disc warped. 4. Clutch hub splines worn or rusty. 5. Diaphragm worn or mal-adjusted.	1. Overhaul or replace clutch hydraulics. 2. Adjust clutch. 3. Replace clutch disc. 4. Replace or lubricate clutch. 5. Replace pressure plate.
Clutch chatter	1. Faulty pressure plate. 2. Faulty clutch disc. 3. Loose or worn engine mounting.	1. Replace pressure plate. 2. Replace clutch disc. 3. Replace mounting.
Clutch noise	1. Insufficient grease on bearing sleeve. 2. Clutch installed incorrectly.	1. Lubricate. 2. Check installation.
Clutch noise (pedal down)	1. Faulty release bearing.	1. Replace bearing.
Clutch grabs	1. Contaminated clutch lining. 2. Clutch worn or loose rivets. 3. Clutch splines worn or rusted. 4. Warped flywheel or pressure plate. 5. Loose mountings on engine or power unit	1. Replace clutch. 2. Replace clutch. 3. Clean or replace. 4. Repair or replace. 5. Tighten or replace.

Front Suspension/Steering

WHEEL ALIGNMENT . . . .[1]

Checking

Ideally, the front wheel alignment should be checked after any overhaul procedure in which a suspension component has been removed, or its location altered. It should also be checked if the suspension has been subjected to heavy impact, as accident damage may disturb one or more settings.

Apart from the toe setting, the suspension geometry may not be altered. The checking of the castor and camber settings requires special optical equipment and for this reason the job should be entrusted to an authorised Ford agent.

The toe setting may be checked using a simple mechanical tracking bar, but should be measured after checking and/or adjusting the castor/camber settings. Incorrect castor and/or camber angles may be due to worn or damaged suspension bushes, ball joints or top mounts, loose or worn wheel bearings, or distorted or damaged suspension components.

Toe Setting

The toe setting of the front wheels should be 0.10 in (2.5 mm) toe-out. The checking range is 0.04 in (1 mm) toe-in to 0.24 in (6 mm) toe-out.

Adjustment of the toe setting is achieved by altering the length of the track rods.

Before attempting to measure or adjust the toe setting, the following pre-checks should be made:
1. Make sure that the car is at its normal kerb weight and height.
2. The vehicle should be standing on a level, horizontal surface.
3. Check that the tyre pressures are to specification.
4. Check the steering and front suspension ball joints, bushes and mountings for excessive wear, looseness or tightness. Rectify any unfavourable condition before proceeding.
5. Roll the car straight forwards and stop it without using the brakes.
6. Bounce the car approximately 2 in (50 mm) in each direction a few times to settle the suspension.
NOTE: Once the ride height has been established, it must not be disturbed by jacking up the car or by someone sitting in it to centralise the steering.

Adjusting

1. Use the tracking bar to measure the distance between the inside edges of the front wheels at a point level with and in front of the wheel axis. Take a second reading of the distance between the wheel rims at a point level with but behind the wheel axis. The difference by which the first reading exceeds the second reading will give the existing toe setting.
2. Move the car forwards sufficiently to rotate the front wheels through 180° and repeat the measuring process. The average of the two results will give the actual wheel alignment.
3. If adjustment is necessary, slacken the locknuts adjacent to the track rod ends of each track rod. Also slacken the small clips on the steering gear bellows (Fig. H:2).
4. Turn both track rods an equal amount in the same direction, i.e. so that the top of both rods moves backwards until the correct toe-out setting is obtained.
NOTE: Both track rods should be approximately the same length after adjustment. If they are appreciably different the wheel angles on turns will be adversely affected.
5. When adjustment is completed, tighten the locknuts at the track rod ends and the clips on the steering gear bellows. Ensure that the wheels are in the straight-ahead position and that each track rod end ball joint is in the middle of its travel before tightening the locknuts.

WHEEL BEARINGS. . . . .[2]

Replacement

1. Slacken the front wheel bolts, then jack up the car

and fit stands. On no account leave the car supported on the jack only.

2. Remove the road wheel and replace two wheel bolts.
NOTE: These bolts should be fitted to prevent any strain being placed on the disc retaining screw caused by the tendency for the disc to turn relative to the hub when releasing or tightening the hub nut.

3. Have an assistant apply the footbrake to prevent the driveshaft from turning then undo the front hub retaining nut and washer.

4. Release the foot brake and remove the wheel bolts.

5. Remove the brake caliper mounting bolts (Fig. H:3), lift the caliper clear of the brake disc and tie it out of the way to prevent putting any strain on the brake hose.

6. Remove the hub and disc assembly. It may be necessary to use a suitable two legged puller for this if the hub is a tight fit.

7. Remove the split pin and locknut from the track rod end ball joint and separate the ball joint from the steering arm with a ball joint separator tool (Fig. H:4).

8. Remove the suspension lower arm by extracting the arm to body mounting bolt and releasing the arm ball joint pinch bolt at the spindle carrier.

9. Remove the two bolts securing the top mounting of the suspension assembly to the body in the engine compartment (Fig. H:5).

10. Support the driveshaft at the outer CV joint and pull the hub carrier clear of the driveshaft. Remove the suspension assembly complete with hub carrier.

11. Fit a pair of 'soft' jaws to a vice and mount the suspension assembly in the vice so that the seals and bearings in the hub carrier are accessible.

12. Use pliers to pull the dust shield from the groove in the spindle carrier. Using a screwdriver, lever out the inner and outer grease retainers from the hub carrier.

13. Lift out the inner and outer bearings.

14. Using a flat ended punch, drift out the bearing cups (Fig. H:6). Make sure the punch is in good condition and take care not to raise any burrs on the cup seats as these may prevent the cups from seating properly and hence will adversely affect the bearing preload.

15. Support the carrier on a block of wood, then drive the new bearing cups into the carrier using one of the old cups as a drift. Check that the cup is seated properly by turning over the spindle carrier and checking the seating face from the rear.

16. The new bearings should be packed with high melting point lithium based grease which should be worked thoroughly between the rollers. Insert the one bearing in one side of the spindle carrier.

17. Apply grease to the sealing lips of the grease retainer, making sure the cavities between the sealing lips are also filled with grease and tap in the new grease retainer (Fig. H:7) using a shaped drift or a smooth wood block.

18. Repeat the previous operation for the remaining bearing and grease retainer.

19. Making sure the cut-out in the dust shield is at the bottom and in line with the ball joint location, gently tap the shield into the groove in the inner face of the hub carrier with a block of wood (Fig. H:8).

20. Lightly grease the drive shaft splines and push the spindle carrier over the end of the shaft, placing the suspension assembly into position.

21. Fit the suspension assembly top mounting to the body with the two mounting bolts.

22. Refit the suspension lower arm, noting that the arm to body mounting bolt should be passed through the mounting bracket from the rear (Fig. H:9).

23. Refit the track rod end ball joint to the steering arm, using a castellated nut and new split pin.

24. Push the hub and disc assembly on to the splined end of the driveshaft by hand. Fit the plain washer and a new nut to draw the hub on to the drive shaft splines. If there is not enough thread showing to allow the fitting of the washer and nut, gently tap the hub flange with a soft hammer to drift the hub into position.

25. Loosely fit the plain washer and new hub retaining nut. It is essential to use a new nut to ensure adequate retention when it is finally staked.

26. Remount the brake caliper and fit two wheel bolts to the hub assembly.

27. With the footbrake applied, tighten the hub retaining nut to a torque figure of 180-200 lb ft (24.0-27.0 kg m).

28. Stake the retaining nut by using a punch to deform its collar into the slot in the driveshaft (Fig. H:10).

29. Release the brakes, remove the wheel bolts and refit the roadwheels.

30. Lower the car to the ground and finally fully tighten the wheel bolts.

DRIVESHAFTS . . . . [3]

Removal - 957/1117 cc Models

1. Remove the hub and disc assembly as described in the previous section. Take care to prevent dirt entering the exposed bearings.

2. Release the track rod end ball joint and both ends of the suspension lower arm as described in the previous section. Take care not to strain the forward mounting of the tie bar by pushing the rear end downwards.

3. Position a suitable container beneath the inner CV joint to catch any oil that may spill when the inner end of the driveshaft is released from the transmission.

4. Use a large screwdriver to release the inner CV joint of the shorter of the two driveshafts. Strike the handle of the screwdriver with the ball of the hand whilst pulling the shaft outwards (Fig. H:11). The longer of the two shafts should be driven out as illustrated in Fig. H:12. Pull the outer end of the driveshaft from the hub carrier.
NOTE: If both driveshafts are to be removed, the differential gears should be secured in position with a plastic cup or plug.

Installation

1. Insert the outer end of the driveshaft through the hub carrier (Fig. H:13).

2. Refit the inner end of the driveshaft to the transmission by applying firm but gentle blows to the weld bead on the CV joint (Fig. H:14). The driveshaft will be felt to

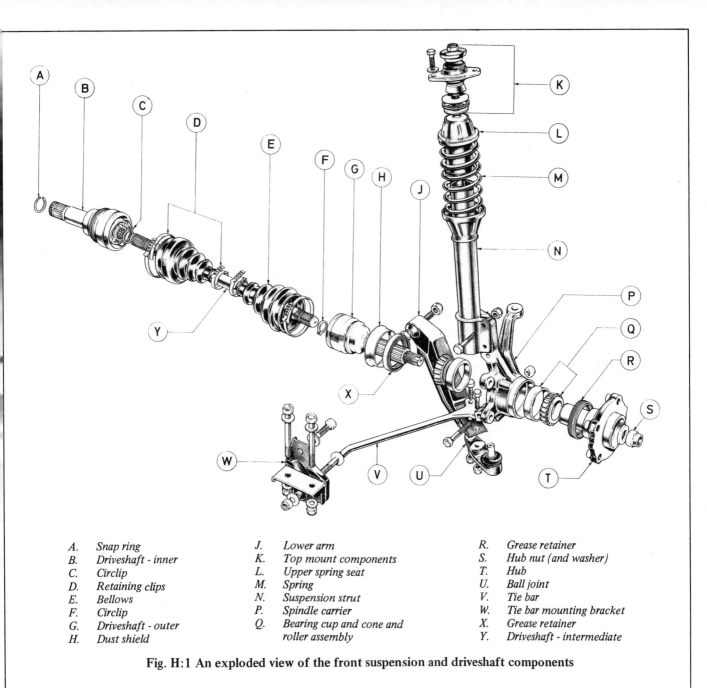

A. Snap ring
B. Driveshaft - inner
C. Circlip
D. Retaining clips
E. Bellows
F. Circlip
G. Driveshaft - outer
H. Dust shield

J. Lower arm
K. Top mount components
L. Upper spring seat
M. Spring
N. Suspension strut
P. Spindle carrier
Q. Bearing cup and cone and
roller assembly

R. Grease retainer
S. Hub nut (and washer)
T. Hub
U. Ball joint
V. Tie bar
W. Tie bar mounting bracket
X. Grease retainer
Y. Driveshaft - intermediate

Fig. H:1 An exploded view of the front suspension and driveshaft components

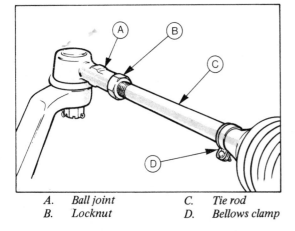

A. Ball joint
B. Locknut
C. Tie rod
D. Bellows clamp

**Fig. H:2 Details of the track rod end ball joint
arrangement**

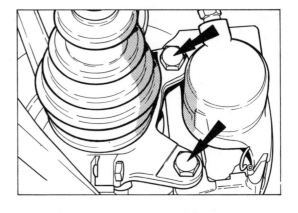

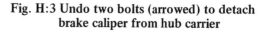

**Fig. H:3 Undo two bolts (arrowed) to detach
brake caliper from hub carrier**

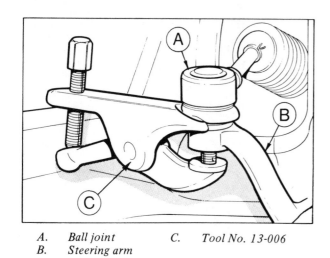

A. Ball joint   C.   Tool No. 13-006
B. Steering arm

Fig. H:4 Disconnecting track rod ball joint from steering arm using separator tool

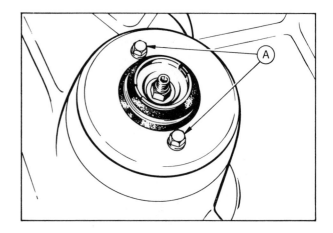

Fig. H:5 Undo two bolts (A) to detach suspension unit from body

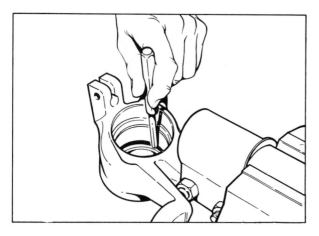

Fig. H:6 Using a thin punch to drift out hub bearing cups

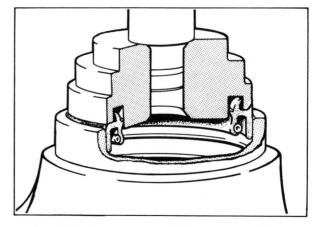

Fig. H:7 Using a recessed drift to press the hub grease retainer into position

Fig. H:8 Make sure dust shield cut-out is at bottom when installing

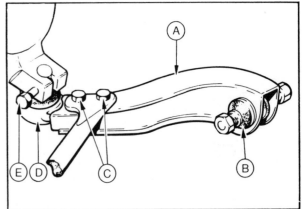

A.   Lower arm
B.   Lower arm to body mounting bolt
C.   Ball joint and tie bar to lower arm retaining bolts
D.   Lower arm ball joint
E.   Ball joint to hub carrier clinch joint

Fig. H:9 Details of the suspension lower arm attachment points

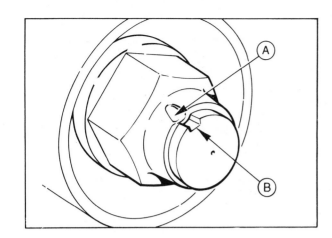

Fig. H:10 Stake hub nut (A) into stub axle groove (B) when refitting

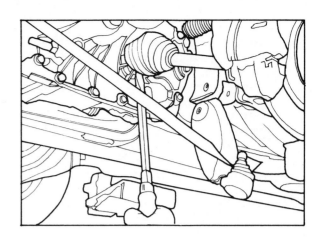

Fig. H:11 Levering out the nearside drive-shaft using a screwdriver as shown

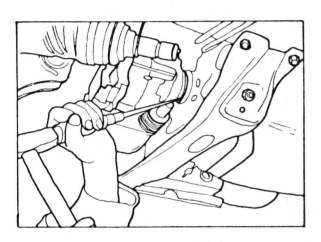

Fig. H:12 Using a screwdriver to drift out the offside driveshaft from transmission

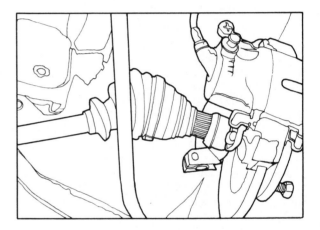

Fig. H:13 Removing/refitting driveshaft in hub carrier

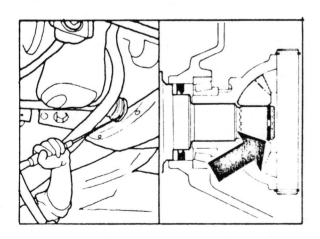

Fig. H:14 Drift driveshaft into position until snap ring (arrowed) engages

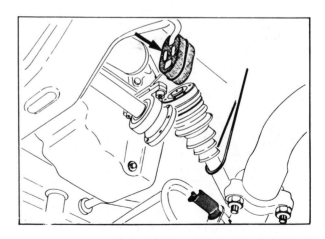

Fig. H:15 Undo exhaust from support (arrowed) then disconnect and support drive shaft

snap into place. If the CV joint has no weld bead, the gaiter should be pulled clear and gentle blows applied to the flange with a plastic headed hammer.

NOTE: A new snap ring should be used at the inner end of the shaft (Fig. H:14).

3. Replace the remaining components as described in the previous section and top up the oil level in the transmission.

Removal - 1300 cc Intermediate Shaft Type

1. Remove the hub and disc assembly as described in the previous section. Take care to prevent dirt entering the exposed bearings.

2. Release the track rod end ball joint and both ends of the suspension lower arm as detailed in the previous section. Take care to avoid straining the forward mounting of the tie bar by pushing the rear end downwards.

3. Position a suitable container under the transmission to collect any oil that may spill out when the driveshafts are disconnected.

4. Disconnect the nearside driveshaft (Fig. H:11) by inserting a large screwdriver behind the CV joint and striking the handle whilst, at the same time, pulling the driveshaft outwards. Detach the outer end of the shaft from the hub carrier.

5. To give extra room, if necessary, detach the exhaust pipe at the manifold connection and disconnect the front rubber insulator (arrowed) in Fig. H:15. Support the exhaust system at a suitable point.

6. Undo and remove the six socket headed bolts and linked washers securing the CV joint to the intermediate shaft. Support the shaft with wire from a suitable point (Fig. H:15), or disconnect the shaft from the hub carrier and remove it from the car.

7. If necessary, remove the intermediate shaft by undoing the two socket headed bolts securing the intermediate shaft support bearing housing to the support bracket. Detach the housing from the bracket, then withdraw the intermediate shaft and CV joint assembly from the transmission.

Installation

1. Refit the nearside driveshaft as detailed for 957/1117 cc models described previously.

2. Smear the splines of the intermediate shaft with a lithium based Moly grease then fit the shaft to the transmission.

3. Slacken the bolts securing the intermediate shaft bearing support bracket to the engine block (Fig. H:16). This will ensure that the support bearing is not under stress when assembled.

4. Fit the bearing housing to the support bracket, making sure that it is correctly aligned in relation to the shaft and the support bracket, then tighten the two socket headed bolts 'A' in Fig. H:16 to a torque of 13-16 lb ft (1.8-2.2 kg m). Then tighten the upper support bracket bolt 'B1' followed by the lower one 'B2' in Fig. H:16.

5. Pack the CV joint flange on the intermediate shaft with 1 oz (30 grams) of lithium based Moly grease, then insert the outer end of the offside driveshaft through the hub carrier and connect the inner CV joint end to the intermediate shaft. Tighten the socket headed bolts to a torque of 28-32 lb ft (3.8-4.4 kg m).

6. Refit the exhaust pipe to the manifold - if previously disconnected.

Constant Velocity (CV) Joint Overhaul

1. Remove the driveshaft as described previously.

2. Slacken the CV joint bellows retaining clamps and slide the bellows along the shaft.

3. Wipe all surplus grease from the CV joint, prise open the retaining circlip (Fig. H:17) and withdraw the driveshaft from the joint.

4. Repeat the procedure for the remaining CV joint.

5. Thoroughly clean the joints, removing all traces of old grease and dirt.

6. Inspect the condition of the circlips and replace them if necessary. Repack each joint with 1.5 oz (40 grams) of grease to Ford specification S-M1C-75-A or SQM-1C-9004-A.

7. Slide the bellows along the shaft and refit the CV joints to the shaft, pushing the shaft into each joint until the circlip is felt to engage.

8. Refit the bellows to the joints. The inner bellows should be fitted in such a way that with the inner joint fully contracted and at an angle of 10-20°, the distance between the inner end of the bellow and the outer mounting flange is 2.75 in (70 mm). See Fig. H:18. The outer bellows should be fitted so that the same dimension is 3.7 in (95 mm).

9. Tighten the bellows retaining clamp until it is held finger tight. Then engage the pipe of the clamp in the next available hole and crimp as shown in Fig. H:19 to tighten it fully.

NOTE: If it is necessary to remove the torsional damper from the offside driveshaft on 957/1117 cc models, make sure it is fitted in its original position on replacement. See Fig. H:20.

Driveshaft Inner Joint Bellows Replacement

The driveshaft inner bellows can be replaced without removing the driveshaft from the car. The track rod end ball joint should be separated from the steering arm on the hub carrier as described previously, both ends of the lower suspension arm released from the body bracket and hub carrier respectively and the bellows clamp released. The bellows can then be moved back along the shaft to reveal the CV joint retaining circlip. Prise open the clip and separate the shaft from the CV joint. Slide the old bellows from the shaft and replace with a new one. Fit the new bellows following the sequence detailed in operations 7-9 in the previous section and then reconnect the driveshaft in the reverse order of removal.

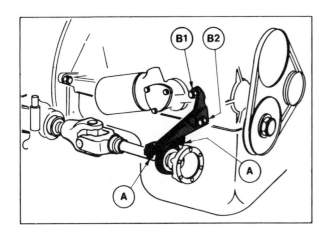

Fig. H:16 Tighten the bolts arrowed (A) and (B) in the correct order - see text

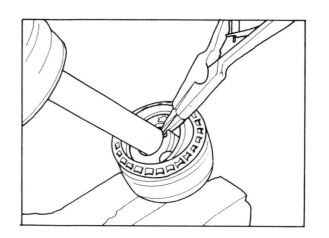

Fig. H:17 Use circlip pliers to prise open the CV joint circlip

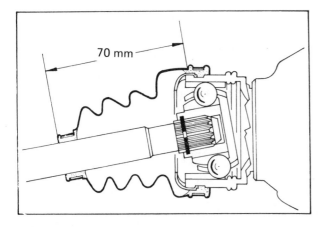

Fig. H:18 The correct positioning of the inner CV joint bellows

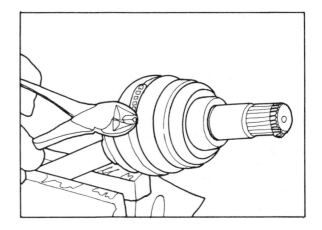

Fig. H:19 Compress bellows retaining clip with pliers until tight

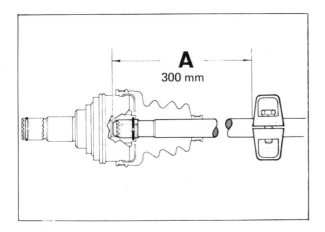

Fig. H:20 If removed, make sure torsional damper is replaced in correct position (A)

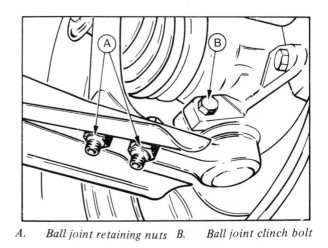

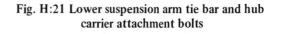

A.   Ball joint retaining nuts   B.   Ball joint clinch bolt

Fig. H:21 Lower suspension arm tie bar and hub carrier attachment bolts

SUSPENSION LOWER ARM . . . . [4]

Removal

1. Jack up the front of the car and fit axle stands. On no account work beneath the car without supporting it adequately.
2. Remove the lower arm inner pivot bolt and the clinch bolt holding the lower arm ball joint to the hub carrier (Fig. H:21).
3. Remove the two nuts holding the lower arm to the tie bar and remove the lower arm (Fig. H:21).

Installation

This is a reversal of the removal procedure, noting that the nut holding the lower arm to the tie bar end should be fully tightened until the inner pivot bolt and the clinch bolt of the balljoint have been tightened to their correct torque. The lower arm inner pivot bolt should be pushed through the body bracket from the rear.

Suspension Arm Bush Replacement

1. Remove the lower suspension arm as detailed previously.
2. Using two pieces of tubing and a heavy duty vice, press the arm inner bush out of the arm (Fig. H:22). One tube should be large enough to receive the rubber bush and the other should be of the same diameter as the bush inner sleeve. Place the larger piece of tube behind the bush. Hold this tube and the lower arm in the jaws of a vice and fit the smaller piece of tube so that it bears upon the other side of the bush. As the vice jaws are closed the small tube will push the bush out of the arm and into the receiver tube (Fig. H:22).

The new bush should be lubricated with a soap solution and assembled to the arm in a similar manner to that by which it was removed. It is important that the vice jaws are wound together quickly so that the bush is deformed for the minimum period of time. Refit the arm as described in the previous section.

Ball Joint Replacement (Fig. H:21)

1. Jack up the car and support on axle stands.
2. Remove the clutch bolt securing the ball joint to the hub carrier.
3. Release the two nuts securing the ball joint to the lower suspension arm and remove the ball joint.
4. Mount the new ball joint to the lower suspension arm, leaving the retaining nuts loose.
5. Insert the ball joint stud in the spindle carrier and secure it with the clinch bolt and nut.
6. Finally, tighten fully the two nuts holding the ball joint to the lower arm.
7. Lower the car to the ground.

TIE BAR . . . . [5]

Removal

1. Jack up the front of the car and fit axle stands.
2. Remove the retaining nut and washer from the forward end of the tie bar (Fig. H:23).
3. Release the two nuts securing the tie bar to the lower suspension arm, remove the bolts and detach the tie bar.

Installation

1. Fit washer to the forward end of the tie bar and insert the end through the mounting bracket.
2. Loosely assemble the rearward end of the tie bar to the lower arm with the two nuts and bolts.
3. Fit the remaining washer and retaining nut to the forward end of the tie bar and tighten it fully.
4. Fully tighten the lower arm mounting nuts and bolts.
5. Lower the car to the ground.
NOTE: The front suspension tie bars are handed and should be fitted so that the 'FORD' mark is uppermost (Fig. H:24).

Tie Bar Front Mounting Bush-Replacement

1. Jack up the front of the car and fit axle stands.
2. Remove the retaining nut and washer from the front end of the tie bar.
3. Remove the three nuts and bolts attaching the tie bar front mounting bracket assembly to the body and withdraw the assembly from the end of the tie bar.
4. Remove the bush from the bracket by using two pieces of tubing and a vice as detailed previously for replacing the lower arm bush (Fig. H:26).
5. Lubricate the new bush with a soap solution and fit it in the mounting bracket using the vice and tubing.
6. Slide the mounting bracket over the end of the tie bar, then fit the bracket to the body and tighten the three mounting bolts.
7. Refit the retaining washer and nut to the tie bar and tighten fully.
8. Lower the car to the ground.

SUSPENSION & HUB CARRIER . . . . [6]

Removal

1. Slacken the wheel bolts, then jack up the front of the car and fit axle stands. Remove the road wheel(s).
2. Undo the two bolts attaching the brake caliper to the hub carrier (Fig. H:3), detach the caliper and suspend it to prevent straining the brake pipe.
3. Remove the three bolts attaching the tie bar front mounting bracket to the body.
4. Remove the split pin and castellated locknut from the track rod end ball joint and separate the joint from the steering arm with a ball joint separator tool (Fig. H:4).
5. Remove the lower suspension arm inner pivot bolt.
6. Position a container beneath the driveshaft inner CV

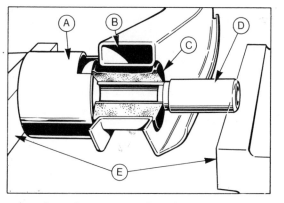

A. Large diameter tube D. Small diameter tube
B. Lower arm   E. Vice jaws
C. Bush

Fig. H:22 Using a vice and tubes to remove and replace the arm inner bush

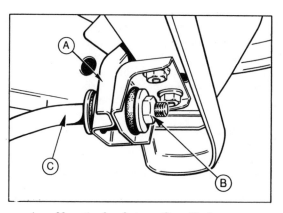

A. Mounting bracket   C. Tie bar
B. Retaining nut

Fig. H:23 Details of the tie bar front bracket attachment

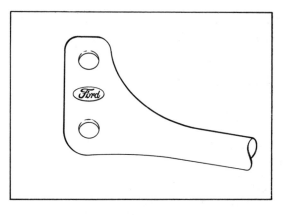

Fig. H:24 Tie bars are handed, make sure they are fitted with FORD mark uppermost

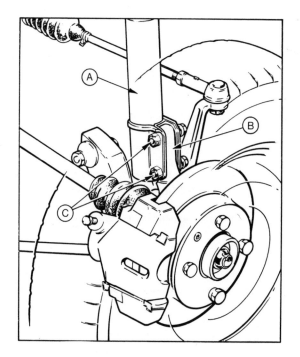

Fig. H:25 Suspension unit (A) is attached to hub carrier (B) by two bolts (C)

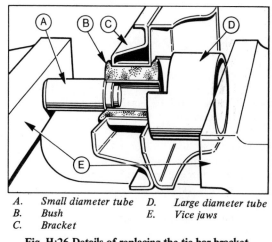

A. Small diameter tube D. Large diameter tube
B. Bush   E. Vice jaws
C. Bracket

Fig. H:26 Details of replacing the tie bar bracket bush using vice and tubes

joint to catch any oil spillage, then disconnect the drive-shaft from the transmission as described previously.

7. Support the suspension assembly underneath, then undo the two bolts holding the suspension top mounting to the body, then remove the complete suspension drive-shaft and hub carrier assembly from the car.

Installation

Replacement of the suspension and hub carrier assembly is a reversal of the removal procedure, noting the following points:

1. Use a new snap ring on the inner CV joint where applicable and drive the joint into place in the transmission by applying firm yet gentle blows to the weld bead of the joint. The driveshaft will be felt to snap into position. On 1300 cc models, reconnect the offside driveshaft to the intermediate shaft.

2. Insert the lower arm inner pivot bolt from the rear of its mounting bracket.

3. Use a new split pin to secure the track rod end ball joint locknut.

4. Ensure wheel bolts are fully tightened after lowering the car to the ground.

5. Top up the transmission with a suitable EP 80 gear oil.

6. Check the front wheel alignment.

SUSPENSION UNIT . . . . [7]

Removal

1. Loosen the road wheel bolts, then jack up the front of the car, fit axle stands and remove the road wheel.

2. Make sure the hub carrier is supported from under-neath.

3. Remove the two nuts and bolts attaching the suspen-sion unit to the hub carrier (Fig. H:25).

4. Remove the two bolts attaching the suspension unit top mounting to the body and lift away the suspension unit.

Suspension Strut-Replacement

1. Mount the suspension unit in a vice and fit spring compressors to the coil spring (Fig. H:27). Tighten gradually and evenly to remove any pressure from the top mounting assembly.

2. Use a 6 mm hexagonal key in the socket at the end the piston rod to hold the rod whilst undoing the top mounting retaining nut (Fig. H:28).

3. Remove the top mounting assembly followed by the coil spring (Fig. H:29).

4. Assemble the spring and top mounting to the new strut in the reverse order of removal.

Installation

1. Refit the suspension unit to the body with the two mounting bolts.

2. Using new special bolts as shown in Fig. H:30 (Ford part number E800615-S72) refit the lower end of the sus-pension unit to the hub carrier.

NOTE: These bolts are essential since the original relation-ship between the suspension unit and the hub carrier is accurately set at the factory using a special jig. Because this jig is not available in service, in order to retain correct suspension alignment it is essential that this relationship is restored by the use of specially ground bolts fitted in place of the original production bolts.

3. Refit the roadwheel, lower the car to the ground and fully tighten the road wheel bolts. Check the toe setting as described previously.

STEERING RACK ASSEMBLY . . . . [8]

Removal (Fig. H:31)

1. Set the steering so that the front wheels are in the straight-ahead position, then jack up the front of the car and support on axle stands.

NOTE: Whilst the front of the vehicle is in the air take care, if it is necessary to turn the steering wheel from lock to lock, to do so only very slowly. Sudden, sharp lock to lock movement will result in damage to the steering rack bellows.

2. Remove the clinch bolt securing the steering gear pinion to the steering shaft coupling (Fig. H:32).

3. Remove the split pins securing the castellated lock nuts of the track rod end ball joints and, using a ball joint separating tool, disconnect the ball joints from the steer-ing arms (Fig. H:4).

4. Bend back the locking tabs and remove the steering rack mounting bolts and clamps from the body (Fig. H:31). Remove the steering rack from inside the engine com-partment.

NOTE: If it is necessary to remove the track rod end ball joints, note the number of turns required to remove them from the threaded track rods or mark their position with tape. This is to ensure correct positioning when replacing them.

Installation

1. Check that the steering wheel is still in the straight-ahead position and set the steering rack in the mid-travel straight ahead position.

2. Refit the steering rack assembly to the body, engag-ing the steering gear pinion in the steering shaft.

3. Refit the steering rack retaining clamps and bolts, using new locking tabs. Bend up the locking tabs.

4. Reconnect the track rod end ball joints to the steer-ing arms, using new split pins to secure the castellated locknuts.

5. Tighten the steering gear pinion to steering shaft coupling clinch bolt.

6. Finally, recheck that the wheels are pointing straight ahead when the steering wheel is in the straight ahead position. Also, check the toe setting as described previous-ly.

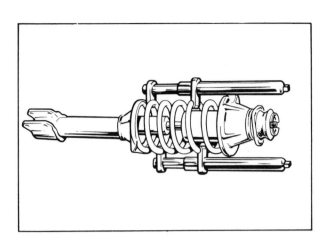

Fig. H:27 Using tool to compress the coil spring
and remove top mounting

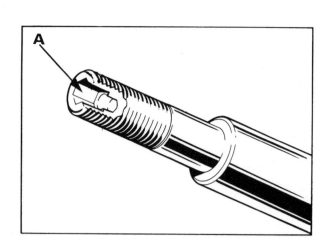

Fig. H:28 Insert Allen key into rod (A) to prevent
rod turning when undoing nut

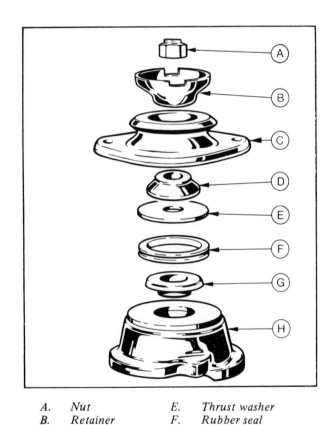

A.	Nut	E.	Thrust washer
B.	Retainer	F.	Rubber seal
C.	Top mount	G.	Phenolic resin bearing
D.	Spacer	H.	Upper spring seat

Fig. H:29 An exploded view of the top mounting
components

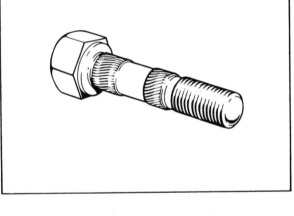

Fig. H:30 Details of the special bolts used when
replacing the suspension unit

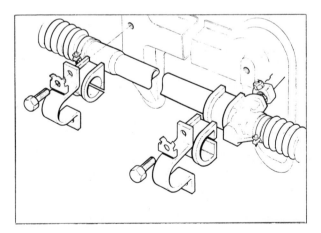

Fig. H:31 The steering rack is attached to the
body by two brackets

Steering Rack Bellows-Replacement (Fig. H:33)

1. Jack up the front of the car and fit axle stands.
2. Release the securing clips at each end of the damaged bellows, remove the castellated locknut and separate the track rod end ball joint from the steering arm with a ball joint separator tool (Fig. H:4).
3. Unscrew the ball joint from the track rod after releasing the locknut. Note the number of turns required to remove the track rod ball joint or mark the position with tape.
4. Slide the damaged bellows off the track rod.
5. Before fitting the new bellows it is necessary to expel steering rack lubricant from the pinion end of the rack tube. If the damaged bellows is at this end, merely turn the steering gear to and fro to expel the lubricant. If the damaged bellows is at the other end of the rack, loosen the inner bellows clamp at the steering pinion end, turn back the bellows and slowly turn the rack to and fro to expel the lubricant. It will not be possible to expel all the lubricant, but any that is expelled in this manner will be sufficient.
6. Smear the inner surface of the new bellows with grease where it contacts the track rod and rack tube and fit the new bellows over the track rod.
7. If the new bellows is to be fitted to the steering pinion end of the rack, leave both ends of the bellows unclamped. If it is to be fitted to the other end of the rack, clamp the inner end of the bellows to the rack tube. Some racks are fitted with soft iron wire clips to retain the bellows, these should not be reused.
8. Replace the track rod end ball joint, screwing it on the same number of turns that were required to remove it. This will ensure correct toe setting. Refit the balljoint to the steering arm, using a new split pin to secure the castellated locking nut.
9. Fit the outer end of the bellows to the groove in the track rod end. Secure with the clip.
10. Adjust the axle stands so that the pinion end of the rack is higher than the other, add 0.14 pt (80 cc) of the specified lubricant to the pinion end of the rack tube. Traverse the rack to ensure easy flow of the lubricant.
11. Refit the inner bellows clamp.
12. Lower the vehicle to the ground.

TRACK ROD END JOINTS . . . . [9]

Replacement (Fig. H:2)

Wear in the track rod end ball joint cannot be removed by adjustment and so replacement of the track rod end ball joint is necessary.

Always replace track rod end ball joints in pairs, even if only one appears to be worn. The method of replacement is as follows:

1. Jack up the front of the car and fit axle stands.
2. Slacken the track rod end ball joint lock nut a few turns.
3. Remove the split pin securing the castellated lock nut that secures the ball joint to the steering arm. Remove the nut.
4. Using a ball joint separator tool, disconnect the ball joint from the steering arm. Do NOT hammer on the ball joint stud to release it.
5. Unscrew the track rod end ball joint, noting the number of turns necessary to remove it. Or mark the track rod end threads with tape to ensure accurate repositioning of the new ball joint.
6. Smear the track rod end thread lightly with grease and screw on the new ball joint, using the same number of turns necessary to remove the old joint.
7. Reconnect the joint to the steering arm, using a new split pin for the lock nut.
8. Lower the car to the ground and check the toe setting. When satisfied that this is correct, finally tighten the ball joint lock nut.

STEERING COLUMN & SHAFT . . . . [10]

Column Removal

1. Disconnect the battery.
2. Carefully lever out the steering wheel centre piece, unscrew the steering wheel retaining nut and lift the steering wheel and direction indicator cam from the end of the column. If may be necessary to use a puller to remove the wheel.
3. Remove the retaining screws from the upper and lower steering column shrouds and detach the shrouds (Fig. H:34).
4. Remove the lower dash insulation panel (Fig. H:35).
5. Unscrew the bolt holding the choke control bracket in place and allow the control to hang free.
6. Unscrew the two retaining screws and remove the multi-function switch from the column (Fig. H:36).
7. Remove the clamp securing the wiring loom to the column.
8. Disconnect the ignition switch multi-way plug.
9. Remove the two steering column mounting clamps (Fig. H:40).The upper clamp has a stud and nut fixing and the lower clamp a nut and bolt fixing.
10. Lift off the steering column tube, being careful not to lose the bearing tolerance ring.
11. Drill out the shear bolts and remove the column lock and ignition switch assembly (Fig. H:37).
12. Drift out the column upper bearing sleeve (Fig. H: 40).

Installation

1. Tap the upper bearing into the column tube.
2. Fit the steering column lock and ignition switch assembly to the column tube, making sure the lock spigot engages the hole in the tube.
3. Secure the lock assembly with two new shear bolts and tighten them until their heads break off.
4. Place the tube over the steering shaft and secure it in position with the steering column clamps. Make sure the tube is positioned as far up the shaft as possible and check that the pins at the foot of the shaft are fully engaged in the steering coupling bushes. Use the upper cowl to gauge

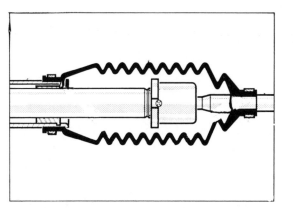

Fig. H:32 Details of the pinion shaft coupling
clamp and bolt

Fig. H:33 The steering rack bellows and retaining clip arrangement

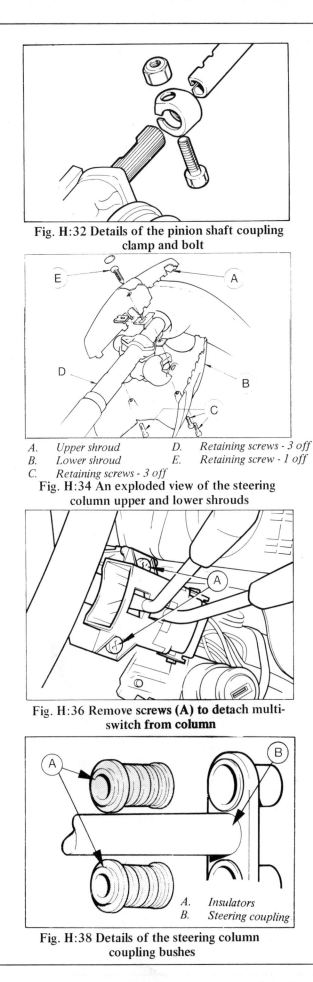

A. Upper shroud
B. Lower shroud
C. Retaining screws - 3 off
D. Retaining screws - 3 off
E. Retaining screw - 1 off

Fig. H:34 An exploded view of the steering
column upper and lower shrouds

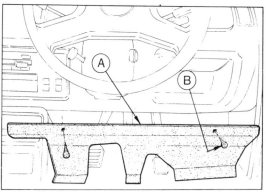

Fig. H:35 Undo screws (B) to remove fascia
insulation panel (A)

Fig. H:36 Remove screws (A) to detach multi-
switch from column

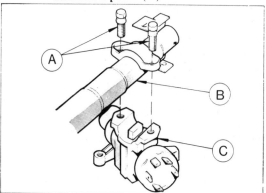

A. Shear-off bolts
B. Steering column tube   C. Steering column lock assembly

Fig. H:37 Steering lock to column attachment,
note 'shear' bolts (A)

A. Insulators
B. Steering coupling

Fig. H:38 Details of the steering column
coupling bushes

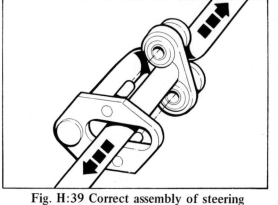

Fig. H:39 Correct assembly of steering
column coupling

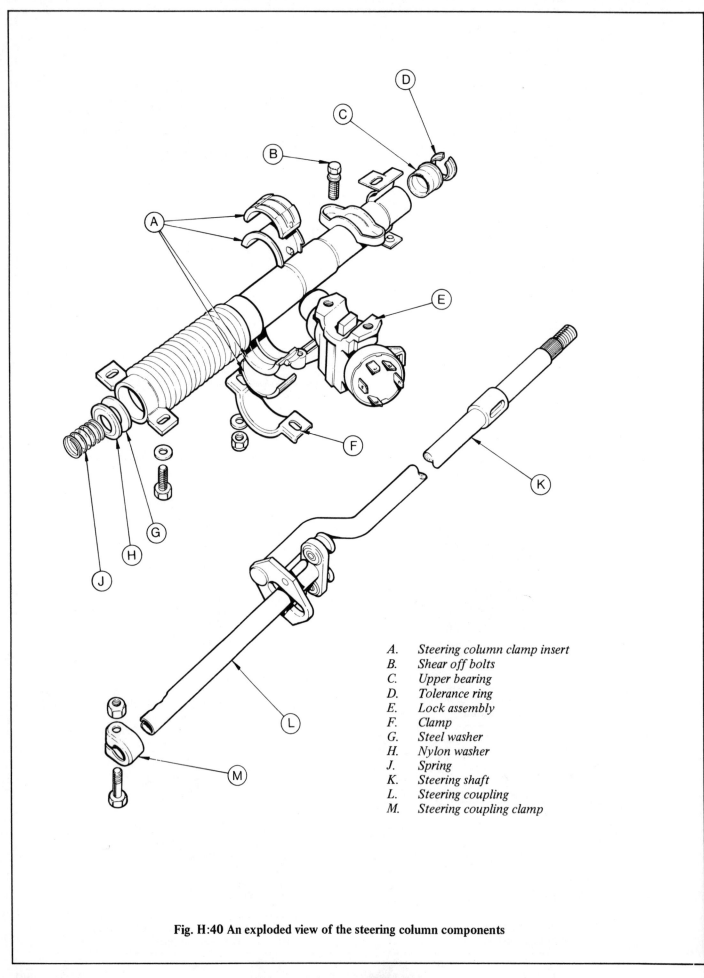

A.   Steering column clamp insert
B.   Shear off bolts
C.   Upper bearing
D.   Tolerance ring
E.   Lock assembly
F.   Clamp
G.   Steel washer
H.   Nylon washer
J.   Spring
K.   Steering shaft
L.   Steering coupling
M.   Steering coupling clamp

Fig. H:40 An exploded view of the steering column components

the axial position; the gap between the shroud and instrument panel should be 0.28 in (7 mm). Adjust the position of the tube to gain this dimension before fully tightening the clamps.

5. Refit the bearing tolerance ring.

6. Reconnect the ignition switch multi plug, refit the multi-function switches and secure the wiring looms to the column with plastic clips.

7. Refit the remaining components in the reverse order of removal, taking care when replacing the steering wheel to make sure that it is in the straight-ahead position when the front wheels are.

Flexible Coupling Bush - Replacement

1. Disconnect the battery.

2. Remove the steering coupling to steering gear pinion clinch bolt and disengage the clamp (Fig. H:32).

3. Remove the dash lower insulation panel (Fig. H:35).

4. Disconnect the coupling from the lower end of the steering shaft by pulling it upwards through the bulkhead seal.

5. Examine the bushes for signs of wear or damage and if necessary replace them. Lubricate the new bushes with paraffin to facilitate installation. Push them into the steering coupling (Fig. H:38).

6. Lubricate the bulkhead seal and push the coupling through the steering shaft plate and through the bulkhead seal. Make sure the upper end of the coupling is properly seated on the steering shaft pins and the lower end is correctly seated on the steering gear pinion. Make sure the coupling is pushed down fully so that the bushes engage the steering shaft end plate (Fig. H:39).

7. Tighten the steering coupling clamp clinch bolt, securely attaching the coupling to the steering gear pinion. Recheck engagement of the steering coupling and shaft.

8. Refit the dash lower insulating panel and reconnect the battery.

Technical Data

Wheel alignment
    Toe setting. . . . . 0.04 in (1 mm) toe-in to
                                0.24 in (6 mm) toe-out

Springs
Colour code
    Standard . . . . Brown
    S . . . . Brown/Red
    Heavy duty . . . . .Brown/Yellow
Free length
    Standard . . . . .10.75 in (273 mm)
    S . . . . 10 in (253 mm)
    Heavy duty . . . . .10.7 in (271 mm)
Shock absorbers
Colour code
    Standard . . . . .Red/Yellow
    S and Heavy duty . . . . Red/Blue
Steering gear
    Capacity . . . . .0.17 pt (95 cc)
Lubricants
    Wheel bearings . . . . High melting point lithium grease
    CV joints. . . . . Ford Spec. S-M1C-75-A/SQM-1C-9004-A
    Steering rack . . . . Ford Spec. S-AM1C-9106-A Fluid grease

STEERING

Trouble Shooter

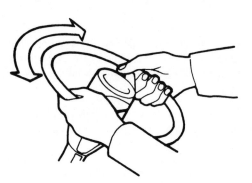

FAULT	CAUSE	CURE
Steering feels stiff	1. Low tyre pressures 2. Incorrect wheel alignment 3. Stiff track rod ends 4. Steering rack needs adjustment	1. Correct tyre pressures. 2. Correct wheel alignment. 3. Check and replace if necessary. 4. Adjust if necessary.
Steering wheel shake	1. Wheels and tyres need balancing 2. Tyre pressures incorrect 3. Incorrect wheel alignment 4. Wheel hub nut loose 5. Wheel bearings damaged 6. Front suspension distorted 7. Steering rack needs adjustment 8. Shock absorbers faulty	1. Balance as necessary. 2. Correct. 3. Correct alignment. 4. Adjust wheel bearings. 5. Replace wheel bearings. 6. Check, repair or replace. 7. Adjust as necessary. 8. Check and rectify.
Steering pulls to one side	1. Uneven tyre pressure 2. Wheel alignment incorrect 3. Wheel bearings worn or damaged 4. Brakes improperly adjusted 5. Shock absorbers faulty 6. Suspension distorted 7. Steering box/rack worn	1. Correct. 2. Correct. 3. Replace and adjust. 4. Adjust brakes. 5. Check and rectify. 6. Check and rectify. 7. Adjust or replace.
Wheel tramp	1. Over-inflated tyres 2. Unbalanced tyre and wheel 3. Defective shock absorber 4. Defective tyre	1. Correct pressure. 2. Check and balance if necessary. 3. Check and rectify. 4. Repair or replace.
Abnormal tyre wear	1. Incorrect tyre pressure 2. Incorrect wheel alignment 3. Excessive wheel bearing play 4. Improper driving	1. Check pressures. 2. Check wheel alignment. 3. Adjust wheel bearings. 4. Avoid sharp turning at high speeds, rapid starting and braking, etc.
Tyre noises	1. Improper tyre inflation 2. Incorrect wheel alignment	1. Correct tyre pressures. 2. Correct wheel alignment.

Rear Suspension

REAR WHEEL BEARINGS . . . . [1]
REAR SPRINGS. . . . . [2]
SUSPENSION LOWER ARM . . . . [3]
STABILISER BAR . . . . [4]
PANHARD ROD. [5]
SHOCK ABSORBERS. . . . . [6]
REAR AXLE & SUSPENSION ASSEMBLY. . [7]
TECHNICAL DATA. . . . . [8]

REAR WHEEL BEARINGS . . . . [1]

Adjustment

1.   Refer to the information on jacking the vehicle contained in ROUTINE MAINTENANCE at the front of the book. Jack up the rear of the car and support it on stands.
2.   Remove the rear wheels.
3.   Remove the grease cup, split pin and nut retainer.
4.   Tighten the locknut to a torque of 27 lbf ft (3.7 kg m) and, whilst rotating the hub, back off the locknut 90º.
5.   Replace the nut retainer, split pin and grease cup, making sure a new split pin is used.
6.   Repeat the operation for the other hub.
7.   Replace the road wheels, lower the vehicle to the ground and finally tighten the wheel bolts.

Bearing Replacement

1.   Jack the rear of the car and support it on stands as mentioned in the previous section.
2.   Remove the rear wheels, grease cup, split pin and nut retainer.
3.   Remove the adjusting locknut, washer and outer bearing.
4.   Making sure the handbrake is fully released, pull the drum and hub assembly from the stub axle.
5.   Ideally, use special tool 21-051 to remove the grease retainer from the hub (Fig. I:3). However, if this is not available, it should be possible to lever out the seal with a screwdriver. Care should be taken, though, not to damage the seal bore.
6.   Lift out the bearing cone.
7.   Use a punch to tap out the bearing cups, tapping at diametrically opposed points on the cup. Make sure it does not tilt in the hub. Also make sure the punch is in good condition. Take care not to raise any burrs on the cup seats as this will adversely affect the bearing pre-load.
8.   Clean all old grease and any dirt from the hub.
9.   Refit the bearing cups with an installer tool (Fig. I:4), or large socket or tubing, drifting each one firmly into position.
10. Pack both bearings with lithium based grease, working it between the rollers. Also, apply a light smear of

grease between the sealing lips of a new grease retainer.
11. Position the inner bearing cone and then fit the new grease retainer with its lip towards the bearing, using either an installer tool (Fig. I:5) or a large socket or piece of tubing.
12. Refit the hub to the spindle followed by the outer bearing cone, washer and locknut.
13. Apply the handbrake and adjust the bearings as described previously.
14. Repeat the procedure for the other hub.
15. Replace the roadwheels, lower the car to the ground and finally tighten the wheel bolts fully.

REAR SPRINGS. . . . . [2]

Removal

1.   Slacken the wheel bolts and jack up the car, referring to the jacking information contained under ROUTINE MAINTENANCE. Remove the rear wheels.
2.   Place a jack beneath the rear axle tube to take its weight.
3.   Open the tailgate, lift the parcel shelf and remove the plastic cap, nut and washer from the shock absorber top mounting.
4.   Remove the through bolt holding the lower arm to the axle assembly.
5.   If a stabiliser bar is fitted, remove the two retaining nuts from the body mounts.
6.   Lower the jack supporting the axle until it is possible to lift out the spring and insulator (Fig. I:6).

Installation

Installation is a reversal of the removal procedure.

SUSPENSION LOWER ARM . . . . [3]

Removal

1.   Jack up both ends of the car, referring to the jacking information contained under ROUTINE MAINTENANCE at the front of the book.
2.   Remove the through bolt from the forward mounting (Fig. I:8).

3. Remove the through bolt from the axle mounting and remove the lower arm.

Installation

Installation is basically a reversal of the removal procedure, noting the following points:

a) Fit the axle end of the lower arm first, making sure that the flanges on the arm point towards the centre line of the car. Don't fully tighten the mounting nut and bolt at this stage.

b) Fit the front end, again not fully tightening the nut and bolt.

c) Tighten the nuts and bolts fully after lowering the car to the ground.

STABILISER BAR . . . . [4]

Removal

1. Raise the rear of the car by running it up on to a pair of ramps.

2. Remove the locknuts from the two through bolts securing the bottoms of the stabiliser bar connecting links to the shock absorber mountings.

3. Remove the circlips from the upper bush locating pin at the upper ends of the stabiliser bar connecting links.

4. Remove the connecting links with their plastic sleeves and washers (Fig. I:9).

5. Remove the two nuts securing the stabiliser bar clamps to the body.

6. Pull the bar downwards, removing the retaining clamps (Fig. I:10).

Bush Replacement

If it is necessary to replace the rubber stabiliser bar bushes, fit them so that the splits in them face outwards and to the rear. The upper bush in the connecting link can be replaced by pushing out the old one and pushing in a new one. However, if the lower bush shows signs of wear, the complete link must be replaced since the lower bush is not serviceable.

Installation

Installation of the stabiliser bar and its connecting links is a reversal of the removal procedure.

PANHARD ROD . . . . [5]

Removal (Fig. I:11)

1. Raise the rear of the car by driving it on to a pair of ramps.

2. Remove the mounting bolt holding the panhard rod to the body.

3. Remove the mounting bolt holding the panhard rod to the axle.

4. Lift away the panhard rod.

Bush Replacement

1. Assemble the rod end in the vice with a pair of sockets or pieces of tubing, one large enough to accept the bush, the other small enough to push it out through the eye of the rod (Fig. I:12).

2. Close the vice jaws, removing the bush.

3. Lubricate the new bush with paraffin and push it into the rod eye with the sockets or tubing in the same way that it was removed.

Installation

1. Fit the panhard rod so that the open side of its U-section faces the axle.

2. Fit the axle mounting bolt and then the body mounting bolt. Tighten both.

3. Lower the car to the ground.

SHOCK ABSORBERS. . . . . [6]

Removal

1. Slacken the rear wheel bolts and jack up the rear of the car, referring to the jacking information contained under ROUTINE MAINTENANCE. Remove the rear wheels.

2. Place a jack beneath the rear axle tube to take the weight of the axle assembly.

3. Open the tailgate, lift the parcel shelf and remove the plastic cap, nut and washer from the upper shock absorber mounting (Fig. I:13). Remove the upper insulator, making a note of which way round it is fitted.

4. Remove the lock nut and bolt from the lower shock absorber mounting and lever the shock absorber lower end from its locating peg. Lift away the shock absorber.

5. Clean off the locating peg.

Inspection

Check the unit visually for any fluid leaks or signs of damage. If any are present it must be replaced.

Clamp the unit vertically in a vice and operate the piston rod to its full length, then compress it. There should be a moderate and even resistance throughout the upward and downward strokes. Any variation or sudden loss of resistance indicates the presence of air in the system, loss of fluid or a faulty valve.

If a lack of resistance or a spring 'feel' is felt at the beginning of each stroke, this usually indicates the presence of air. In this case leave the unit in the vertical position for a few minutes to allow the air bubbles to collect at the top of the pressure chamber, then give the piston rod a few short strokes from the fully compressed position, followed by a few slow full strokes to remove all air from the chamber. Repeat the test.

If the resistance is still slight or erratic and free movement cannot be eliminated, then the shock absorber must be replaced.

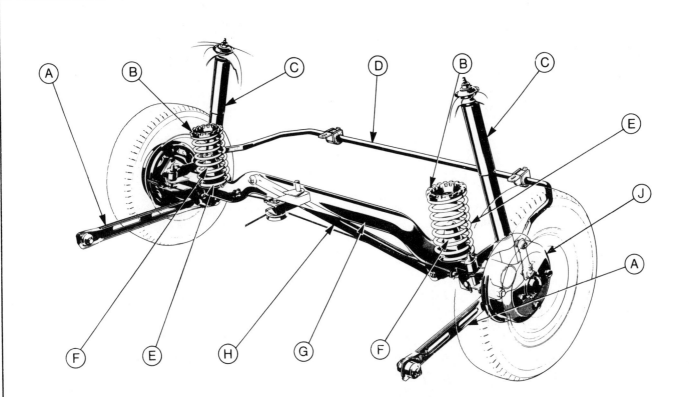

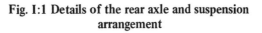

A. Lower arms
B. Spring insulator pads
C. Shock absorbers
D. Stabiliser bar (where fitted)
E. Springs
F. Bump rubbers
G. Axle
H. Panhard rod
J. Integral hub and brake drum

Fig. I:1 Details of the rear axle and suspension arrangement

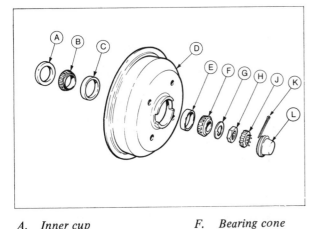

A. Inner cup
B. Bearing cone
C. Grease retainer
D. Drum and hub assembly
E. Outer cup
F. Bearing cone
G. Tab washer
H. Locknut
J. Nut retainer
K. Split pin
L. Grease cup

Fig. I:2 An exploded view of the rear hub bearing components

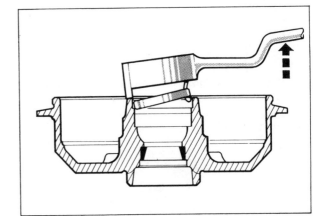

Fig. I:3 Levering out the hub bearing inner oil seal

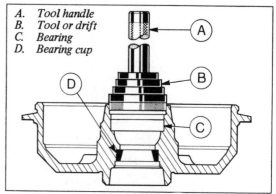

A. Tool handle
B. Tool or drift
C. Bearing cups

Fig. I:4 Fit the new bearing cups using an installer tool or tubular drift

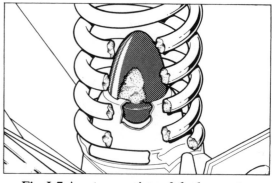

A. Tool handle
B. Tool or drift
C. Bearing
D. Bearing cup

Fig. I:5 Fit the new oil seal, making sure that the seal lips are not damaged

Fig. I:6 Details of the coil spring insulator pad

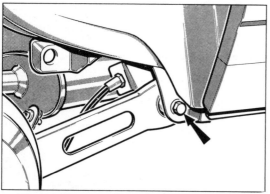

Fig. I:7 A cut-away view of the bump stop attachment to the body

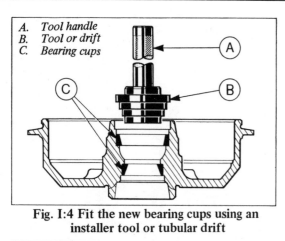

Fig. I:8 Remove through bolt (arrowed) to detach suspension lower arm from body

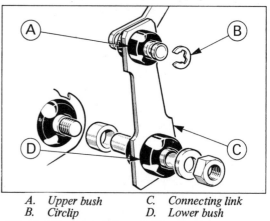

A. Upper bush   C. Connecting link
B. Circlip   D. Lower bush

Fig. I:9 Details of the stabiliser bar connecting link mounting arrangement

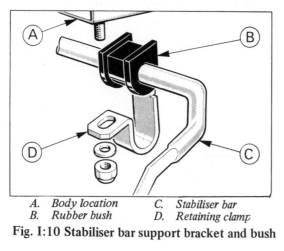

A. Body location   C. Stabiliser bar
B. Rubber bush   D. Retaining clamp

Fig. I:10 Stabiliser bar support bracket and bush

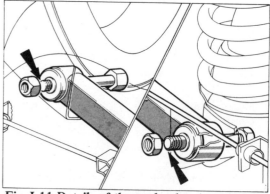

Fig. I:11 Details of the panhard rod mounting arrangement

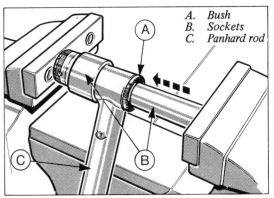

A. Bush
B. Sockets
C. Panhard rod

Fig. I:12 Method of removing and replacing panhard rod bush

Fig. I:13 Shock absorber mounting nut inside luggage compartment

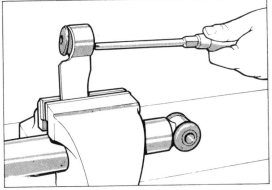

Fig. I:14 Support shock absorber in vice then remove/replace arm bush

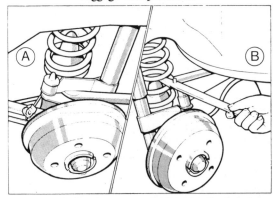

Fig. I:15 Using lever to refit the shock absorber arm (A) to its peg (B)

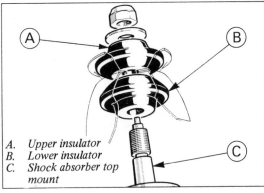

A. Upper insulator
B. Lower insulator
C. Shock absorber top mount

Fig. I:16 Details of the shock absorber upper mounting components

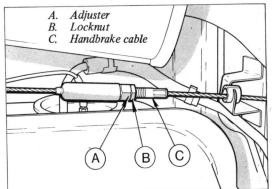

A. Adjuster
B. Locknut
C. Handbrake cable

Fig. I:17 Disconnect the handbrake cable at the adjuster when removing rear suspension

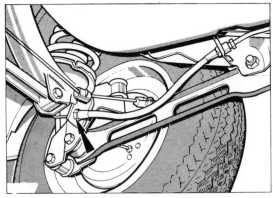

Fig. I:18 Disconnect the brake pipes at the axle bracket union (arrowed)

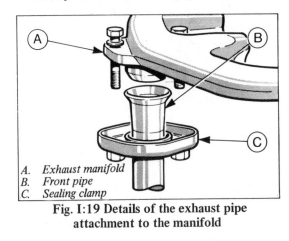

A. Exhaust manifold
B. Front pipe
C. Sealing clamp

Fig. I:19 Details of the exhaust pipe attachment to the manifold

Bush Replacement

Using a vice and suitable piece of tubing, press out the metal spacer tubes from the centre of the rubber shock absorber lower mounts. With these removed the rubber bushes can be removed by hand (Fig. I:14). The new bushes should be lubricated with a water/soap solution and pressed into the shock absorber lower eye. Refit the metal spacer tubes by the method used to remove them.

The shock absorber arm bush can be pushed out with a screwdriver or some similar tool. The new bush should be lubricated with soap and water and pushed into place using a vice.

Installation

1. Lubricate the shock absorber arm bush and its locating peg with a soap and water solution and, using a flat lever, washer and piece of tube or large socket, lever the arm on to the peg. See Fig. I:15. A steady force will need to be applied to the bush so that it gradually 'creeps' on to the peg.
2. Set the shock absorber lower mounting in place and secure it with the through bolt and nut.
3. Position the shock absorber upper insulator (Fig. I: 16) and then secure the upper mounting with the locknut and washer. Replace the plastic cap.
4. Refit the road wheels, remove the jack beneath the axle and lower the car to the ground.
5. Finally, fully tighten the road wheel bolts.

REAR AXLE & SUSPENSION ASSEMBLY.. [7]

Removal

1. Raise the rear of the car, referring to the jacking information contained under ROUTINE MAINTENANCE.
2. Disconnect the handbrake cable from its adjuster (Fig. I:17).
3. Remove the panhard rod as described previously.
4. Place a brake pipe clamp on each flexible brake pipe then disconnect the pipes at the axle bracket (Fig. I:18) and plug the open ends to prevent the ingress of dirt.

5. Disconnect the exhaust pipe from the exhaust manifold in the engine compartment (Fig. I:19).
6. Disconnect the rear exhaust pipe mountings and lift away the exhaust pipe assembly.
7. Position a trolley jack beneath the axle tube to take the weight of the axle assembly.
8. Remove the through bolts holding the lower suspension arms to the body and the nuts holding the stabiliser bar clamps to the body (if fitted).
9. Open the tailgate, lift the parcel tray and remove the plastic cap, nut and washer from the top shock absorber mounting. Lift off the insulator.
10. Lower the axle assembly on to its wheels and roll it out from under the car.

Installation

This is basically a reversal of the removal procedure, noting the following points:
a) The handbrake should be adjusted as described in the BRAKES chapter.
b) Bleed the brake system as detailed in the BRAKES chapter.
c) Tighten the lower arm body mounting bolts after the car has been lowered to the ground.

Axle Tube-Replacement

1. Remove the rear axle and suspension as detailed previously, then support the axle assembly on stands.
2. Remove the brake drum/hub assembly and brake carrier plates. See BRAKES chapter.
3. Remove the handbrake equaliser and guides.
4. Remove the bump stop rubber.
5. Remove the back plate studs.
6. Clean and check all parts for damage and wear. Replace if necessary.
7. Fit the components to the new tube in the reverse order of removal adjusting the wheel bearings as described previously after making sure the spindle and seal diameter are clean.
8. Fit the axle and suspension assembly to the car as detailed previously.

Technical Data

Springs
  Colour code
    Standard . . . . .Blue/yellow
    Heavy duty . . . . .Green/yellow
    'S' . . . . Green/blue
  Free length
    Standard . . . . .10.5 in (270 mm)
    Heavy duty . . . . .11.1 in (282 mm)
    'S' . . . . .10.2 in (260 mm)

NOTE: Spring free lengths are nominal and may vary by up to 0.39 in (10 mm)

Shock absorbers
  Colour code
    Standard . . . . .Red/yellow
    Heavy duty . . . . Red/blue
    'S' . . . . .Red/green

Brakes

BLEEDING THE BRAKES . . . . [1]

The fluid level in the master cylinder reservoir (Fig. J:1) must be maintained at a reasonable level throughout the bleeding operation as, if it is allowed to drop excessively, air may be drawn into the system. Use only fresh hydraulic fluid of the type specified in Technical Data at the end of this section. Never re-use fluid which has already been passed through the system. Take care when topping up the master cylinder with fluid since it is an effective paint stripper, and any spilt on the bodywork should be washed off with cold water immediately.

1. Jack up both ends of the car, referring to the jacking information contained under ROUTINE MAINTENANCE at the front of the book.
2. Remove the reservoir cap and top up the reservoir, making sure both chambers are topped up with the recommended fluid.
3. Remove the rubber dust cap from the bleed nipple (Fig. J:2) on the left hand front brake caliper and attach a bleed tube.
4. Immerse the other end of the tube in a clean jar containing a small quantity of clean brake fluid (Fig. J:3). Throughout the bleeding operation, the end of the tube must remain immersed in this fluid.
5. Slacken the bleed valve approximately half a turn and then depress the brake pedal fully, allowing it to return to the fully released position. Brake fluid and/or air should have been pumped into the jar. If not, slacken the bleed valve further until fluid and/or air can be pumped into the jar.
6. Continue depressing the brake pedal, pausing briefly (about three seconds) after each stroke, until the fluid coming from the bleed tube is completely free of air bubbles and is completely clean.
7. Finally, with the brake pedal in the fully depressed position, close the bleed valve. Take care not to over-tighten the valve; tighten it only enough to seal it.
8. Remove the bleed tube and refit the rubber dust cap.

9. If a brake pressure control valve is fitted to the car, bleed the upper valve in a similar manner. See Fig. J:4. Close the bleed valve after the operation.
10. Then bleed the right hand rear brake with the handbrake applied. Release the handbrake.
11. Repeat the process with the right hand front brake, the lower valve on the brake pressure control valve (if fitted) and finally the left hand rear brake with the handbrake applied. Release the handbrake.
12. Top up the master cylinder reservoir with approved fluid and replace the cap, after first checking that the vent hole in it is clear. Do not fill the reservoir above the MAX mark on the side.
13. Check the operation of the brakes. If, after bleeding, the brake pedal is still 'spongy', or goes right down to the floor, this indicates that air is still present in the system, and the bleeding operation must be repeated. If subsequent attempts at bleeding still fail to produce a satisfactory result, the system should be checked for leaks, as air is obviously being drawn into the system.

DISC PADS . . . . [2]

Replacement

The brake pads should be renewed if they are worn below the minimum safe thickness of 0.060 in (1.5 mm), or if they are the cause of braking problems.

Whenever one or more brake pads require replacement, BOTH pads at BOTH front brakes should be replaced to maintain even braking balance.

1. Slacken the wheel bolts, jack up the front of the car, fit axle stands and remove the front wheels.
2. Remove the piston housing retaining pins and discard them. Apply slight pressure to the housing against the caliper tension springs and slide out the keys (Fig. J:5). Discard them.

3. Remove the piston housing (Fig. J:6) and suspend it from the body with a piece of wire. Make sure the piston assembly is securely suspended.

4. Withdraw the anti-rattle clips and brake pads.

5. Brush any dirt or dust from the caliper, taking care not to inhale any since it is asbestos based and is harmful. Ideally use a vacuum cleaner to remove the dust, or use a brush or rag with care.

6. Check that the replacement pads are of the correct type and that the pads, anti-rattle clips, keys and disc are free from grease, oil or dirt.

7. Before fitting the new pads, push the caliper piston back into its bore to provide adequate clearance. This should be done by carefully applying pressure to the face of the piston. It will be necessary to suck out some of the brake fluid from the master cylinder reservoir during this operation since the level will rise as the piston is pushed back into its bore. Take care not to remove too much otherwise air will enter the system and the brakes will have to be bled as described previously.

8. Fit the new pads (Fig. J:8) and anti-rattle clips into the pad housing, making sure that both are fitted correctly. The anti-rattle clips should be fitted at the tops of the pads.

9. Replace the piston housing, fitting it above the caliper tension springs. Apply pressure to the housing against the tension springs and slide in new keys. Make sure the retaining pin holes in the keys and piston housing are properly aligned.

10. Fit new key retaining pins from the disc side and secure them (Fig. J:9).

11. Operate the brake pedal several times to bring the brake pads into their correct operating position.

12. Repeat the operation for the other front brake.

13. Refit the road wheels and lower the car to the ground. Fully tighten the road wheel bolts and check the fluid level in the master cylinder reservoir.

DISC BRAKES . . . . [3]

Calipers

Removal

1. Slacken the wheel bolts, jack up the front of the car, fit axle stands and remove the road wheel.

2. Disconnect the brake flexible hose from the caliper and plug the end to prevent fluid loss.

3. Release the two caliper retaining bolts (Fig. J:10) and lift away the caliper.

Installation

1. Refit the caliper assembly, tightening the two retaining bolts to a torque of 37-45 lb.ft (5.1-6.1 kg m).

2. Unplug the brake flexible hose and reconnect it to the caliper inlet port. Tighten the connector to a torque of 8-11 lb.ft (1.2-1.5 kg m). Make sure the hose is not twisted and will be clear of the body and suspension components during steering and suspension movement.

3. Bleed the brake circuit as described previously.

4. Replace the road wheel, lower the car to the ground and fully tighten the road wheel bolts.

NOTE: If the caliper is being removed to allow removal of the front hub/disc assembly to gain access to the suspension components, it will not be necessary to disconnect the flexible brake hose. All that will be necessary will be to support the caliper from the body with a piece of wire, making sure the hose is not strained in any way.

Caliper Overhaul (Fig. J:7)

1. Remove the piston housing as described under DISC PADS, disconnecting the flexible brake hose and plugging it to allow complete removal from the car.

2. Make sure the working conditions are spotlessly clean.

3. Remove the rubber bellows from around the piston.

4. Apply an air line to the brake fluid inlet port. This will force the piston from its bore.

5. Using a blunt instrument, such as a plastic needle, remove the piston seal from the annular groove in the piston housing. Take great care not to scratch the cylinder bore during this operation.

6. Wash the piston and piston bore in methylated spirits or clean brake fluid. Do NOT use petrol or paraffin.

7. Make sure the piston and its bore are free from score marks. This is important.

8. Fit a new piston seal to the annular groove in the piston housing.

9. Lubricate the piston with clean brake fluid and push it into the housing as far as it will go. Take care not to damage the piston seal.

10. Fit new rubber bellows between the piston and housing.

11. Refit the housing to the caliper and reconnect the brake hose.

12. Bleed the brake circuit as described previously.

13. Refit the road wheel, lower the car to the ground and fully tighten the road wheel bolts.

Brake Disc - Runout Check

To check the disc runout, jack up the car and remove the road wheel. Refit the wheel bolts with 0.75 in (19 mm) spacers between the bolt heads and discs. Mount a dial gauge so that its pointer rests on the disc face and then rotate the disc through one complete revolution. (Figs. J:11 and J:12). The disc runout figure should be within 0.006 in (0.15 mm) of the total indicator reading. If a reading in excess of this is found, the cause should be sought and rectified.

Disc Removal

1. Slacken the wheel bolts, jack up the car, fit axle stands and then remove the road wheel.

2. Remove the brake caliper assembly as described previously, suspending it securely from the suspension.

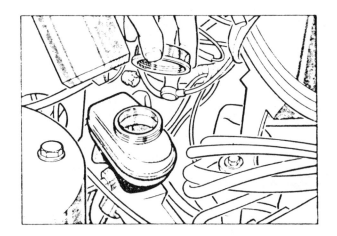

Fig. J:1 Make sure fluid is kept full during the
bleeding operation

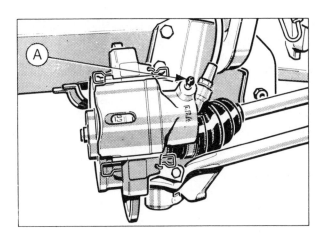

Fig. J:2 The location of the front brake caliper
bleed screw (A)

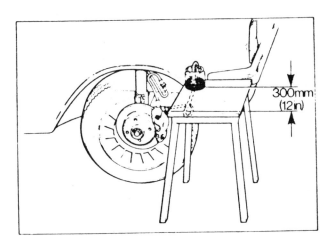

Fig. J:3 Make sure the bleed jar is at least 300
mm above the caliper nipple

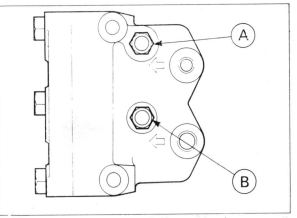

A.   L.H. front – R.H. rear circuit
B.   R.H. front – L.H. rear circuit

Fig. J:4 The position of the bleed nipples on the
brake pressure control valve

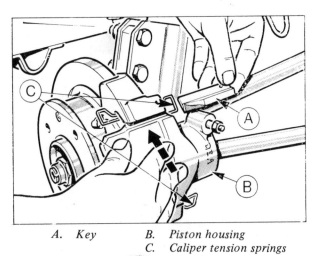

A.   Key   B.   Piston housing
                  C.   Caliper tension springs

Fig. J:5 Remove retaining pins, then withdraw
key (A) to detach piston housing

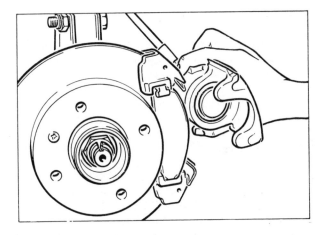

Fig. J:6 Withdraw piston housing to expose brake
pads in pad housing

3. Remove the disc retaining screw from the hub (Fig. J:13) and lift away the disc (Fig. J:15).

Inspection

Inspect the disc friction surfaces. Moderate scoring is permissible, but heavy scoring or grooving, cracking or pitting of the surface, or excessive corrosion build up necessitates replacement of the disc.

The disc may be trued up by grinding down to within the minimum permissible thickness specified in Technical Data, but replacement is preferable.

Make sure all disc/hub mating surfaces are free from dirt and dust. Also make sure the friction surface of the disc is free from dirt, oil and brake fluid.

Installation

1. Make sure the mating face of the hub and disc are spotlessly clean then refit the disc assembly and replace the retaining screw.
2. Replace the caliper assembly, tightening the retaining bolts to the specified torque.
3. Replace the road wheel, lower the car to the ground and fully tighten the road wheel bolts.

BRAKE SHOES .... [4]

The brake shoes in the rear brakes (Fig. J:14) should be renewed if the linings are worn to or approaching the minimum wear thickness of 0.06 in (1.5 mm), or if they are the cause of braking problems.

Brake shoes should be renewed in axle sets, i.e. BOTH sides of BOTH rear brakes to maintain braking balance.

Removal

1. Slacken the rear wheel bolts, jack up the rear of the car, fit axle stands and remove both rear wheels.
2. Fully release the handbrake and release the handbrake cable from the brake assembly by prising off the spring clip and withdrawing the clevis pin (Fig. J:16).
3. Slide the handbrake operating lever rubber dust cover from the operating lever.
4. Remove the hub nut dust cover, split pin, nut retainer, adjusting nut, washer and outer bearing from the spindle.
5. Slide the brake drum/hub assembly from the spindle.
6. Use a pair of pliers to depress the spring retaining washer on the leading shoe retaining spring. Turn the spring washer through 90° so that the slots in the pin hole coincide with the lugs on the retaining pin. Remove the washer and spring and then remove the pin from the carrier plate. Take care not to lose the spring.
7. Twist the leading shoe outwards and upwards away from the carrier plate until it is possible to detach the shoe and remove the springs (Fig. J:17).
8. Remove the trailing shoe hold down spring in the same manner as the leading shoe spring assembly.
9. Slide the lower end of the spacer strut from the slot in the carrier plate (Fig. J:18) and move the trailing shoe

upwards and away from the carrier plate (Fig. J:19). Withdraw the handbrake operating lever and shoe assembly from the carrier plate.
10. Prise the spring washer from the long ratchet lever spigot and remove the ratchet lever from the leading shoe.
11. Prise the spring washer from the short ratchet lever spigot and remove the spring and ratchet lever from the leading shoe.
12. Remove the spacer strut from the trailing shoe by twisting it and removing the spring.

Installation

1. Fit the handbrake lever return spring to the trailing shoe. Then hook the spacer strut to the spring and lever it into position on the shoe (Fig. J:21).
2. Fit the smaller of the two ratchet levers to the shoe pivot on the leading shoe. Place two 0.008 in (0.2 mm) feeler gauges between the shoe and ratchet lever and fit a new spring washer, making sure the retaining tabs are properly fitted. Remove the feeler gauges and check that the ratchet lever turns freely on the pivot and returns under spring's pressure.
3. Fit the longer ratchet lever to the brake shoe with a new spring washer, making sure no clearance exists between the ratchet lever and shoe.
4. Position the two ratchets relative to each other and with an overlap as shown in Fig. J:22.
5. Insert the handbrake operating lever through the carrier plate and locate the trailing shoe against the wheel cylinder and upper pivot position. Slide the spacer strut into the slot in the carrier plate.
6. Refit the hold down spring, washer and pin to the trailing shoe, turning the washer through 90° so that the slots in the washer are at right angles to the lugs on the retaining pin.
7. Fit the stronger of the two shoe return springs between the trailing and leading shoes at the upper pivot point.
8. Hook the upper end of the leading shoe under the upper pivot position and fit the shoe against the carrier plate. Make sure the slot in the long ratchet lever is engaged with the spacer strut and then locate the lower end of the shoe with the wheel cylinder.
9. Refit the leading shoe hold down spring, washer and pin.
10. Attach the second shoe return spring to the leading shoe and then to the trailing shoe using a pair of pliers.
11. Bend up a stout wire hook and use it to pull back the spring loaded ratchet lever against its spring (Fig. J:23).
12. Refit the handbrake lever rubber boot to the back of the carrier plate.
13. Reconnect the handbrake cable to the operating lever.
14. Refit the hub/drum assembly to the spindle, replacing the outer bearing, retaining washer and adjusting nut. Tighten the latter to 27 lbf.ft (3.6 kg m), whilst rotating the drum (Fig. J:24). Then back off the nut 90°. Fit the nut retainer, a new split pin and the dust cap.
15. Depress the foot brake pedal several times to adjust the brakes.
16. Repeat the procedure for the other brake assembly.

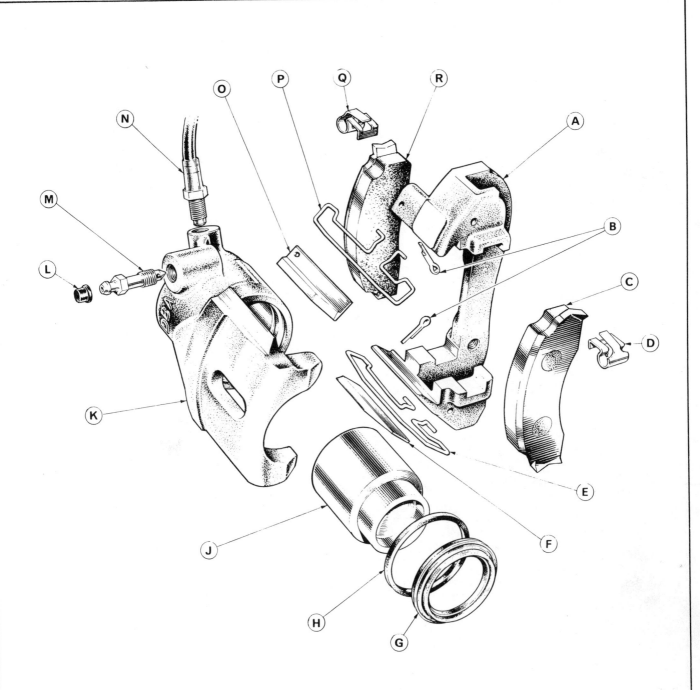

A. Pad housing
B. Retaining pins
C. Brake pad
D. Anti-rattle clip
E. Caliper tension spring

F. Key
G. Rubber bellows
H. Piston seal
J. Piston
K. Piston housing
L. Dust cap

M. Bleed screw
N. Fluid hose
O. Key
P. Tension spring
Q. Anti-rattle clip
R. Brake pad

Fig. J:7 An exploded view of the front brake caliper components

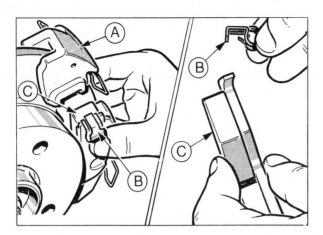

A. *Pad housing* B. *Anti-rattle clip* C. *Brake pad*

Fig. J:8 Fit anti-rattle clips (B) then assemble pads (C) to housing (A)

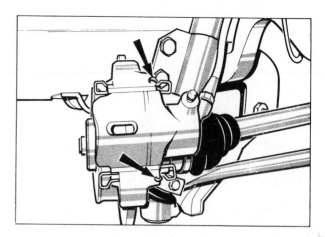

Fig. J:9 Fit the retaining pins, making sure holes in key and housing are aligned

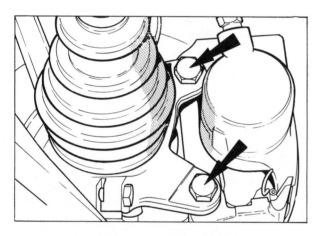

Fig. J:10 Undo the two bolts (arrowed) to remove caliper from hub carrier

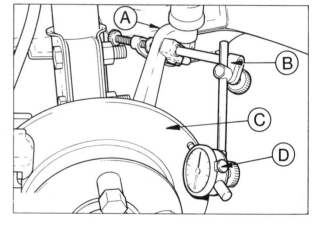

A. *Steering arm* C. *Disc*
B. *Holding fixture* D. *Dial indicator*

Fig. J:11 Mount a clock gauge on the disc face to measure run out

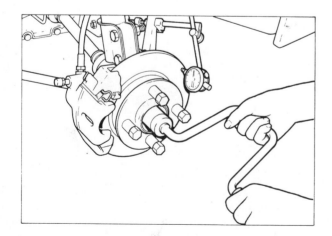

Fig. J:12 Rotate the disc using a wrench and socket to measure run out

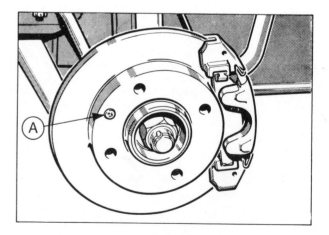

Fig. J:13 To remove brake disc from hub assembly, first undo screw (A)

Brakes

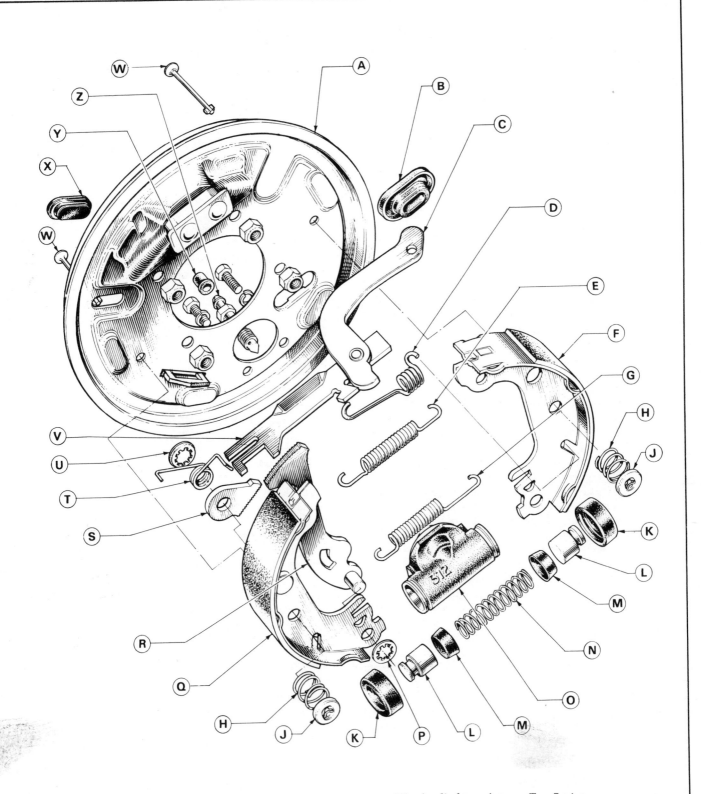

A.	Carrier plate	G.	Shoe return spring
B.	Rubber boot	H.	Spring
C.	Handbrake actuating lever	J.	Shoe holding down washer
D.	Lever return spring	K.	Dust cover
E.	Shoe return spring	L.	Piston
F.	Trailing brake shoe	M.	Piston seal

N.	Wheel cylinder spring	T.	Spring
O.	Wheel cylinder	U.	Spring retainer washer
P.	Spring retainer washer	V.	Spacer strut
Q.	Leading shoe	W.	Pin
R.	Large ratchet	X.	Inspection plug
S.	Small ratchet	Y.	Dust cover
		Z.	Bleed nipple

Fig. J:14 An exploded view of the rear brake assembly components

17. Refit the road wheel, lower the car to the ground and fully tighten the road wheel bolts.
18. Road test the vehicle.

WHEEL CYLINDERS .... [5]

Removal

1. Remove the rear brake shoe assembly as described previously.
2. Disconnect the brake pipe from the cylinder inlet port and plug the pipe to prevent loss of brake fluid.
3. Release the two retaining bolts at the back of the carrier plate (Fig. J:25) and remove the wheel cylinder.

Installation

This is a reversal of the removal procedure, noting that the brake circuit should be bled as described previously at the beginning of this chapter.

Overhaul (Fig. J:26)

1. Remove the wheel cylinder as described previously.
2. Pull the rubber boots from the ends of the cylinder and withdraw the piston assemblies. Separate the boots from the pistons.
3. Slide out the piston seals and then remove the spring from the centre of the cylinder bore.
4. Unscrew the brake bleed nipple.
5. Clean all components with clean brake fluid or methylated spirits, wiping them dry with a lint free cloth. Check the pistons and cylinder bore for scoring - this is important. If any component is badly scratched or scored, it must be replaced.
6. Screw in the bleed nipple, tightening it sufficiently to prevent leaks.
7. Assemble the rubber boots to the pistons.
8. Lubricate the piston, seal and cylinder bore with clean brake fluid.
9. Fit one piston and boot into the cylinder.
10. From the open end of the cylinder, slide in a NEW piston seal, spring and second seal, making sure the open ends of the seals face the spring.
11. Fit the second piston and rubber boot.
12. Refit the cylinder to the carrier plate, reconnect the brake hose and replace all the remaining components.
13. Bleed the brake circuit as described previously.

MASTER CYLINDER .... [6]

Reservoir Removal

1. Remove the reservoir cap and empty the reservoir of brake fluid. This may be sucked out using a length of clear plastic tubing. Take care that no fluid is spilt on the bodywork since it is a very effective paint stripper. Any that is spilt should be washed off with cold water immediately.
2. Pull the reservoir from the master cylinder body,

tilting it sideways at the same time (Fig. J:27).
3. Prise out the two rubber seals in the master cylinder. Inspect their condition and replace if necessary.

Replacement

1. Lubricate the rubber seals with clean brake fluid and press them into the master cylinder, making sure they are seated properly.
2. Push the reservoir spigots fully home through the rubber seals.
3. Bleed the brake system as described previously.

Master Cylinder Removal

1. Remove the reservoir cap and suck out the fluid using a length of clear plastic tubing.
2. Disconnect the fluid pipes from the master cylinder, plugging the ends to prevent fluid spillage and ingress of dirt.
3. Disconnect the wiring from the fluid level indicator switch (if fitted).
4. Prise off the spring clip and remove the clevis pin and bushes holding the master cylinder pushrod to the pedal (Fig. J:28) on bulkhead fitted cylinders.
5. Release the two nuts and spring washers holding the master cylinder to the bulkhead or servo cylinder and lift away the master cylinder (Fig. J:30).

Installation

This is a reversal of the removal procedure, noting that the brake line union nuts should be tightened to a torque of 8-11 lb.ft (1.2-1.5 kg m) and that the brakes should be bled afterwards as described previously.

Master Cylinder Overhaul (Fig. J:29)

1. Remove the master cylinder from the car as described previously.
2. Carefully prise the reservoir from the body of the master cylinder and remove the rubber seals from the inlet ports.
3. Clamp the master cylinder in a vice fitted with 'soft' jaws.
4. Depress the operating rod, to release any pressure on the stop pin and remove the stop pin through the forward inlet port.
5. Pull back the operating rod rubber boot to expose the piston retaining circlip. Use circlip pliers to remove the clip.
6. Slide out the operating rod, boot and washer.
7. Remove the rubber boot from the operating rod.
8. Withdraw the primary piston assembly from the master cylinder bore (Fig. J:31).
9. Tap the master cylinder against the palm of the hand or a block of wood or similar soft surface to remove the secondary piston assembly (Fig. J:32).
10. Unscrew the primary piston spring retaining screw and remove the screw and retaining sleeve from the spring. Remove the spring, retainer and seal from the primary

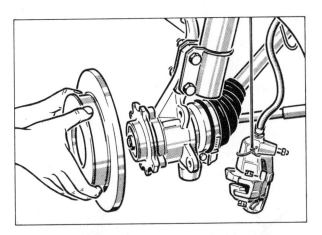

Fig. J:15 Remove and support caliper, then withdraw brake disc from hub assembly

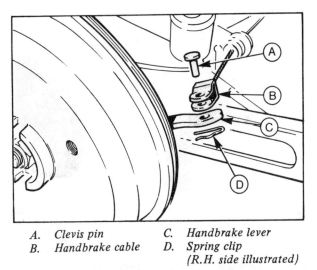

A.	Clevis pin	C.	Handbrake lever
B.	Handbrake cable	D.	Spring clip
			(R.H. side illustrated)

Fig. J:16 Details of the handbrake cable to brake lever clevis connection

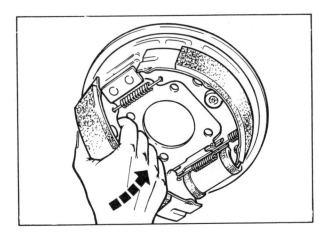

Fig. J:17 Method of removing the right-hand leading brake shoe

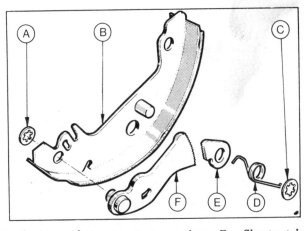

A.   Spacer strut
B.   Slot

Fig. J:18 Release the lower end of the spacer strut from slot in back plate

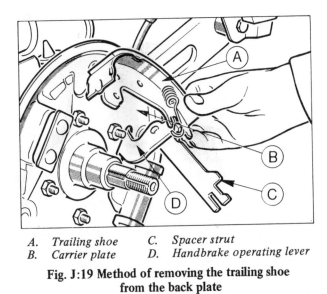

A.	Trailing shoe	C.	Spacer strut
B.	Carrier plate	D.	Handbrake operating lever

Fig. J:19 Method of removing the trailing shoe from the back plate

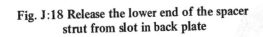

A.	Spring washer	C.	Spring washer	E.	Short ratchet
B.	Leading shoe	D.	Spring	F.	Long ratchet

Fig. J:20 Exploded view of the leading shoe components

piston and, taking great care not to damage the piston, gently lever the remaining seal from the piston.

11. Remove the secondary piston spring, retainer and seal and then gently lever the remaining seal from the piston.

12. Clean the master cylinder and pistons with methylated spirits or clean brake fluid. Do NOT use mineral based oils such as petrol or paraffin. Dry the components with a lint free cloth or blow them dry with an air line.

13. Inspect the pistons and master cylinder bore for visible score marks, ridges or corrosion. This is important. If any of these conditions is evident, the component must be renewed.

14. Fit new seals to the secondary piston and secure them with the spring and retainer. Make sure the seals are fitted correctly.

15. Lubricate the secondary piston with clean brake fluid and gently insert it into the cylinder bore, the spring leading.

16. Fit new seals to the primary piston securing them with the retainer, spring, sleeve and screw. Make sure they are fitted correctly.

17. Lubricate the primary piston assembly with clean brake fluid and gently insert it in the cylinder bore, spring leading.

18. Slide a new rubber boot on to the operating rod and then fit the rod in the master cylinder securing it with a new circlip fitted in front of the rod washer.

19. Fit the operating rod rubber boot to the end of the master cylinder.

20. Fit new rubber seals to the inlet ports of the master cylinder and then gently push the reservoir into place.

21. Refit the master cylinder assembly as described previously and bleed the brakes. After bleeding, depress the brake pedal and hold it depressed for approximately ten seconds. Examine the master cylinder to ensure that there are no signs of fluid leakage.

BRAKE SERVO . . . . [7]

Removal (Fig. J:33)

1. Prise the spring clip from the clevis pin securing the servo actuating rod to the brake pedal and remove the clevis pin.

2. Unfasten the hose clip and remove the vacuum hose from the servo non return valve.

3. Disconnect the brake pipes from the master cylinder, plugging the ends to prevent undue loss of brake fluid. By placing a piece of adhesive tape over the reservoir cap vent hole, fluid loss will be kept to a minimum when disconnecting the brake pipes. Any fluid that is spilt on the bodywork must be washed off immediately with cold water since it will damage the paintwork.

4. Remove the two nuts and washers holding the master cylinder to the servo and remove the master cylinder.

5. Remove the four nuts and washers holding the servo to its mounting bracket and remove the servo complete.

Installation

Installation of the servo unit is basically a reversal of the removal procedure, noting that the brake pipe union nuts should be tightened to a torque of 8-11 lb ft (1.2-1.5 kg.m). If adhesive tape was used to block the reservoir cap vent hole it should be removed and the brakes bled as described earlier in this chapter.

Operating Linkage - Removal (Fig. J:34)

1. Remove the spring clip and clevis pin securing the brake pedal actuating rod to the servo linkage and disconnect the actuating rod from the linkage.

2. Remove the spring clip and clevis pins securing the servo actuating rod to the operating linkage and disconnect the actuating rod from the linkage.

3. Remove the servo unit as described previously.

4. Remove the six bolts holding the servo operating linkage to the bulkhead and lift away the linkage.

Linkage Bush Replacement

1. Slide the right-hand bracket from the end of the linkage rod and push out the bush.

2. Slide the left-hand bracket from the end of the linkage rod and push out the bush.

3. Fit the new bushes in the brackets so that their shoulders abut the insides of the brackets.

4. Slide the brackets back on to the linkage rod.

Installation

1. Mount the linkage to the bulkhead with the six mounting bolts.

2. Refit the servo unit as described previously.

3. Refit the right hand lower pivot to the brake pedal actuating rod with the clevis pin and spring clip.

4. Connect the left-hand lower pivot to the servo actuating rod with the clevis pin and spring clip.

5. Check the position of the brake pedal. It should hang 1-1.2 in (25-30 mm) below the level of the clutch pedal with the brake pedal pulled back towards the driver's seat. If necessary, the position can be adjusted by disconnecting the actuating rod from the servo operating linkage, slackening the locknut and rotating the rod to achieve the correct dimension. When the dimension is correct, tighten the locknut and reconnect the actuating rod to the servo operating linkage.

6. Bleed the brakes as described at the beginning of this chapter.

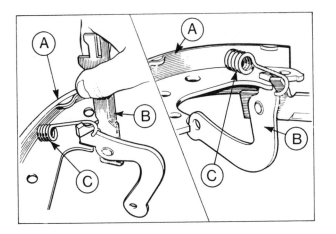

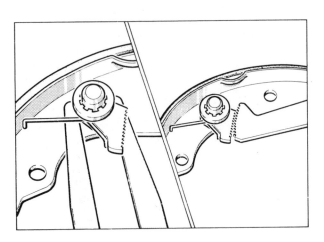

A. *Trailing shoe*   C. *Handbrake lever return spring*
B. *Spacer strut*

Fig. J:21 Method of fitting the handbrake lever to the trailing shoe

Fig. J:22 Assembling the ratchet levers to the leading shoe

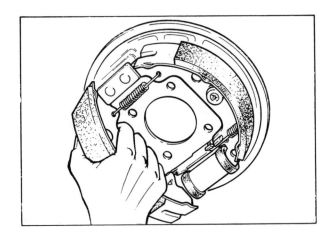

Fig. J:23 Pulling the spring loaded ratchet back against spring

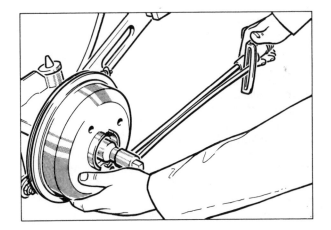

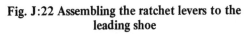

Fig. J:24 Using a torque wrench to tighten rear hub bearing nut

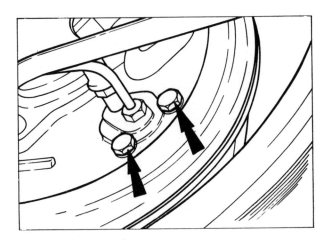

Fig. J:25 Undo two bolts (arrowed) to detach wheel cylinder from backplate

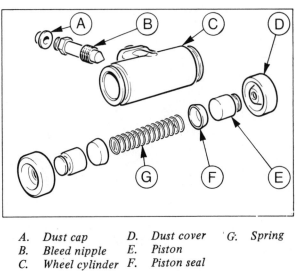

A. *Dust cap*   D. *Dust cover*   G. *Spring*
B. *Bleed nipple*   E. *Piston*
C. *Wheel cylinder* F. *Piston seal*

Fig. J:26 An exploded view of the rear wheel cylinder components

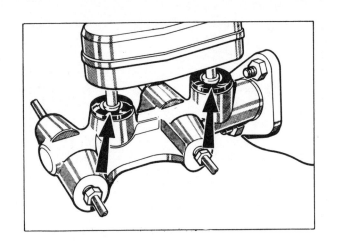

Fig. J:27 Removing the reservoir from the master cylinder, note seals (arrowed)

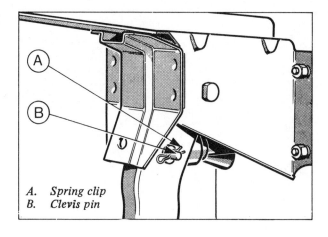

A. Spring clip
B. Clevis pin

Fig. J:28 Remove clip and pin to disconnect operating rod from brake pedal

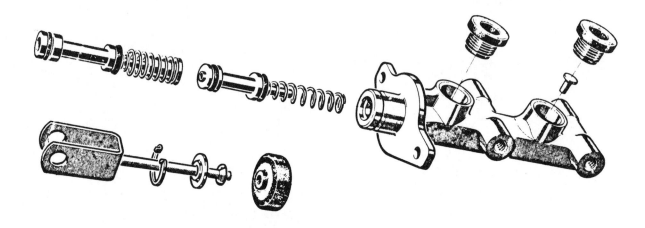

Fig. J:29 An exploded view of the master cylinder components

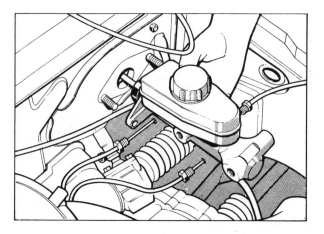

Fig. J:30 Withdrawing master cylinder assembly from bulkhead

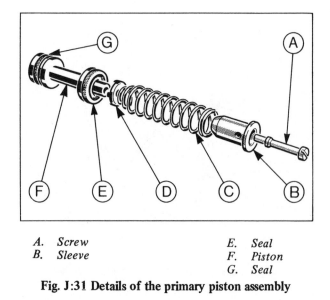

A.	Screw	E.	Seal
B.	Sleeve	F.	Piston
		G.	Seal

Fig. J:31 Details of the primary piston assembly

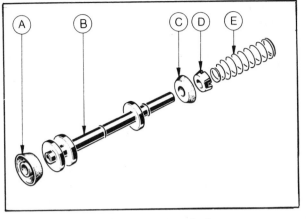

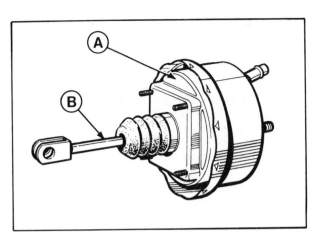

A. Seal   C. Seal
B. Piston   D. Retainer
E. Spring

Fig. J:32 Details of the secondary piston assembly

A. Servo unit   B. Actuating rod

Fig. J:33 Details of the brake servo unit

Fig. J:34 The brake servo installation and connecting linkage

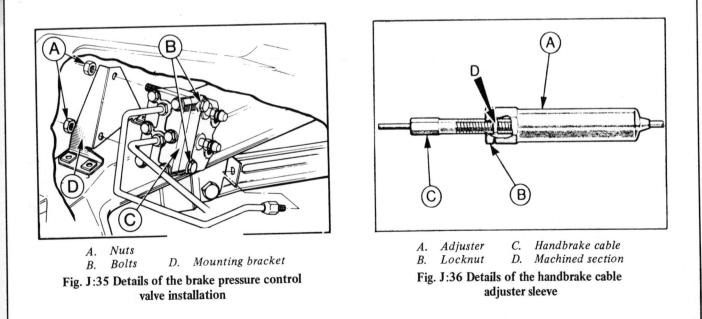

A. Nuts
B. Bolts   D. Mounting bracket

Fig. J:35 Details of the brake pressure control valve installation

A. Adjuster   C. Handbrake cable
B. Locknut   D. Machined section

Fig. J:36 Details of the handbrake cable adjuster sleeve

BRAKE PEDAL . . . . [8]

Removal

1. Disconnect the clutch cable from the clutch pedal as described in the CLUTCH & GEARBOX chapter.
2. Remove the four nuts holding the pedal box assembly to the forward bulkhead.
3. Remove the two screws securing the dash lower insulating panel (if fitted).
4. Remove the bolt connecting the pedal box to the front upper panel.
5. Disconnect the master cylinder pushrod or servo connecting linkage from the brake pedal by removing the spring clip and clevis pin.
6. Disconnect the brake light switch wires from the switch on the pedal bracket.
7. Pull the pedal box rearwards and remove it.
8. Remove the pedal shaft circlip and withdraw the clutch pedal and pedal shaft together with the flat and wave washers.
9. Remove the brake pedal and bushes.

Installation

1. If a new pedal is being fitted, apply an adhesive such as Bostik to the centre and edges of the pedal pad and fit the pad to the pedal, making sure the lug on the pad engages with the cutout in the pedal.
2. Replacement of the pedal is a reversal of the removal procedure.

BRAKE PRESSURE CONTROL VALVE . . [9]

Removal (Fig. J:35)

1. Jack up the car and fit axle stands. Refer to the jack-ing information contained under ROUTINE MAINTENANCE at the front of the book.
2. Remove the brake pipes from the valve, plugging the ends to prevent fluid loss.
3. Remove the two nuts and bolts holding the valve to its mounting bracket and lift away the valve.

Installation

1. Fit the valve to its mounting bracket, tightening the nuts and bolts to a torque of 15-18.5 lb ft (2.0-2.5 kg m).
2. Reconnect the brake pipes and tighten their unions to a torque of 9-11 lb ft (1.2-1.5 kg m).
3. Bleed the brakes as described at the beginning of this chapter.
4. Lower the car to the ground.

HANDBRAKE . . . . [10]

Adjustment

1. Jack up the car and support it on axle stands. Release the handbrake.
2. Make sure the handbrake cable follows its correct run and is properly located in its guides.
3. Slacken the adjuster locknut and then rotate the adjuster to loosen the cable (Fig. J:36).
4. Turn the adjuster to tighten the cable until all slack has been removed. A noticeable change in the cable tension will be apparent as the slack is taken up and the handbrake levers just begin to move.
5. As soon as the handbrake levers are seen to move rotate the adjuster a further three full turns and then secure it with the locknut. When adjustment is completed the machined section at the threaded end of the cable must not protrude beyond the adjuster locknut.
6. Lower the car to the ground.

Technical Data

Brake fluid. . . . . .SAM-6C-9101A or C-Amber

FRONT BRAKES

Disc diameter
    inner. . . . . .5.8 in (148 mm)
    outer. . . . . .8.7 in (221 mm)
Disc thickness. . . . . .0.39 in (10 mm)
Minimum disc thickness . . . . 0.34 in (8.7 mm)
Disc run-out (incl. hub) . . . . 0.006 in (0.15 mm)
Pad material. . . . . .Mintex M175

REAR BRAKES

Drum diameter . . . . .7 in (177.8 mm)
Shoe width. . . . . .1.18 in (30 mm)
Lining material . . . . Mintex M79/1

BRAKES

Trouble Shooter

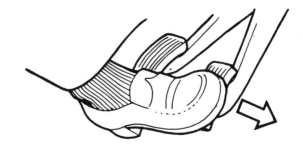

FAULT	CAUSE	CURE
Excessive brake pedal travel	1. Brakes need adjusting or replacement. 2. Air in system. 3. Leaking or contaminated fluid. 4. Faulty master cylinder.	1. Adjust or renew brake shoes. 2/3. Bleed hydraulic system. 4. Fit new master cylinder.
Brake fade	1. Incorrect pad or lining material. 2. Old or contaminated fluid. 3. Excessive use of brakes or car overloaded.	1. Fit new pads or shoes. 2. Renew brake fluid. 3. Check vehicle load.
Spongy brake pedal	1. Air in hydraulic system. 2. Shoes badly lined or distorted. 3. Faulty hydraulic cylinder.	1. Bleed system. 2. Fit new pads or shoes. 3. Check hydraulic circuit.
Brake pedal too hard	1. Seized wheel cylinder or caliper piston. 2. Glazed friction material.	1. Replace seized component. 2. Fit new shoes/pads.
Brake pedal requires pumping or loss of pedal	1. Brakes wrongly adjusted. 2. Air in hydraulic system. 3. Fluid leak from component or brake pipe. 4. Loss of fluid from master cylinder.	1. Adjust brakes. 2. Bleed system. 3/4. Check hydraulic circuit and replace parts as necessary.
Brakes grab when applied	1. Contaminated friction material. 2. Wrong linings fitted. 3. Scored drums or discs.	1/2. Replace (don't clean) pads or shoes. 3. Fit new drum or disc.
Brake squeal	1. Worn retaining pins (disc). 2. Faulty damping shims or shoe retaining clips. 3. Dust in drum. 4. Loose backplate or caliper.	1. Fit new pins. 2. Fit new shims or clips. 3. Remove dust from drums and shoe. 4. Tighten caliper or backplate.
Brake judder	1. No clearance at master cylinder operating rod. 2. Shoe tension springs either broken or weak. 3. Wheel cylinder or caliper piston seizing. 4. Faulty self-adjusting mechanism. 5. Seized handbrake mechanism.	1. Adjust rod if possible. 2. Replace tension springs. 3. Fit new caliper or cylinder. 4. Check mechanism. 5. Check handbrake operation.

Cont'd over

FAULT	CAUSE	CURE
Brake pull to one side only	1. Contaminated friction material on one side (grease, oil or brake fluid). 2. Loose backplate. 3. Seized cylinder. 4. Faulty suspension or steering.	1. Replace shoes/pads all round. 2. Tighten backplate. 3. Replace seized cylinder. 4. Check suspension and steering.
Handbrake ineffective	1. Worn rear shoes or pads. 2. Brakes require adjusting. 3. Faulty handbrake linkage. 4. Cable or rod requires adjustment.	1. Fit new pads/shoes. 2. Adjust brakes. 3. Check linkage and operating mechanism. 4. Adjust cable or rod.
Servo (where fitted) late in operation	1. Blocked filter. 2. Bad vacuum sealing or restricted air inlet.	1. Clean or replace filter. 2. Tighten vacuum hose connections and check hoses.
Loss of servo action when braking heavily	1. Air leak in servo - vacuum low.	1. Either overhaul servo or replace.
Loss of fluid (Servo only)	1. Seal failure. 2. Scored servo bores. 3. Damaged or corroded fluid pipes.	1/2. Replace or overhaul servo. 3. Inspect and fit new pipes.

General Electrics

HEADLAMPS. . . . . [1]

Alignment

Ideally the alignment of the headlamps should be set using suitable optical beam setting equipment. However, as it is unlikely that the average owner/driver will have access to such equipment, it is suggested that the method described below is utilised.

1. A suitable aiming board should be made up marked with horizontal and vertical lines as shown in Fig. K:1. This should be placed at right angles to the car and 33 ft (10 metres) in front of it in a suitably darkened area.
2. Make sure the car is parked on level ground, is unladen and has the tyres inflated to the correct pressures.
3. Bounce the car a few times to settle the suspension.
4. Use a wax crayon to mark the centre line of both front and rear windows and place the aiming board so that its vertical centre line is in alignment with the car centre line when viewed through the rear window. The horizontal line on the board should be at a height from the ground equal to the height from the ground to the centre of the headlamps minus 7 in (170 mm).
5. Switch on the headlamps with the beams set to the dipped position. Open the bonnet to give access to the headlamp adjusters.
6. Cover the left-hand headlamp.
7. Using the two headlamp adjusting screws, adjust the right-hand headlamp so that the intersection of the horizontal and angled light patterns coincides with the vertical line on the aiming board and the vertical alignment so that the light/dark boundary of the beam pattern coincides with the dotted line on the aiming board.
8. Cover the right-hand headlamp and repeat the operation to align the left-hand headlamp.
9. Switch off the headlamps and remove the wax marks from the front and rear windows.

Headlamp Unit Replacement

1. Disconnect the battery.
2. Unclip the indicator unit as described under the appropriate heading in this chapter and allow it to hang free of the front panel.
3. Pull off the headlamp wiring multi-plug and disconnect the parking lamp wiring (Fig. K:2).
4. Depress the two projections on the upper headlamp adjuster (Fig. K:3) and remove the headlamp unit by tilting it forwards and downwards.
5. Remove the parking lamp bulb holder by twisting it clear of the unit.
6. Pull the rubber gaiter from the back of the lamp assembly and then remove the bulb by releasing its retaining clip. On no account should the headlamp bulb be touched with the fingers and if it is touched accidentally it should be washed in methylated spirits and dried with a soft dust free cloth.
7. Unclip the headlamp adjuster units. Unclip the lower headlamp locating guide (Fig. K:4).
8. Installation is a reversal of the removal procedure, noting that care should be taken to ensure the correct location of the two adjuster units, that the three bulb terminals protrude through the appropriate holes in the rubber gaiter and that the headlamps are aligned as described previously.

Headlamp Bulb Replacement

1. Disconnect the battery.
2. Unclip the wiring plug and remove the rubber gaiter.
3. Unclip the spring clip and remove the headlamp bulb (Fig. K:5).
4. Installation is a reversal of the removal procedure, noting that care should be taken to ensure that the three bulb terminals protrude through the appropriate holes in the rubber gaiter.

Parking Lamp - Bulb Replacement (Fig. K:6)

1. Disconnect the battery.
2. Unclip the parking lamp bulb holder from the head-lamp unit by twisting it anti-clockwise and pulling it free.
3. Remove the bulb, which has a bayonet type fitting, from the holder.
4. Fit a new bulb to the holder and replace the latter in the headlamp unit.
5. Reconnect the battery and check the operation of the lamp unit.

FRONT INDICATORS.................[2]

Bulb Replacement

1. Disconnect the battery.
2. Remove the bulb holder from the lamp unit by twisting it and then pulling it free.
3. Remove the bayonet type bulb from the holder and replace it with a new one.
4. Replace the bulb holder in the lamp unit and reconnect the battery.
5. Check the operation of the indicator unit.

Indicator Unit Replacement (Fig. K:7)

1. Disconnect the battery.
2. Remove the indicator bulb holder as described previously.
3. Unclip the lamp from the body at the radiator end hinging it outwards.
4. Installation is a reversal of the removal procedure, noting that the rubber locating cushion and the metal retaining clip should be positioned as shown in Fig. K:8.

Side Repeater Light Unit Removal (Fig. K:9)

1. Disconnect the battery.
2. Turn the steering on to full lock to give access to the rear of the repeater unit.
3. Carefully pull the bulb holder from the repeater unit. The bulb has a bayonet fitting and is simply replaced.
4. Depress the lamp retaining clips and push the lamp out through the wing.
5. To refit the repeater unit simply push it home in the wing mounting hole and then push in the bulb holder from behind.

REAR LAMP UNIT ....[3]

Bulb Replacement

1. Disconnect the battery.
2. Remove the spare wheel cover and internal trim panel as described under BODY FITTINGS.
3. Pull the bulb holder from the lamp body and remove the bulb by twisting and pulling.
4. Fit a new bulb to the holder, replace the holder, trim

panel and spare wheel cover.

Lamp Unit Replacement

1. Remove the bulb holders from the unit as described previously.
2. Release the three retaining nuts and lift the lamp assembly away from the body.
3. Installation is a reversal of the removal procedure, noting that if the foam lamp sealing gasket has been damaged or distorted it should be replaced.

REVERSING LAMPS..................[4]

Bulb Replacement

1. Disconnect the battery.
2. Remove the spare wheel cover and spare wheel.
3. Unclip the bulb holder from the body of the lamp and pull it clear.
4. Remove the old bulb by twisting it free and replace it with a new one.
5. Refit the bulb holder, spare wheel and spare wheel cover.
6. Reconnect the battery and check the lamp operation.

Lamp Unit Replacement

1. Disconnect the battery.
2. Remove the spare wheel cover and spare wheel.
3. Disconnect the bulb holder as described above.
4. Release the two retaining nuts and washers and remove the lamp unit from the body (Fig. K:10).
5. Installation is a reversal of the removal procedure.

NUMBER PLATE LAMP ....[5]

Bulb Replacement (Fig. K:11)

1. Disconnect the battery.
2. Depress the two retaining clips and push the lamp from the bumper.
3. Prise the lens cover from the lamp and remove it together with the lens. The cover is secured by two lugs.
4. Remove the bayonet type bulb by twisting it anti-clockwise.
5. Installation is a reversal of the removal procedure.

WINDSCREEN WIPERS.................[6]

Blade Replacement

1. Lift the wiper arm away from the screen through 90°. Turn the wiper blade so that it is at 90° to the arm (Fig. K:12).
2. Depress the retaining spring clip and slide the blade down the wiper arm clear of the retaining hook. Lift the wiper blade away from the arm.

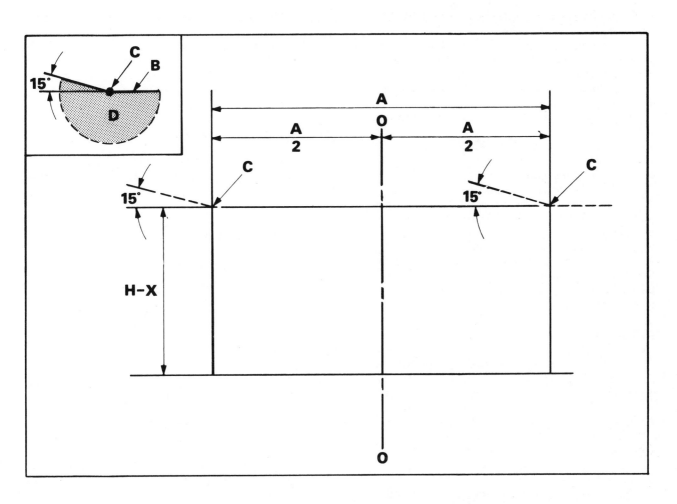

A. Distance between headlamp centre
B. Light/dark boundary
C. Dipped beam centre
OO. Vehicle centre line
D. Dipped beam pattern
H. Height from ground to centre of headlamps
X. 17 cm (7.0 in)

Fig. K:1 Mark the aiming board to the dimensions shown to align headlamps

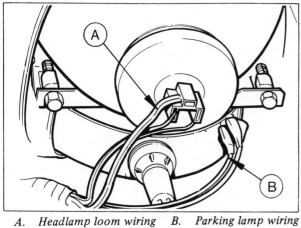

A. Headlamp loom wiring   B. Parking lamp wiring

**Fig. K:2 Details of the headlamp and parking
lamp wiring**

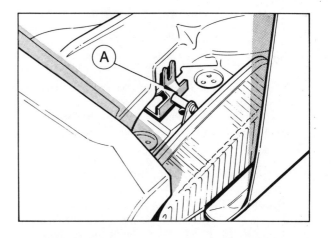

**Fig. K:3 The position of the headlamp upper
adjuster (retaining screw removed)**

3. Remove the metal inserts from the blade rubber and remove the rubber from the blade.

4. Hook the new rubber to the wiper blade, sliding the metal inserts along the channels in the rubber. Make sure the cutouts in the metal inserts face inwards (Fig. K:13).

5. Clip the assembled wiper blade to the wiper arm and then check the operation.

6. Repeat the procedure for the remaining wiper arm(s).

Front Motor Removal (Fig. K:14)

1. Disconnect the battery.

2. Pull off the two wiring plugs from the wiper motor.

3. Remove the three retaining bolts and pull the wiper motor mounting bracket from the bulkhead aperture.

4. Disengage the wiper linkage operating arm from the wiper linkage and remove the motor assembly.

5. Unscrew the operating arm retaining nut and remove the arm from the motor.

6. Release the three bolts and remove the motor from its mounting bracket.

Installation

This is a reversal of the removal procedure, noting that the sealing grommet between the motor and the mounting bracket should be positioned correctly and that a light mastic like sealer should be applied to the mating surfaces of the mounting bracket and its aperture.

Rear Motor Removal (Fig. K:15)

1. Disconnect the battery.

2. Remove the wiper arm retaining nut and pull the arm and blade assembly from the pivot shaft.

3. Remove the nut securing the pivot shaft.

4. Carefully prise the rear trim panel clips from the rear door and remove the trim panel.

5. Remove the two bolts holding the wiper motor mounting bracket to the rear door and pull the motor assembly clear of the door.

6. Unscrew the earth lead retaining screw and disconnect the wiring multi plug.

7. Remove the motor assembly and linkage from the door.

Installation

Installation is a reversal of the removal procedure, noting that the bracket mounting rubbers should be positioned correctly before finally securing it with the two retaining bolts. Check the operation of the wipers before replacing the door trim panel.

Wiper Linkage Removal (Front)

1. Disconnect the battery.

2. Remove the wiper motor as described previously.

3. Remove the wiper arm retaining nuts and remove arm and blade assemblies from the pivot shafts.

4. Remove one coil retaining bolt and loosen the other

to allow it to be swung clear of the bonnet catch retaining plate.

5. Remove the six bolts holding the bonnet catch mounting plate to the bulkhead and remove the plate.

6. Remove the nuts holding the spindle arms to the scuttle and remove the linkage assembly through the bonnet catch mounting plate aperture (Fig. K:16).

Installation

This is a reversal of the removal procedure, noting that a light mastic type sealer should be applied to the mating surfaces of the bonnet catch mounting plate and its aperture.

Pivot Shaft Replacement

1. Remove the wiper operating linkage as described previously.

2. Prise the linkage from the pivot shaft ball joint.

3. Remove the retaining circlip and then dismantle the pivot shaft bush and housing from the pivot shaft (Fig. K: 17).

4. Installation is a reversal of the removal procedure.

WINDSCREEN WASHERS...............[7]

Nozzles - Replacement (Front)

1. Disconnect the battery.

2. Remove one coil retaining bolt and loosen the other to allow the coil to be swung clear of the bonnet catch mounting plate.

3. Remove the six bolts holding the bonnet catch mounting plate in place and remove the plate.

4. Using a screwdriver, and taking great care not to damage the paintwork, prise the washer nozzle from the scuttle.

5. Pull the washer tube from the nozzle.

6. Installation is a reversal of the removal procedure, noting that care should be taken to ensure that the washer tube is not kinked. Apply a light mastic type sealer to the mating surfaces of the bonnet catch mounting plate and its aperture. Check the operation of the washers.

Washer Pump Replacement (Front)

1. Disconnect the battery.

2. Pull the wiring multi plug from the pump.

3. Pull the washer hose from the pump.

4. Position a suitable container beneath the washer reservoir to catch any overflow and prise the washer pump from the reservoir (Fig. K:18).

5. Installation is a reversal of the removal procedure.

Nozzle Replacement (Rear)

1. Open the rear door, remove the weatherstrip and pull down the headlining to give access to the nozzle.

2. Pull the washer tube from the nozzle.

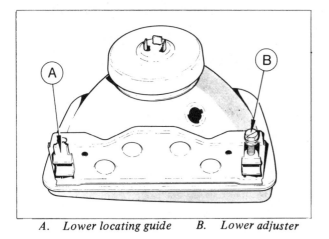

A. Lower locating guide   B. Lower adjuster

Fig. K:4 Headlamp lower locating guide and adjuster

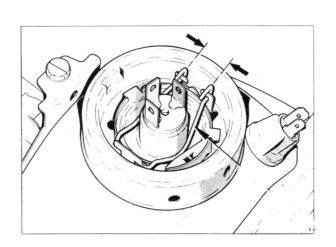
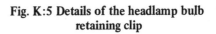

Fig. K:5 Details of the headlamp bulb retaining clip

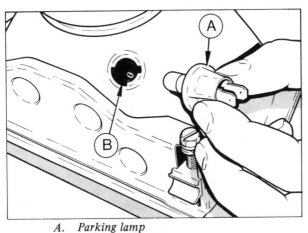

A. Parking lamp
B. Parking lamp aperture
   (Headlamp removed for clarity)

Fig. K:6 Removing and refitting the parking lamp bulb

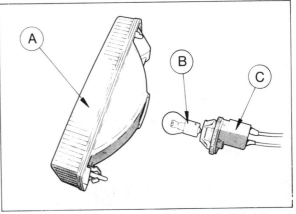

A. Lens and body assembly   C. Bulbholder
B. Bulb

Fig. K:7 Details of the front indicator lamp assembly

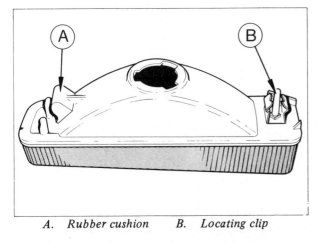

A. Rubber cushion   B. Locating clip

Fig. K:8 The front indicator lamp retaining clip and lug

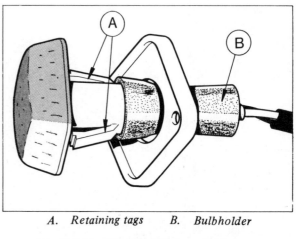

A. Retaining tags   B. Bulbholder

Fig. K:9 Details of the side repeater lamp assembly

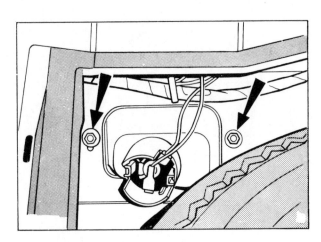

Fig. K:10 The position of the reversing lamp unit retaining bolts

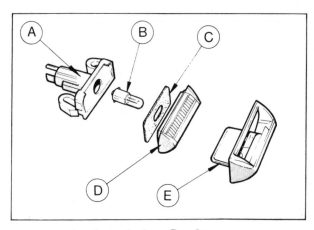

A. Lamp body   D. Lens
B. Bulb   E. Lens cover
C. Gasket

Fig. K:11 An exploded view of the rear number plate lamp unit

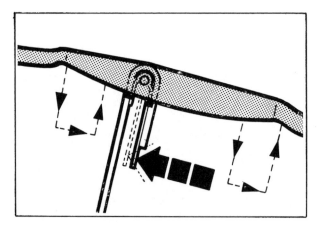

Fig. K:12 Removing the wiper blade from the wiper arm

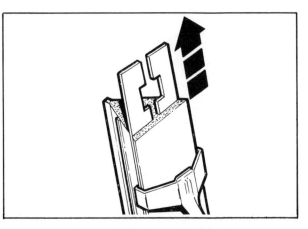

Fig. K:13 Details of the metal insert position when fitting new blade rubbers

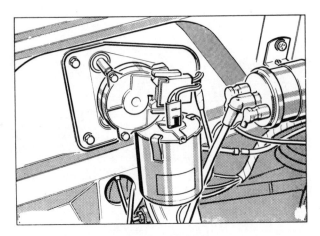

Fig. K:14 Details of the front screen wiper motor installation

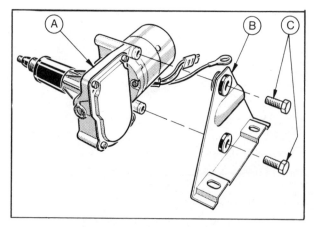

A. *Rear wiper motor* B. *Bracket* C. *Fixing bolts*

Fig. K:15 An exploded view of the rear wiper motor and support bracket assembly

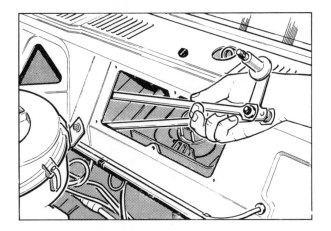

Fig. K:16 Removing the front wiper linkage
through bulkhead aperture

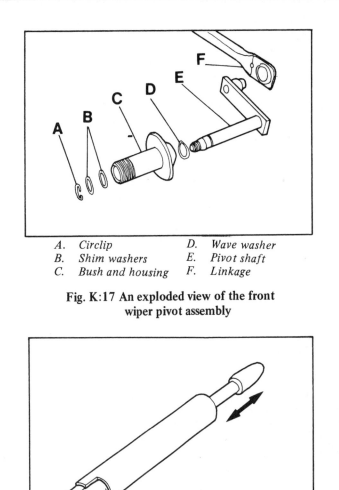

A. Circlip
B. Shim washers
C. Bush and housing
D. Wave washer
E. Pivot shaft
F. Linkage

Fig. K:17 An exploded view of the front
wiper pivot assembly

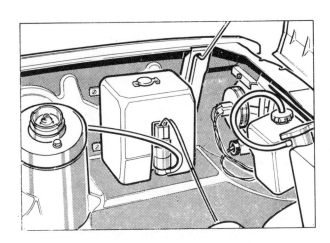

Fig. K:18 The location of the front screen
washer reservoir and pump

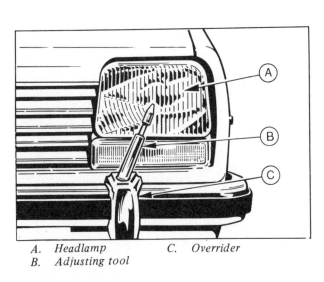

A. Headlamp
B. Adjusting tool
C. Overrider

Fig. K:20 Adjusting the headlamp washer
nozzle with tool

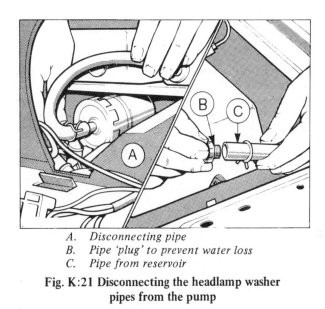

A. Disconnecting pipe
B. Pipe 'plug' to prevent water loss
C. Pipe from reservoir

Fig. K:21 Disconnecting the headlamp washer
pipes from the pump

Fig. K:19 Details of the tool used to adjust
the headlamp washer nozzle alignment

3. Unscrew the nozzle retaining nut, remove the shakeproof washer and seal and remove the nozzle.
4. Installation is a reversal of the removal procedure.

Washer Pump Replacement (Rear)

1. Disconnect the battery.
2. Remove the spare wheel cover.
3. Unhook the rubber holding strap and remove the reservoir from its mounting bracket.
4. Disconnect the wiring multi plug from the pump and pull off the washer tube.
5. Empty the contents of the reservoir into a suitable container and then unclip the pump from the side of the reservoir.
6. Installation is a reversal of the removal procedure.

HEADLAMP WASHERS. . . . . [8]

Nozzle Replacement

The headlamp washer nozzles are integral parts of the bumper overriders and therefore if replacement of the nozzles is necessary for any reason the entire overrider unit must be replaced. See **BODY FITTINGS** for the appropriate removal and replacement procedure.

Nozzle Adjustment

There is a special Ford tool for this purpose (32-001) (Fig. K:19) which is inserted into the slots round the circumference of the nozzle and turned until the point of the tool is aligned with the centre of the headlamp lens (Fig. K:20). However, it should be possible to use a suitably modified piece of tubing to do the same job. Make sure the nozzles are clear of dirt or other foreign matter.

Washer Pump Replacement

1. Disconnect the battery.
2. Pull off the windscreen washer pump multi plug.
3. Remove the reservoir cap and the headlamp washer pump bypass return pipe.
4. Pull the windscreen washer tube from the pump.
5. Disconnect the large bore pipe that runs from the reservoir to the headlamp washer pump at the pump end (Fig. K:21). Plug it to prevent emptying the reservoir.
6. Remove the washer reservoir from the car by unscrewing the retaining screws.
7. Disconnect the pipe from the headlamp washer pump outlet.
8. Remove the two headlamp washer pump mounting screws, pull off the multi plug and lift the pump and return pipe from the car.
9. Pull the return pipe from the pump.
10. Installation is a reversal of the removal procedure.

INSTRUMENT CLUSTER . . . . [9]

Removal

1. Disconnect the battery.
2. Remove the screw holding the steering column upper shroud in place and lift away the shroud.
3. Remove the fascia lower panel (if fitted) by removing the two retaining screws (Fig. K:22).
4. Disconnect the speedometer cable from behind the cluster by depressing the grooved section of the cable locking catch and pulling away the cable.
NOTE: Another method of disconnecting the cable is to disconnect it at the transmission, remove the strap holding the speedometer cable to the choke cable and pull the cable through into the passenger compartment sufficiently to allow removal of the instrument cluster. When the cluster has been removed, the cable can be disconnected from the back.
5. Pull the instrument bezel from the face of the instrument cluster (Fig. K:23), using the fingertip access provided in the major instrument aperture rims.
6. Remove the four screws holding the instrument cluster in place, pull it forward and disconnect the multi wiring plug, direction indicator warning light and, if fitted, the brake failure warning light. Lift away the instrument cluster (Fig. K:24).

Installation

This is a reversal of the removal procedure, noting that the speedometer cable should be slid on to the speedometer drive spigot until it snaps home. Check for correct fitting by pulling the cable without releasing the locking catch.

Printed Circuit Removal (Fig. K:25)

1. Remove the instrument cluster as described previously.
2. Remove the three nuts and washers from the combined fuel and temperature gauge assembly.
3. Remove the screw and washer securing the voltage regulator and remove the voltage regulator.
4. Remove the three warning lamp bulb holders and remove the printed circuit.

On models equipped with a tachometer, remove the two screws, three nuts and washers from the tachometer. Then remove the nuts and washers holding the radio suppressor in place and remove the suppressor. Remove the nuts and washers from the fuel and temperature gauges and the various warning lamp bulbs.

Installation

Installation is a reversal of the removal procedure.

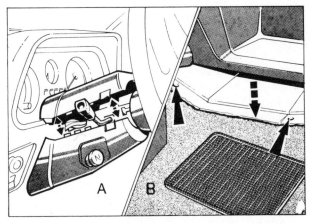

A. Steering column upper shroud   *B. Lower panel*

**Fig. K:22 Method of removing the fascia
lower panel**

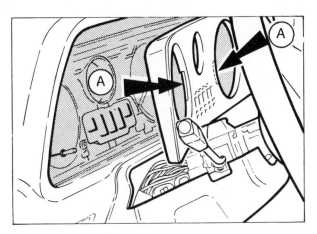

A. Finger tip access

**Fig. K:23 Removing the instrument panel
bezel from the fascia**

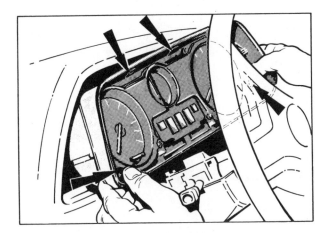

**Fig. K:24 Withdrawing the instrument panel
assembly from the fascia**

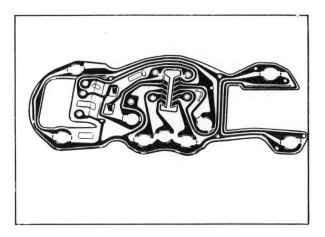

**Fig. K:25 Details of the instrument panel
printed circuit board**

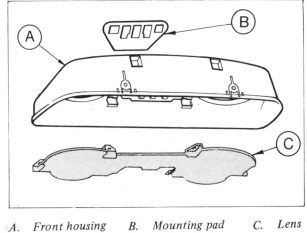

A. Front housing   B. Mounting pad   C. Lens

Fig. K:26 An exploded view of the instrument panel lens fitting

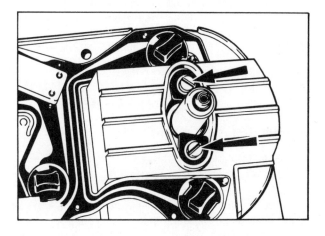

**Fig. K:27 The location of the speedometer
retaining screws**

General Electrics

135

SPEEDOMETER . . . .[10]

Removal

1. Remove the instrument cluster as described previously.
2. Remove the six securing screws and remove the lens, front housing and mounting pad (Fig. K:26).
3. Remove the two screws from the rear of the cluster and remove the speedometer head (Fig. K:27).

Installation

Installation is a reversal of the removal procedure.

CLOCK . . . .[11]

Removal (Fig. K:28)

1. Disconnect the battery.
2. Remove the centre console as described under FITTINGS.
3. Remove the two screws from the rear of the clock and remove the clock bezel.
4. Detach the two illumination bulb holders and disconnect the clock wiring.
5. Push the clock out through the front of the console.

Installation

Installation is a reversal of the removal procedure.

CIGAR LIGHTER . . . .[12]

Removal (Fig. K:29)

1. Disconnect the battery.
2. Remove the ashtray and heater control knobs.
3. Remove the four screws from the switch panel and pull the bezel forwards. Disconnect the wiring and heater illumination holder and then remove the switch bezel.
4. Pull out the cigar lighter element and then press out the body and illumination ring from the bezel or switch panel.
5. Press the body from its illumination ring.

Installation

Installation is a reversal of the removal procedure.

Lighter Coil Replacement

1. Pull out the lighter element.
2. Depress the locknut to expose the coil locknut (Fig. K:30).
3. Use a pair of thin nosed pliers to grip the shaft and then unscrew the locknut to release the coil.
4. Screw home a new coil, securing it with the locknut. Remove the pliers and release the knob.

SWITCHES . . . .[13]

Ignition Switch Unit - Removal (Fig. K:31)

1. Disconnect the battery.
2. Remove the steering column assembly as described under FRONT SUSPENSION & STEERING.
3. Centre punch and drill out the two steering column lock retaining bolts and then remove the lock.

Installation

1. Position the lock on the column and fit two new 'shear' bolts. Tighten them until their heads break off.
2. Refit the steering column assembly and reconnect the battery.
3. Check the switch for correct operation.

Ignition Key Barrel - Replacement

1. Disconnect the battery.
2. Remove the single screw securing the upper steering column housing and remove the housing.
3. Remove the three screws from the lower column shroud and ease the shroud carefully over the choke control to remove it.
4. Turn the key to position 1 (Accessories).
5. Insert the blade of a small electrician's screwdriver into the cut-out in the underside of the ignition switch housing and push upwards against the barrel retaining clip. (Fig. K:32). Pull out the key and barrel assembly.
6. Installation is a reversal of the removal procedure.

Lighting Switch - Removal

1. Disconnect the battery.
2. Remove the single screw securing the upper column shroud and remove the shroud.
3. Remove the three screws securing the lower column shroud and remove the shroud, easing it carefully over the choke control.
4. Disconnect the wiring multi plugs from the switch (Fig. K:33).
5. Remove the two switch securing screws and lift away the switch.

Installation

Installation is a reversal of the removal procedure.

Brake Light Switch - Removal

1. Disconnect the battery.
2. Disconnect the wiring at the switch on the brake pedal bracket, remove the switch locknut (Fig. K:34) and remove the switch.

Installation

1. Wind back the switch adjusting nut fully, fit the switch in position and loosely fit the locknut.

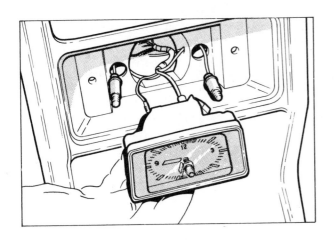

Fig. K:28 Removing the clock unit from the centre console

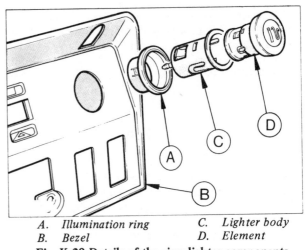

A. Illumination ring   C. Lighter body
B. Bezel   D. Element

Fig. K:29 Details of the cigar lighter components and fitting

Fig. K:30 Undoing the cigar lighter coil locknut

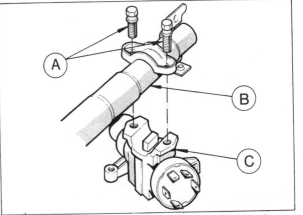
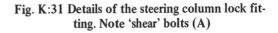

A. Shear-off bolts   C. Steering column lock assembly
B. Steering column tube

Fig. K:31 Details of the steering column lock fitting. Note 'shear' bolts (A)

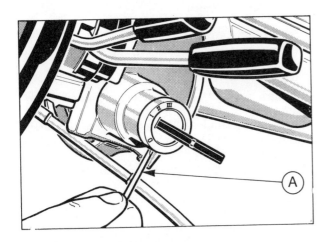

Fig. K:32 Removing ignition key barrel by inserting screwdriver (A) into housing

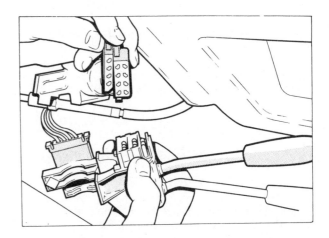

Fig. K:33 Disconnecting the lighting switch wiring multi-connector

2. Adjust the switch position so that it does not operate for the first 0.2 in (5 mm) of brake pedal travel, but does operate within 0.8 in (20 mm). Travel is measured at centre line of foot pad.
3. Tighten the switch locknut and reconnect the wiring.
4. Reconnect the battery and check the operation of the switch.

Reversing Lamp Switch - Replacement

1. Disconnect the battery.
2. Inside the engine compartment, on the near side, disconnect the wiring from the switch and then unscrew the switch from the left-hand side of the gearbox housing (Fig. K:35).
3. Installation is a reversal of the removal procedure.

Handbrake Warning Light Switch - Replacement

1. Disconnect the battery.
2. Remove the left-hand front seat as described under BODY FITTINGS.
3. Pull the switch cover from the handbrake warning light switch (Fig. K:37) and pull the carpet aside.
4. Slacken the screw holding the back of the switch to the handbrake and then remove the screw holding the front of the switch to the handbrake.
5. Disconnect the switch wiring and remove the switch.
6. Installation is a reversal of the removal procedure, noting that the operation of the switch should be checked by switching on the ignition and then applying the handbrake. The warning light bulb should light up if the switch is functioning properly.

Flasher Relay - Replacement

1. Disconnect the battery.
2. Remove the dashboard lower insulation panel (if fitted).
3. Disconnect the wiring from the appropriate relay.
4. Unclip the relay from the bracket welded to the dash panel on the right of the steering column (Fig. K:36).
5. Installation is a reversal of the removal procedure.

Oil Pressure Warning Light Switch - Replacement

1. Disconnect the battery.
2. Disconnect the wiring and unscrew the switch from its location in the cylinder block below the inlet manifold (Fig. K:38).
3. Installation is a reversal of the removal procedure.

Temperature Gauge Sender Unit Removal

1. Disconnect the battery.
2. Make sure the cooling system is not pressurised by releasing the radiator cap and then replacing it. This will ensure that the minimum of coolant is lost when the sender unit is removed.
3. Disconnect the sender wiring and then unscrew the sender (Fig. K:40) from its location in the cylinder head.

Installation

Installation is a reversal of the removal procedure, making sure that a suitable sealer is smeared on the threads of the sender unit before installation. Check the operation of the gauge afterwards.

HEATER ASSEMBLY . . . . [14]

Control Adjustment

1. Remove the left hand lower dash insulating panel. There are two retaining screws.
2. Release the two bolts holding the Bowden cables to the heater assembly.
3. Slide the temperature control lever to the right and position so that it is 0.2 in (5 mm) from the right-hand stop.
4. At the heater assembly, move the temperature control valve to the cold position. Secure the Bowden cable in this position, making sure the retaining clamps are not twisted. Check the control valve for easy action and the lever for free movement along the whole distance between the two stops (Fig. K:41).
5. With the distribution valve in the closed position, make sure the marks on the valve gear are aligned with the mark on the toothed quadrant. If these marks do not align, pull off the control along with the quadrant and refit them in the correct position.
6. Slide the distribution control lever to the left and position it so that it is 0.2 (5 mm) from the left-hand stop. Make sure the distribution valve at the heater assembly is closed.
7. Secure the Bowden cable on the housing in this position, making sure the retaining clamp is not twisted during tightening. Check the valve for free operation and correct operation in each position of the control lever (Fig. K: 42).
NOTE: *Make sure the Bowden cables are not twisted when fitting them to the control pivot pins.*
8. Refit the dash insulating panel.

Heater Control Removal

1. Disconnect the battery.
2. Remove the two screws securing the dashboard lower insulating panel.
3. Remove the two bolts holding the Bowden cables to the heater assembly and unbolt the cables from the temperature and distribution valves.
4. Pull out the ashtray and then remove its bracket by releasing the two retaining screws.
5. Remove the four screws holding the heater control panel cowl in place (if fitted).
6. Pull the knobs from the ends of the control levers.
7. Remove two screws holding the heater control panel and remove complete with Bowden cables (Fig. K:43).

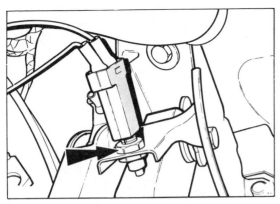

Fig. K:34 Details of the brake light switch on pedal bracket

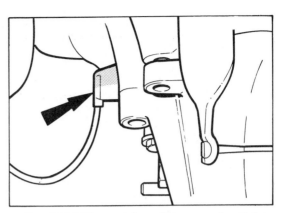

Fig. K:35 The position of the reversing light switch on the end of the gearbox

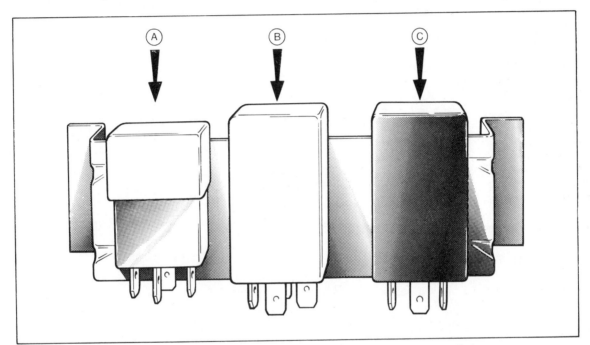

A. Heated rear screen   B. Intermittent wash/wipe   C. Indicator flasher

Fig. K:36 The relay mounting bracket is located under the fascia on right of steering column

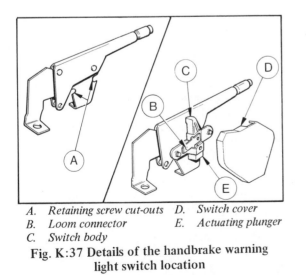

A. Retaining screw cut-outs   D. Switch cover
B. Loom connector   E. Actuating plunger
C. Switch body

Fig. K:37 Details of the handbrake warning light switch location

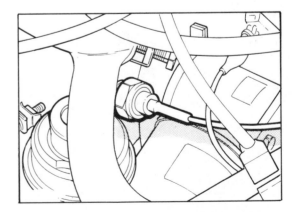

Fig. K:38 Details of the oil pressure switch location on side of engine block

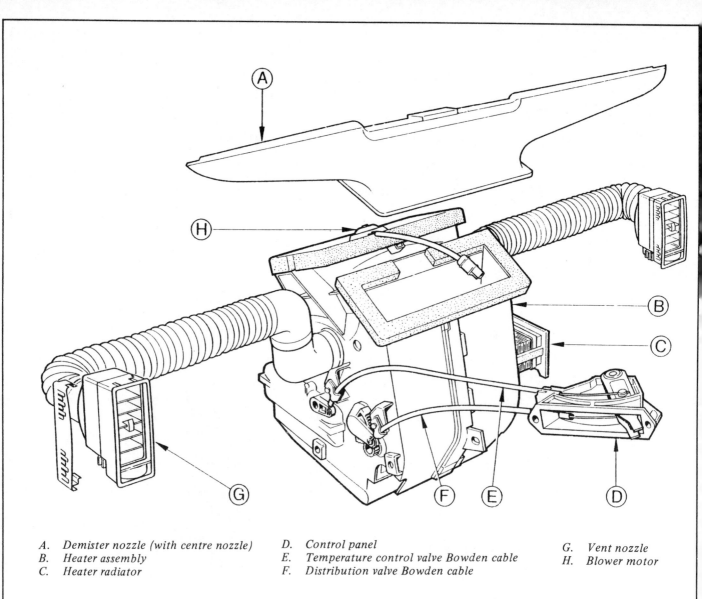

A. *Demister nozzle (with centre nozzle)*
B. *Heater assembly*
C. *Heater radiator*

D. *Control panel*
E. *Temperature control valve Bowden cable*
F. *Distribution valve Bowden cable*

G. *Vent nozzle*
H. *Blower motor*

Fig. K:39 An exploded view of the heater assembly and vent pipes

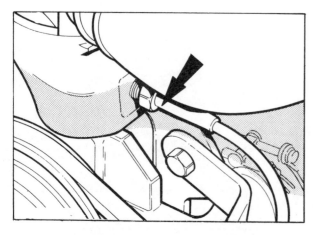

Fig. K:40 The temperature gauge sender unit is screwed into front of cylinder head

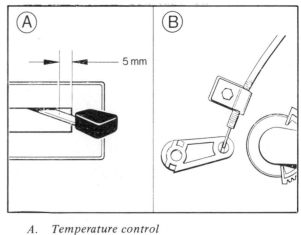

A. *Temperature control*
B. *Temperature control valve in cold position*

Fig. K:41 Details of the temperature control adjustment

140   General Electrics

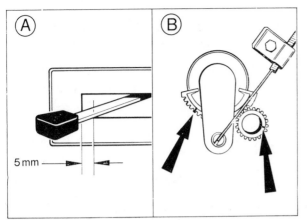

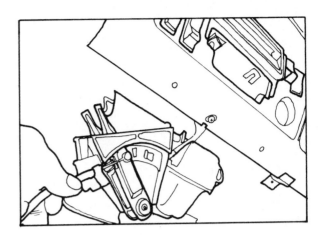

A. Air distribution control
B. Distribution valve closed
   Note alignment marks (arrowed)

Fig. K:42 Details of the air distribution
control adjustment

Fig. K:43 Refitting the heater control panel from
the underside of fascia

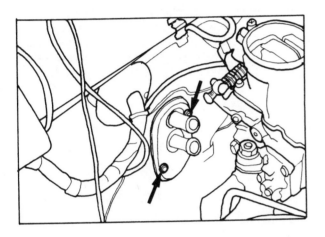

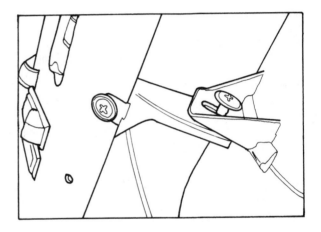

Fig. K:44 Undo two screws (arrowed) to remove
heater pipe bulkhead cover plate

Fig. K:45 Details of the heater unit to fascia
mounting bracket

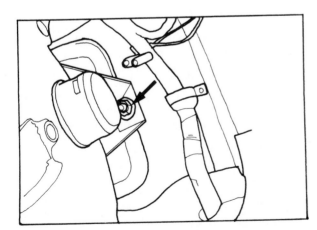

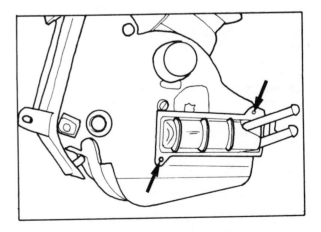

Fig. K:46 Undo nut (arrowed) to detach
heater unit from bulkhead

Fig. K:47 Undo screws (arrowed) and
withdraw heater radiator from body

Installation

Installation is a reversal of the removal procedure, noting that new knobs should be fitted to the heater control levers and the control cables should be adjusted as described previously.

Heater Assembly - Removal

1. Disconnect the battery and set the heater controls to HOT.
2. Inside the engine compartment, slacken the clips securing the heater hoses to the heater radiator at the bulkhead. Pull off the lower hose first and drain the coolant into a suitable container. Then pull off the upper hose. Secure both hoses with their open ends pointing upwards.
3. Remove the two screws securing the cover plate and heater radiator neck gasket to the bulkhead and remove the plate and gasket (Fig. K:44). Seal the ends of the heater radiator inlet and outlet pipes with adhesive tape or plug them in some way to prevent any coolant in the heater radiator from leaking into the interior of the car as the heater assembly is removed.
4. Remove the four screws securing the left and right-hand dash lower trim panels and remove the panels.
5. Remove the ashtray and then remove its mounting bracket by releasing the two securing screws.
6. Pull the vent nozzle hoses from the heater assembly necks.
7. Disconnect the Bowden cables from the heater assembly and unhook them from the temperature and distribution control valves.
8. Remove the two screws securing the bracket between the heater assembly and instrument panel. Remove the bracket (Fig. K:45).
9. Remove the two nuts holding the heater assembly to the cowl top panel (Fig. K:46).
10. Pull the heater assembly inwards until the heater radiator inlet and outlet pipes clear the bulkhead aperture. Disconnect the wiring plug from the heater assembly and then remove the entire assembly to the right.
11. With the assembly removed, drain any remaining coolant from the radiator.

Dismantling

1. Remove the two screws holding the heater radiator in place and slide the radiator from the heater assembly (Fig. K:47).
2. Use a knife to separate the foam gaskets at the joint between the two halves of the heater housing.
3. Press the motor retaining clamps from the motor mounting.
4. Use a screwdriver to split the two halves of the heater assembly. Carefully separate the two halves of the assembly by hand (Fig. K:48), placing the half with the control valves facing downwards. Lift out the blower motor.
5. Remove the centre heater assembly cover plates.
6. Remove the control valves and prise the valve controls from the heater assembly (Fig. K:49).

Reassembly

1. Press the valve controls into the left-hand half of the heater housing. Fit the control valves (Fig. K:50), making sure the mark on the distribution valve shaft gear is aligned with the mark on the toothed quadrant.
2. Fit the centre assembly cover plates to the left-hand half of the housing. Apply plastic sealing compound to the contact points on the two small cover plates for better adhesion.
3. Fit the blower motor with the lead to the rear and then assemble the two halves of the heater assembly, inserting the control valve shafts into their locations in the right-hand housing. Make sure the straps on the flange between the two halves are fully engaged. Additional straps should be used to ensure good retention of the two halves.
4. Refit the motor retaining clips and heater radiator.

Installation

Installation of the heater assembly is basically a reversal of the removal procedure, noting the following points:
a) Make sure the air inlet foam gaskets are correctly installed and positioned.
b) Adjust the control Bowden cables as described previously.
c) Top up cooling system and check operation of heater controls and blower.

Face Level Vent - Removal (Fig. K:51)

1. Remove the dashboard lower trim panel securing screws and remove the panel.
2. Pull the vent hose from the spigot behind the dashboard.
3. Prise out the vent nozzle insert carefully with a screwdriver.
4. Remove the knurled ring and then cut the retaining link.
5. Using a screwdriver push out the four retaining clips and withdraw the vent nozzle.

Installation

To refit the new nozzle assembly, push it on to the hose and press it into the instrument panel aperture. The retaining clips must engage behind the instrument panel.

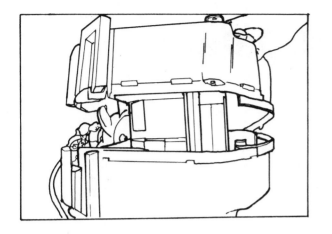

Fig. K:48 Separating the heater body sections

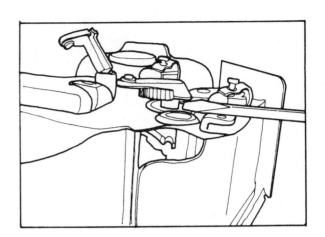

Fig. K:49 Using a screwdriver to lever off the flap valve controls

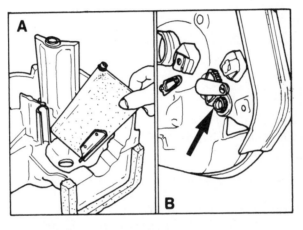

A.   Fit control valves
B.   Ensure alignment of marks (arrowed)

Fig. K:50 Fitting the heater flap valve and controls

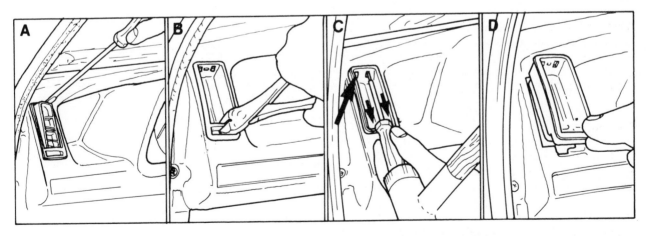

A.   Prise out vent nozzle insert
B.   Remove knurled ring and cut retaining link

C.   Push out retaining clamps on 4 rectangular slots
D.   Withdraw vent nozzle

Fig. K:51 Method of removing the face level vent from the fascia

Technical Data

	Quantity	Wattage
Headlamp		
Halogen	2	60/55W
Tungsten	2	50/45W
Parking lamp	2	4W
Stop/tail lamp	2	21/5W
Reversing lamp	1	21W
Licence plate lamp	2	4W
Indicators	4	21W
Side repeater flasher	2	4W
Warning lamps	8	1.3
Panel illumination	3 (4 Sport/Ghia)	2.6
Clock	2	1.4
Cigar lighter	1	1.4
Glove compartment	1	1
Interior light	1	10

FUSES

The following circuits are protected by fuses:

1.   8 amp: Interior light, hazard flashers, horn, clock, cigar lighter, glove box light.

2.   16 amp: Stop lamps, heater motor, engine cooling fan, indicators, reversing lamps, windscreen washers.

3.   8 amp: Windscreen wipers, instrument cluster, brake warning system, rear window wiper/washer.

4.   8 amp: LH side light, RH tail light, rear fog lamp.

5.   8 amp: RH side light, LH tail light, instrument panel illumination, number plate lamps, clock illumination, cigar lighter illumination.

6.   8 amp: RH main beam headlamp, LH main beam headlamp.

7.   8 amp: RH dipped beam headlamp, LH dipped beam headlamp.

8/9   Export territories only.

ELECTRICAL

Trouble Shooter

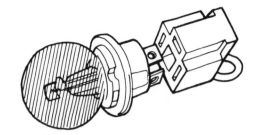

FAULT	CAUSE	CURE
STARTER		
Starter doesn't turn (lights dim)	1. Battery flat or worn. 2. Bad connection in battery circuit	1. Charge or fit new battery. 2. Check all feed and earth connections.
Starter doesn't turn (lights stay bright)	1. Faulty ignition switch 2. Broken starter circuit	1. Check switch. 2. Check starter circuit.
Solenoid switch chatters	1. Flat battery	1. Charge or replace battery.
Starter just spins	1. Bendix gear sticking	1. Remove starter and clean or replace Bendix gear.
CHARGING CIRCUIT		
Low or no charge rate	1. Broken or slipping drive belt 2. Poor connections on or faulty alternator	1. Fit new belt. 2. Check and replace alternator.
LIGHTING CIRCUIT		
No lights (or very dim)	1. Flat or faulty battery, bad battery connections	1. Check battery and connection.
Side and rear lights inoperative although stoplights and flashers work	1. Fuse blown	1. Fit correct value fuse.
One lamp fails	1. Blown bulb 2. Poor bulb contact 3. Bad earth connection. 4. Broken feed	1. Fit new bulb. 2/3. Check connections. 4. Check feed.
Flasher warning bulb stays on or flashers twice as fast	1. Faulty bulb or connection on front or rear of offending side	1. Fit new bulb, make good connection.
Lights dim when idling or at low speed	1. Loose drive belt 2. Flat battery 3. Faulty charging circuit	1. Tighten belt. 2/3. Check charge output and battery.
One dim light	1. Blackened bulb 2. Bad earth 3. Tarnished reflector	1/3. Fit new bulb or sealed-beam. 2. Check earth connections.
WINDSCREEN WIPERS		
Wipers do not work	1. Blown fuse 2. Poor connection 3. Faulty switch 4. Faulty motor	1. Fit fuse. 2. Check connections. 3. Check switch. 4. Remove and examine motor.
Motor operates slowly	1. Excessive resistance in circuit or wiper drive 2. Worn brushes	1. Check wiper circuit. 2. Remove motor and check brushes.

Wiring Diagram

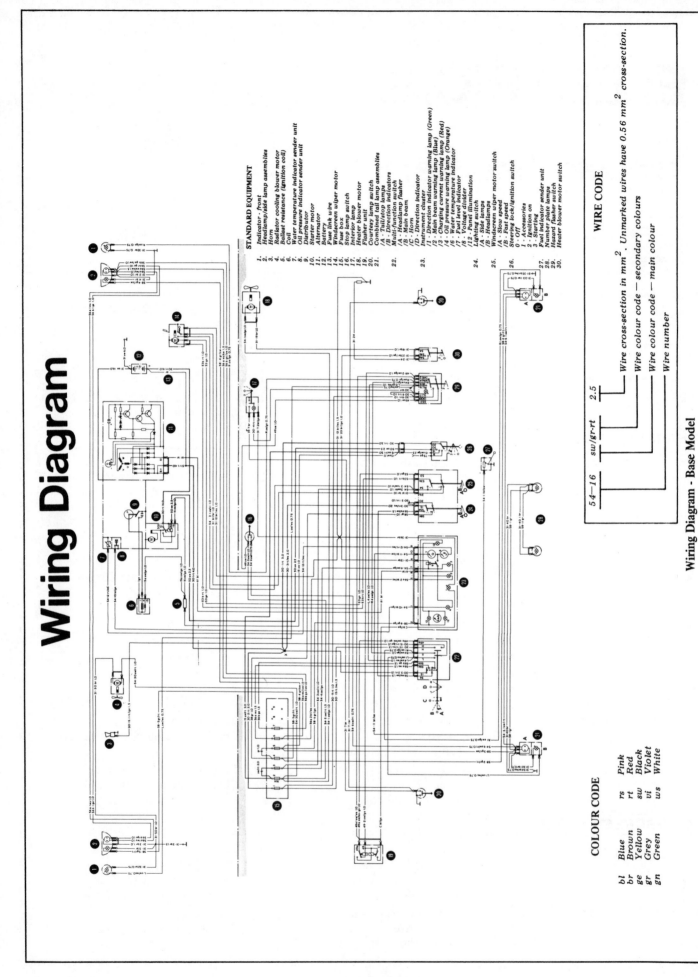

STANDARD EQUIPMENT

1. Indicator - front
2. Headlamp/side lamp assemblies
3. Horn
4. Radiator cooling blower motor
5. Ballast resistance (ignition coil)
6. Coil
7. Water temperature indicator sender unit
8. Oil pressure indicator sender unit
9. Distributor
10. Starter motor
11. Alternator
12. Battery
13. Fuse link wire
14. Windscreen wiper motor
15. Fuse box
16. Stop lamp switch
17. Interior lamp
18. Heater blower motor
19. Heater unit
20. Flasher unit
21. Courtesy lamp switch
22. Combined tail lamp assemblies
    - /A - Tail/stop lamps
    - /B - Direction indicators
23. Multi-function switch
    - /A - Headlamp flasher
    - /B - Main beam
    - /C - Horn
    - /D - Direction indicator
    Instrument cluster
    - /1 - Direction indicator warning lamp (Green)
    - /2 - Main beam warning lamp (Blue)
    - /3 - Charging current warning lamp (Red)
    - /4 - Oil pressure warning lamp (Orange)
    - /5 - Water temperature indicator
    - /6 - Fuel level indicator
    - /7 - Voltage divider
    - /8 - Panel illumination
24. Lighting switch
    - /A - Side lamps
    - /B - Headlamps
25. Windscreen wiper motor switch
    - /A - Slow speed
    - /B - Fast speed
26. Steering lock/ignition switch
    - 0 - Off
    - 1 - Accessories
    - 2 - Ignition on
    - 3 - Starting
27. Fuel indicator sender unit
28. Number plate lamps
29. Hazard flasher switch
30. Heater blower motor switch

WIRE CODE

Wire cross-section in mm². Unmarked wires have 0.56 mm² cross-section.

```
54-16   sw/gr-rt   2.5
```

— Wire cross-section in mm². Unmarked wires have 0.56 mm² cross-section.
— Wire colour code — secondary colours
— Wire colour code — main colour
— Wire number

Wiring Diagram - Base Model

COLOUR CODE

bl	Blue	rs	Pink
br	Brown	rt	Red
ge	Yellow	sw	Black
gr	Grey	vi	Violet
gn	Green	ws	White

Wiring Diagram

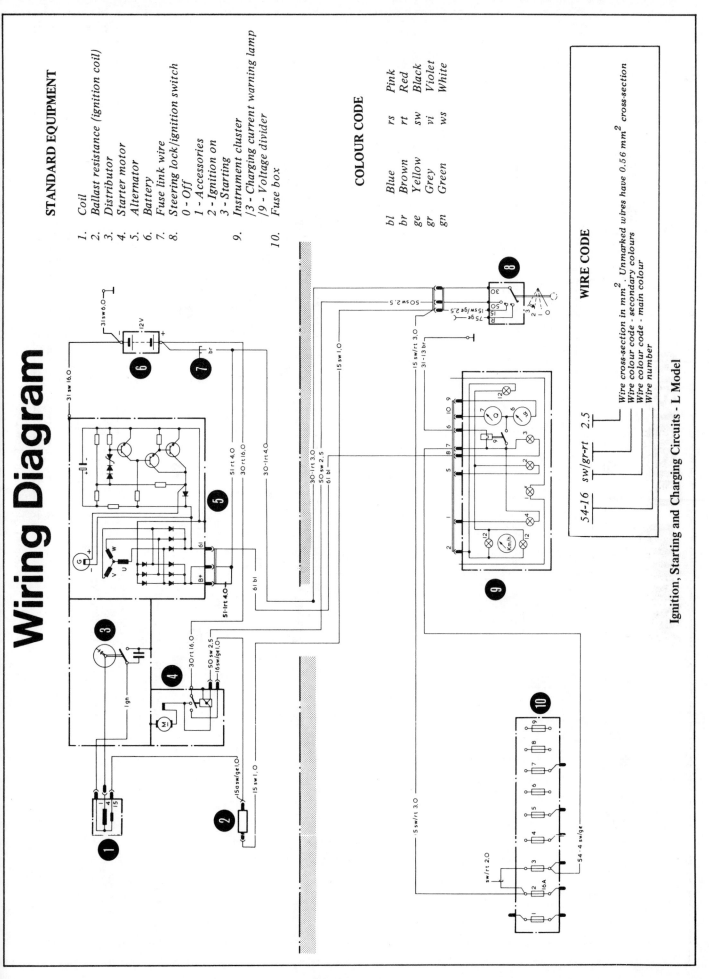

STANDARD EQUIPMENT

1. Coil
2. Ballast resistance (ignition coil)
3. Distributor
4. Alternator
5. Battery
6. Fuse link wire
7. Steering lock/ignition switch
   0 - Off
   1 - Accessories
   2 - Ignition on
   3 - Starting
8. Instrument cluster
   /3 - Charging current warning lamp
   /9 - Voltage divider
9.
10. Fuse box

COLOUR CODE

bl	Blue	rs	Pink
br	Brown	rt	Red
ge	Yellow	sw	Black
gr	Grey	vi	Violet
gn	Green	ws	White

WIRE CODE

54-16   sw/gr-rt   2.5

Wire cross-section in mm². Unmarked wires have 0.56 mm² cross-section
Wire colour code - secondary colours
Wire colour code - main colour
Wire number

Ignition, Starting and Charging Circuits - L Model

Wiring Diagram

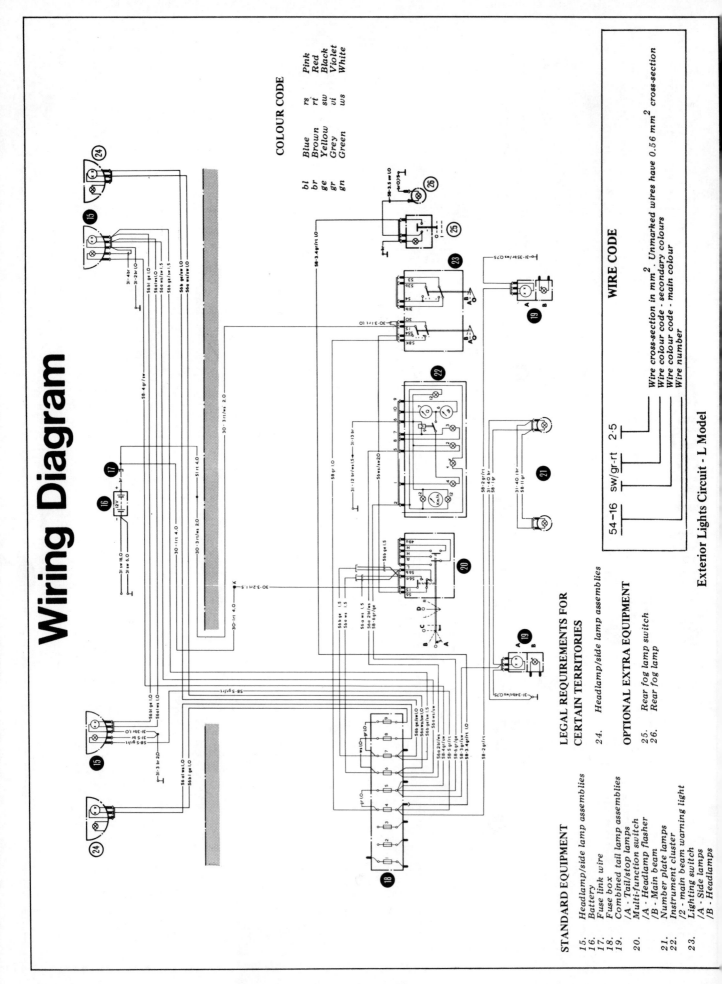

COLOUR CODE

bl	Blue	rs	Pink
br	Brown	rt	Red
ge	Yellow	sw	Black
gr	Grey	vi	Violet
gn	Green	ws	White

WIRE CODE

Wire cross-section in mm². Unmarked wires have 0.56 mm² cross-section
Wire colour code - secondary colours
Wire colour code - main colour
Wire number

Exterior Lights Circuit - L Model

STANDARD EQUIPMENT

15. Headlamp/side lamp assemblies
16. Battery
17. Fuse link wire
18. Fuse box
19. Combined tail lamp assemblies
   /A - Tail/stop lamps
20. Multi-function switch
   /A - Headlamp flasher
   /B - Main beam
21. Number plate lamps
22. Instrument cluster
   /2 - main beam warning light
23. Lighting switch
   /A - Side lamps
   /B - Headlamps

LEGAL REQUIREMENTS FOR CERTAIN TERRITORIES

24. Headlamp/side lamp assemblies

OPTIONAL EXTRA EQUIPMENT

25. Rear fog lamp switch
26. Rear fog lamp

Wiring Diagram

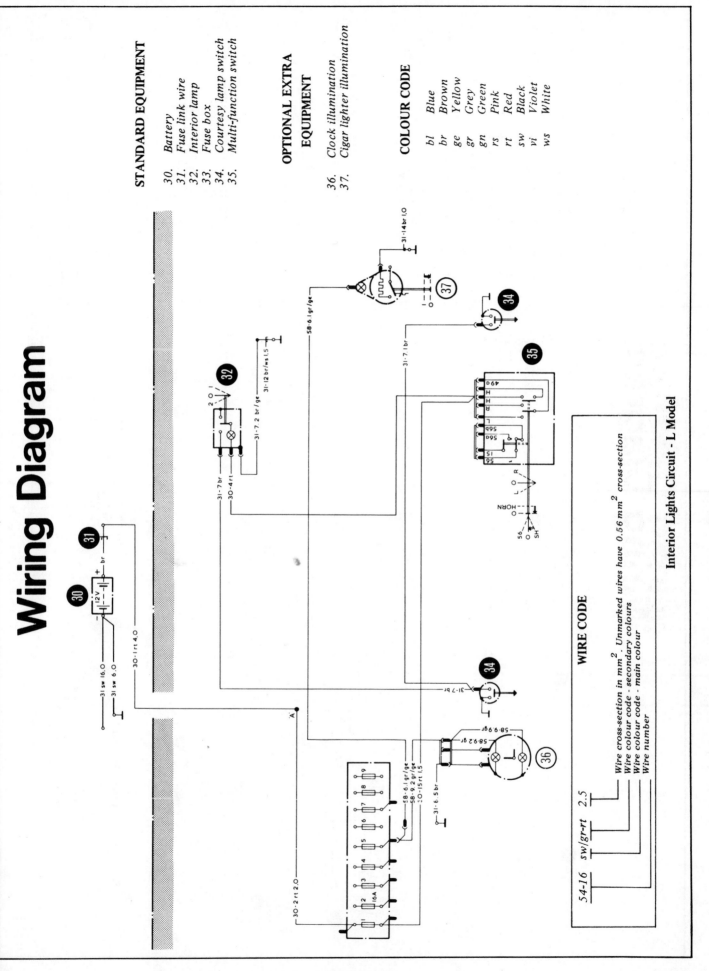

STANDARD EQUIPMENT

30. Battery
31. Fuse link wire
32. Interior lamp
33. Fuse box
34. Courtesy lamp switch
35. Multi-function switch

OPTIONAL EXTRA EQUIPMENT

36. Clock illumination
37. Cigar lighter illumination

COLOUR CODE

bl	Blue
br	Brown
ge	Yellow
gr	Grey
gn	Green
rs	Pink
rt	Red
sw	Black
vi	Violet
ws	White

WIRE CODE

54-16 sw/gr-rt 2.5

Wire cross-section in mm². Unmarked wires have 0.56 mm² cross-section
Wire colour code - secondary colours
Wire colour code - main colour
Wire number

Interior Lights Circuit - L Model

Wiring Diagram

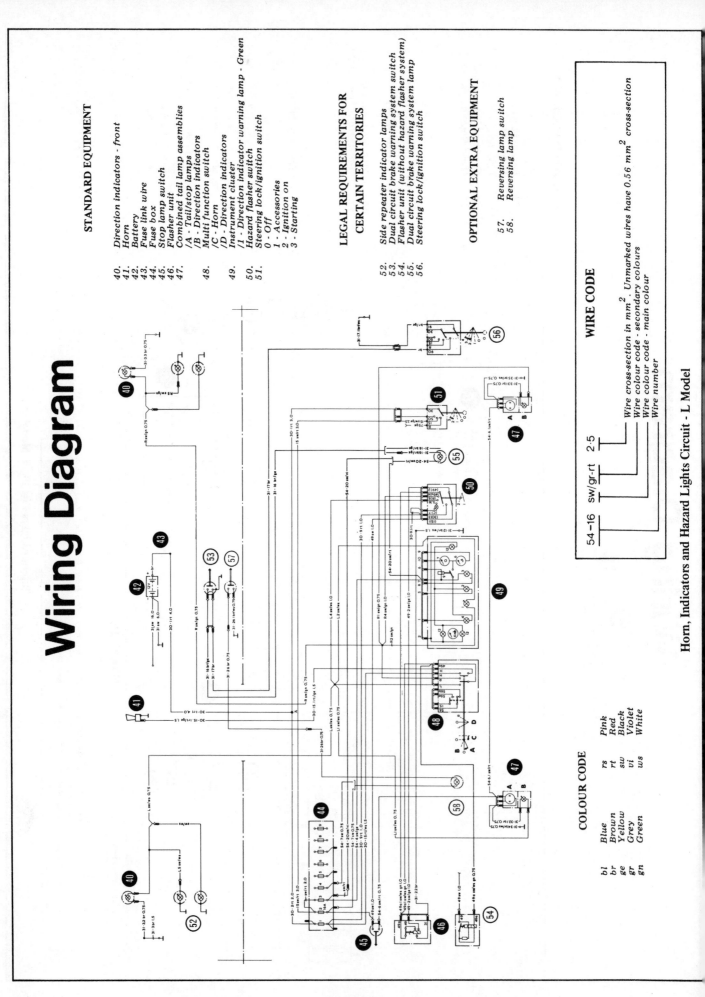

STANDARD EQUIPMENT

40. Direction indicators - front
41. Horn
42. Battery
43. Fuse link wire
44. Fuse box
45. Stop lamp switch
46. Flasher unit
47. Combined tail lamp assemblies
    /A - Tail/stop lamps
    /B - Direction indicators
48. Multi function switch
    /C - Horn
    /D - Direction indicators
49. Instrument cluster
    /I - Direction indicator warning lamp - Green
50. Hazard flasher switch
51. Steering lock/ignition switch
    0 - Off
    1 - Accessories
    2 - Ignition on
    3 - Starting

LEGAL REQUIREMENTS FOR CERTAIN TERRITORIES

52. Side repeater indicator lamps
53. Dual circuit brake warning system switch
54. Flasher unit (without hazard flasher system)
55. Dual circuit brake warning system lamp
56. Steering lock/ignition switch

OPTIONAL EXTRA EQUIPMENT

57. Reversing lamp switch
58. Reversing lamp

WIRE CODE

54 –16	sw/gr-rt	2·5

Wire cross-section in mm². Unmarked wires have 0.56 mm² cross-section
Wire colour code - secondary colours
Wire colour code - main colour
Wire number

Horn, Indicators and Hazard Lights Circuit - L Model

COLOUR CODE

bl	Blue	rs	Pink
br	Brown	rt	Red
ge	Yellow	sw	Black
gr	Grey	vi	Violet
gn	Green	ws	White

Wiring Diagram

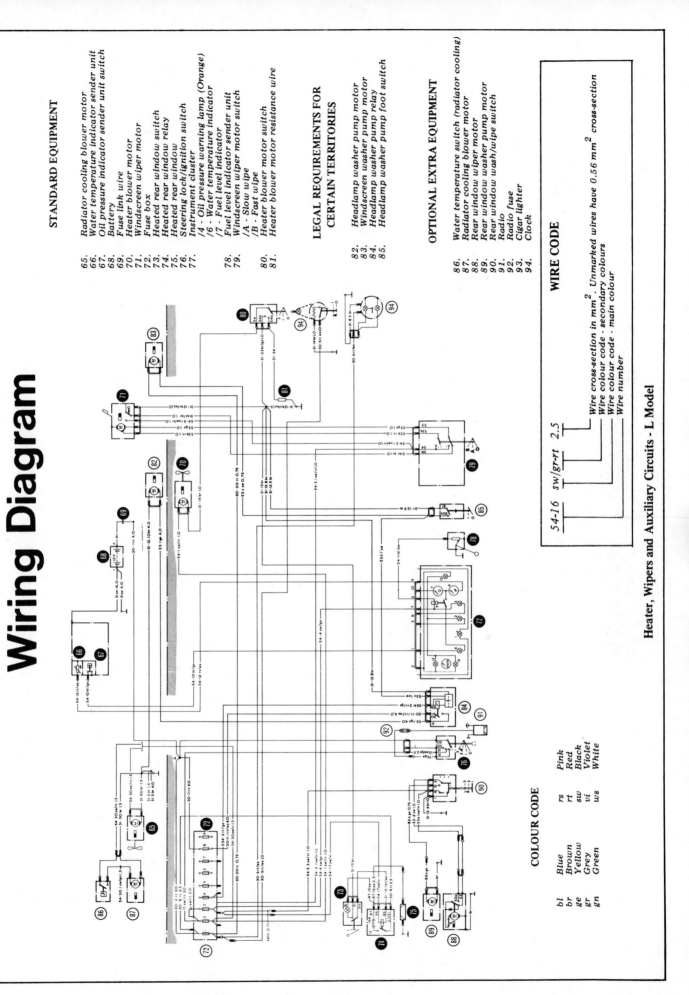

Heater, Wipers and Auxiliary Circuits - L Model

Wiring Diagram

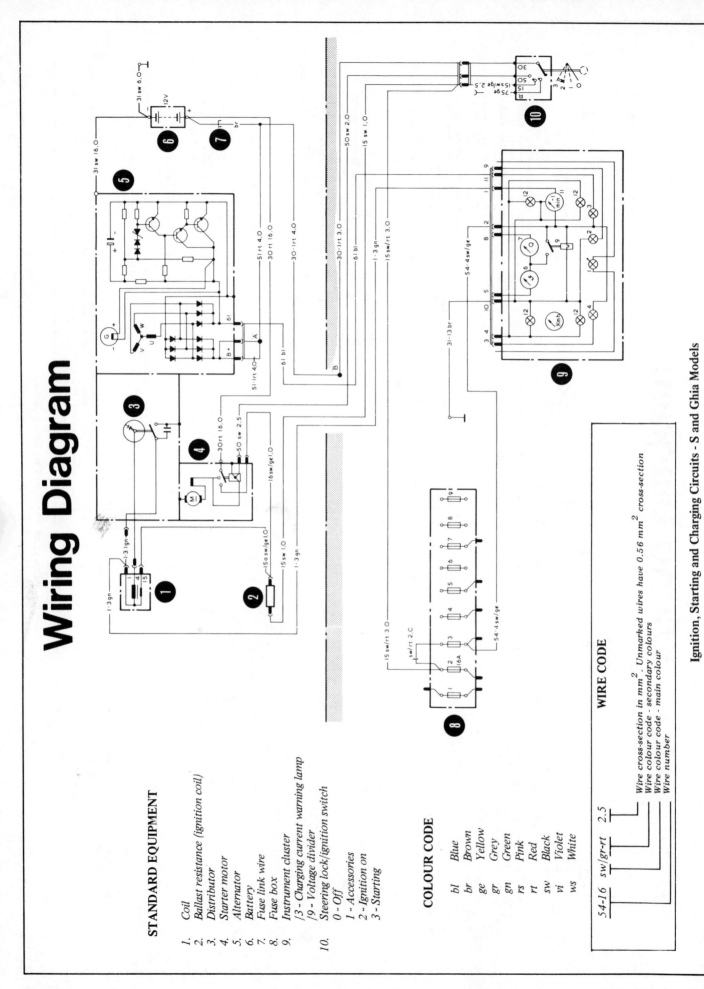

STANDARD EQUIPMENT

1. Coil
2. Ballast resistance (ignition coil)
3. Distributor
4. Starter motor
5. Alternator
6. Battery
7. Fuse link wire
8. Fuse box
9. Instrument cluster
   /3 - Charging current warning lamp
   /9 - Voltage divider
10. Steering lock/ignition switch
    0 - Off
    1 - Accessories
    2 - Ignition on
    3 - Starting

COLOUR CODE

bl	Blue
br	Brown
ge	Yellow
gr	Grey
gn	Green
rs	Pink
rt	Red
sw	Black
vi	Violet
ws	White

WIRE CODE

54-16 sw/gr-rt 2.5

Wire cross-section in mm². Unmarked wires have 0.56 mm² cross-section
Wire colour code - secondary colours
Wire colour code - main colour
Wire number

Ignition, Starting and Charging Circuits - S and Ghia Models

Wiring Diagram

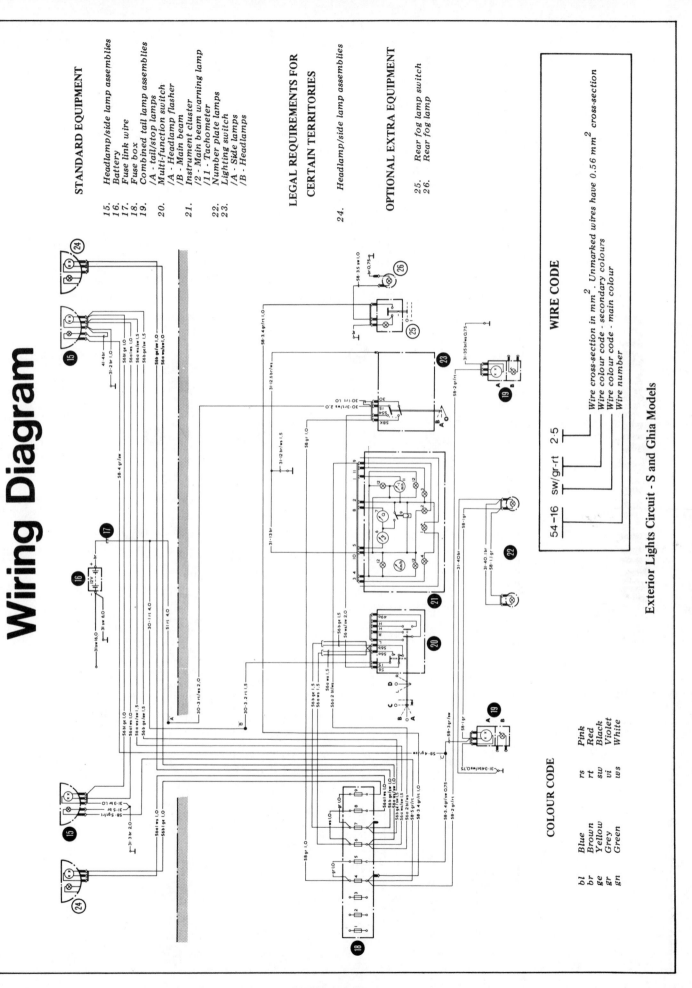

STANDARD EQUIPMENT

15. Headlamp/side lamp assemblies
16. Battery
17. Fuse link wire
18. Fuse box
19. Combined tail lamp assemblies
    /A - tail/stop lamps
20. Multi-function switch
    /A - Headlamp flasher
    /B - Main beam
21. Instrument cluster
    /2 - Main beam warning lamp
    /11 - Tachometer
22. Number plate lamps
23. Lighting switch
    /A - Side lamps
    /B - Headlamps

LEGAL REQUIREMENTS FOR CERTAIN TERRITORIES

24. Headlamp/side lamp assemblies

OPTIONAL EXTRA EQUIPMENT

25. Rear fog lamp switch
26. Rear fog lamp

WIRE CODE

54-16 sw/gr-rt 2.5

Wire cross-section in mm^2. Unmarked wires have 0.56 mm^2 cross-section
Wire colour code - secondary colours
Wire colour code - main colour
Wire number

Exterior Lights Circuit - S and Ghia Models

COLOUR CODE

bl	Blue	rs	Pink
br	Brown	rt	Red
ge	Yellow	sw	Black
gr	Grey	vi	Violet
gn	Green	ws	White

Wiring Diagram

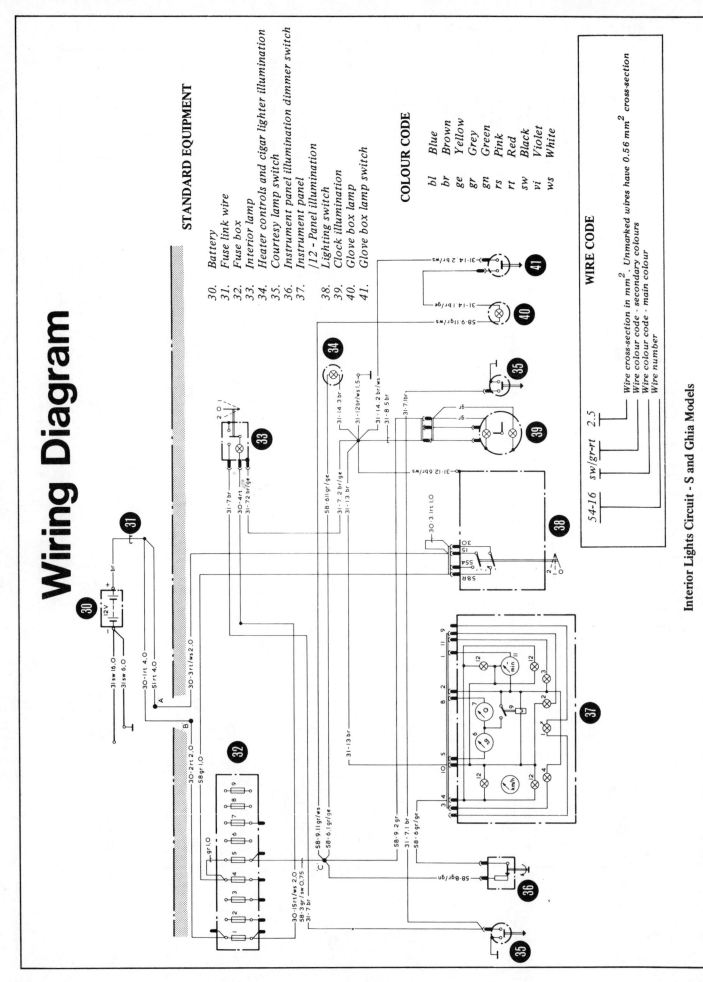

STANDARD EQUIPMENT

30. Battery
31. Fuse link wire
32. Fuse box
33. Interior lamp
34. Heater controls and cigar lighter illumination
35. Courtesy lamp switch
36. Instrument panel illumination dimmer switch
37. Instrument panel
/12 - Panel illumination
38. Lighting switch
39. Clock illumination
40. Glove box lamp
41. Glove box lamp switch

COLOUR CODE

bl	Blue
br	Brown
ge	Yellow
gr	Grey
gn	Green
rs	Pink
rt	Red
sw	Black
vi	Violet
ws	White

WIRE CODE

Wire cross-section in mm². Unmarked wires have 0.56 mm² cross-section
Wire colour code - secondary colours
Wire colour code - main colour
Wire number

Interior Lights Circuit - S and Ghia Models

Wiring Diagram

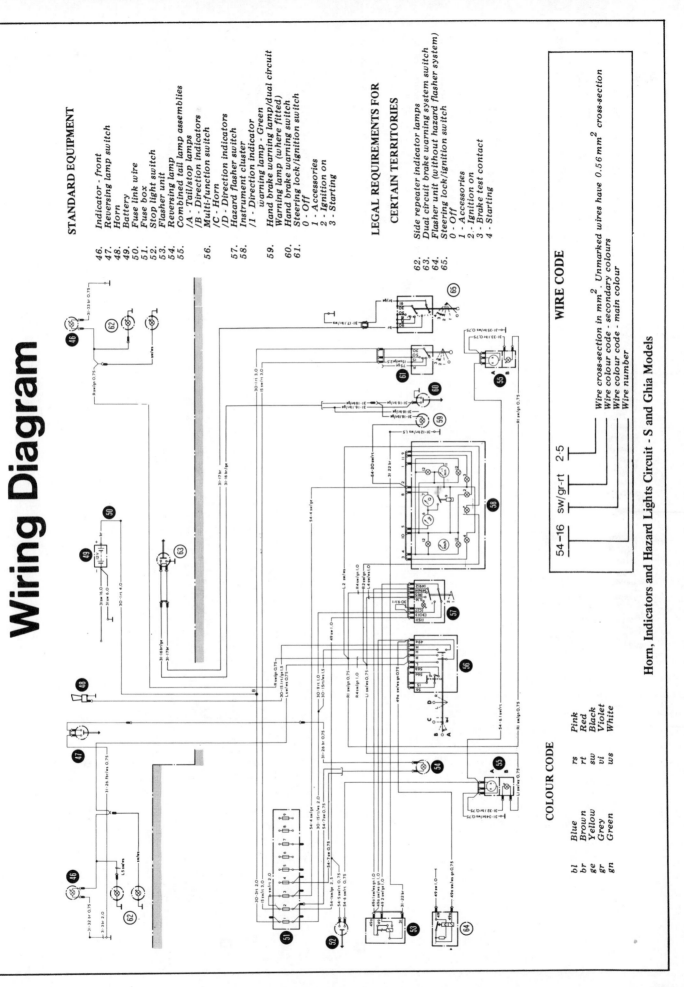

STANDARD EQUIPMENT

46. Indicator - front
47. Reversing lamp switch
48. Horn
49. Battery
50. Fuse link wire
51. Fuse box
52. Stop light switch
53. Flasher unit
54. Reversing lamp
55. Combined tail lamp assemblies
     /A - Tail/stop lamps
     /B - Direction indicators
     /C - Horn
     /D - Direction indicators
56. Multi-function switch
57. Hazard flasher switch
58. Instrument cluster
     /1 - Direction indicator
          warning lamp - Green
59. Hand brake warning lamp/dual circuit
60. Warning lamp (where fitted)
61. Hand brake warning switch
     Steering lock/ignition switch
     0 - Off
     1 - Accessories
     2 - Ignition on
     3 - Starting

LEGAL REQUIREMENTS FOR
CERTAIN TERRITORIES

62. Side repeater indicator lamps
63. Dual circuit brake warning system switch
64. Flasher unit (without hazard flasher system)
65. Steering lock/ignition switch
     0 - Off
     1 - Accessories
     2 - Ignition on
     3 - Brake test contact
     4 - Starting

WIRE CODE

54–16	sw/gr-rt	2·5

Wire cross-section in mm² Unmarked wires have 0.56 mm² cross-section
Wire colour code - secondary colours
Wire colour code - main colour
Wire number

Horn, Indicators and Hazard Lights Circuit - S and Ghia Models

COLOUR CODE

bl	Blue	rs	Pink
br	Brown	rt	Red
ge	Yellow	sw	Black
gr	Grey	vi	Violet
gn	Green	ws	White

Wiring Diagram

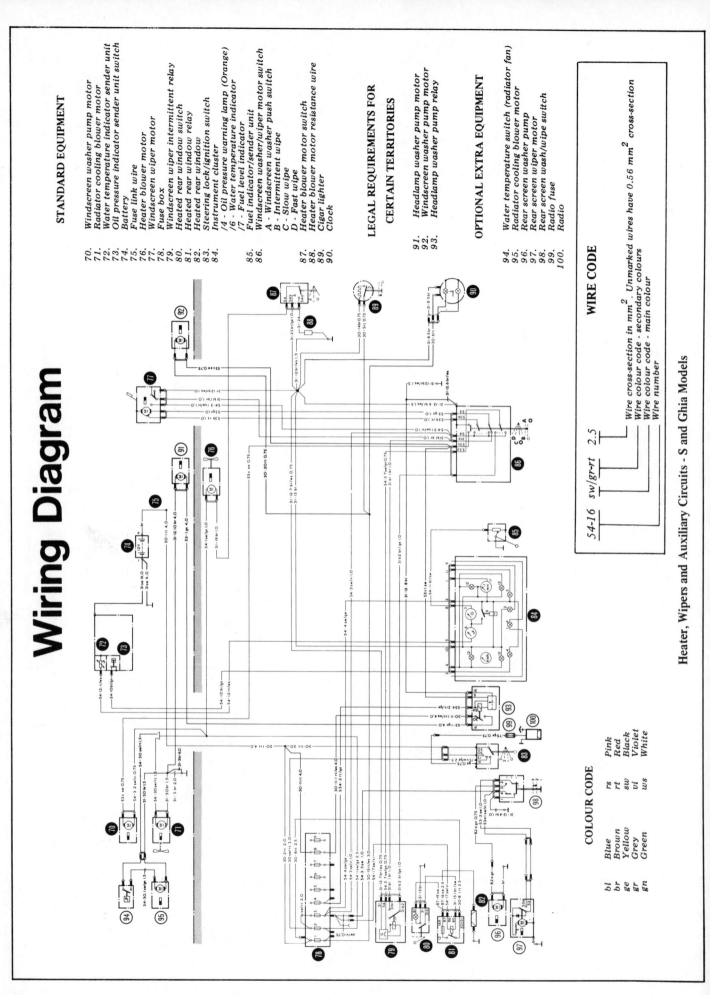

STANDARD EQUIPMENT

70. Windscreen washer pump motor
71. Radiator cooling blower motor
72. Water temperature indicator sender unit
73. Oil pressure indicator sender unit switch
74. Battery
75. Fuse link wire
76. Heater blower motor
77. Windscreen wiper motor
78. Fuse box
79. Windscreen wiper intermittent relay
80. Heated rear window switch
81. Heated rear window relay
82. Heated rear window
83. Steering lock/ignition switch
84. Instrument cluster
    /4 - Oil pressure warning lamp (Orange)
    /6 - Water temperature indicator
    /7 - Fuel level indicator
85. Fuel indicator/sender unit
86. Windscreen washer/wiper motor switch
    A - Windscreen washer push switch
    B - Intermittent wipe
    C - Slow wipe
    D - Fast wipe
87. Heater blower motor switch
88. Heater blower motor resistance wire
89. Cigar lighter
90. Clock

LEGAL REQUIREMENTS FOR CERTAIN TERRITORIES

91. Headlamp washer pump motor
92. Windscreen washer pump motor
93. Headlamp washer pump relay

OPTIONAL EXTRA EQUIPMENT

94. Water temperature switch (radiator fan)
95. Radiator cooling blower motor
96. Rear screen washer pump
97. Rear screen wiper motor
98. Rear screen wash/wipe switch
99. Radio fuse
100. Radio

WIRE CODE

54-16   sw/gr-rt   2.5

Wire cross-section in mm². Unmarked wires have 0.56 mm² cross-section
Wire colour code - secondary colours
Wire colour code - main colour
Wire number

COLOUR CODE

bl	Blue	rs	Pink
br	Brown	rt	Red
ge	Yellow	sw	Black
gr	Grey	vi	Violet
gn	Green	ws	White

Heater, Wipers and Auxiliary Circuits - S and Ghia Models

Body Fittings

Removal - Glass Panel Type (Fig. L:1)

1. Depress the two catch retainers to disengage the handle from the bracket, raise the roof panel, disengage the stop clip and lift away the panel.
2. Remove each of the two hinge plates from their pedestal blocks by releasing the retaining screws.
3. Remove the single screw from each pedestal block and remove the two halves of each block from the glass.
4. Remove each handle retainer screw and lift the handle and retainers from the glass.
5. Lift the spacers and washers from the handle screw block and lift it from the glass.
6. Pull the seal from the panel edge.

Installation

Installation is a reversal of the removal procedure, noting that adjustment of the hinge plates may be necessary to ensure correct operation of the roof panel. Each plate has elongated fixing holes for this purpose (Fig. L: 2).

Removal - Solid Panel Type

1. Depress the two catch retainers to release the handle from its bracket and lift the panel from the roof.
2. Remove the two hinges by releasing the two screw securing each to the panel.
3. Pull the seal from the edge of the panel.
4. Unscrew the two screws holding the handle to the panel and lift the handle away.

Installation

1. Making sure the panel edge is free from traces of old adhesive sealer, refit the new seal with a rubber mallet. The ends of the seal should meet in the middle of the front flange. The ends should be cut to length as necessary and pushed down on to the front flange.
2. Fit the panel hinges with the screws and spring washers.
3. Refit the handle with the two screws and spring washers.
4. Fit the panel to the roof by inserting the hinges in their retainers in the front of the roof aperture. Engage the handle with the roof bracket by depressing the retainers and then push the handle to close the roof panel.
5. Check the position of the panel visually, making sure it is flush with the roof. If it is not, the position can be adjusted by adding or removing washers from beneath the handle screws (Fig. L:3).

Handle Bracket - Removal

1. Lift out the sun roof panel.
2. Remove the single screw holding the handle cup in place. Remove the cup.
3. Remove the two screws holding the bracket to the roof and lift away the bracket.

Installation

This is a reversal of the removal procedure, noting that prior to replacing the handle cup, the adjustment of the panel flush to the roof should be carried out by adding or removing washers under the bracket bolts. When adjustment is satisfactory, replace the handle cup.

Hinge Retainer - Replacement

1. Lift out the sun roof panel.
2. Carefully pull the sun roof aperture weather seal from around the aperture.
3. Prise the headlining clips from the aperture flange and carefully pull the headlining clear of the flange in the area of the retainer.
4. Remove the two retainer securing screws and press the retainer forward out of its location. Withdraw the retainer from between the headlining and roof (Fig. L:4).

5. Fit a new seal around the new retainer and insert the assembly into its roof location. Secure with the two screws.

6. Refit the headlining, securing it to the aperture flange with the spring clips.

7. Refit the aperture weather seal, starting in the centre of the rear flange where the join in the strip should be positioned.

8. Refit the roof panel, adjusting the height if necessary and as described under the appropriate heading previously.

BONNET...........................[2]

Removal

1. Open the bonnet and prop it open with a length of wood or something similar.

2. Remove the screw holding the stay retainer to the underside of the bonnet and remove the retainer and stay.

3. Remove the radiator grille as described under the appropriate heading in this chapter.

4. Draw round the hinge plates with a felt tip pen or similar to ensure correct positioning or replacement and then remove hinge retaining bolts and washers (Fig. L:5).

5. Lift the bonnet from the body.

Installation

1. Fit the bonnet in the approximate correct position and loosely secure the hinges with their bolts and washers.

2. Align the hinge plates with the drawn outlines and fully tighten the retaining bolts.

3. If a new bonnet is being fitted, its position should be adjusted as follows:

4. Slacken the two bolts holding the bonnet catch to the plate on the bulkhead.

5. Refer to Fig. L:6, and move the bonnet on its hinges until the gaps between the side of the bonnet and the front wings are correct and the gap between the rear edge of the bonnet and cowl is correct.

6. Raise or lower the bonnet catch as necessary until the rear surface of the bonnet is flush with the cowl and rear upper surfaces of the front wings. Tighten the bonnet catch retaining bolts.

Bonnet Release Cable Replacement

1. Inside the car, remove the two screws holding the bonnet release handle to the cowl (Fig. L:7).

2. In the engine compartment, pull the cable grommet from the bracket at the catch and then disengage the cable nipple from the catch operating lever.

3. Pull the cable through the bulkhead into the car to remove.

4. Fit the new cable in the reverse order of removal.

Bonnet Catch Removal

1. Disconnect the battery.

2. Pull the cable grommet from its bracket at the catch and disconnect the cable nipple from the operating lever.

3. Remove the two bolts holding the catch to the plate on the bulkhead and remove the catch (Fig. L:8).

Installation

Installation is a reversal of the removal procedure, noting that the position of the catch should be adjusted vertically and horizontally to correct positioning of the bonnet when closed.

RADIATOR GRILLE..................[3]

Removal

1. Remove the screw and washer assemblies holding the grille to the front panel and remove the grille.

Installation

1. Make sure that the retaining nuts are correctly located in their holes in the front panel and that the spire clip is in position on the upper mounting tab.

2. Fit the grille, aligning the mounting holes with the special nuts and secure it with the screws and washers.

TAILGATE..........................[4]

Removal

1. Open the tailgate and prop it with a length of wood or similar.

2. Remove the screws holding the dampers to the tailgate brackets. Disengage the dampers.

3. Pull the weatherstrip from around the tailgate aperture.

4. Prise the clips holding the headlining to the flange and pull the flange headlining down in the area of the tailgate hinges.

5. Draw round the hinge plates with a felt tip pen or similar to aid correct positioning on replacement and remove the nuts and washers holding the hinges in place (Fig. L:9) and lift away the tailgate complete with hinges.

Installation

1. Make sure the paper gaskets are fitted to the hinge leaves. Fit the tailgate in position, inserting the hinge studs through the holes in the header bar. Secure them loosely with the nuts and washers.

2. Reconnect the dampers to the tailgate.

3. Realign the hinges with the drawn outlines, checking that the gap between the top of the tailgate and the roof is as shown in Fig. L:10. Fully tighten the hinge retaining nuts.

4. Replace the headlining and weatherstrip, making sure the join in the latter is positioned at the mid point of the lower aperture flange.

5. Close the tailgate and check that the gaps between it and the sides of the body are equal and even top to bottom. Check the opening and closing operation, adjusting

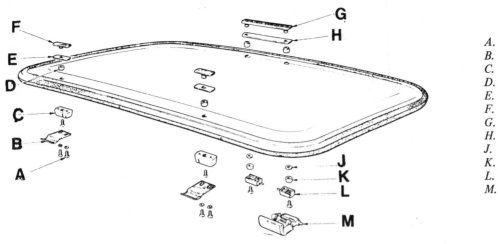

A. Screw
B. Hinge plate
C. Pedestal block
D. Spacer
E. Shim
F. Pedestal block
G. Handle screw block
H. Shim
J. Spacer
K. Spacer
L. Pivot block
M. Handle

Fig. L:1 An exploded view of the glass sunroof components

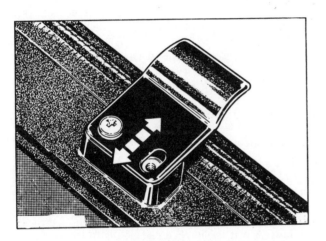

Fig. L:2 Sunroof hinge plate adjustment arrowed

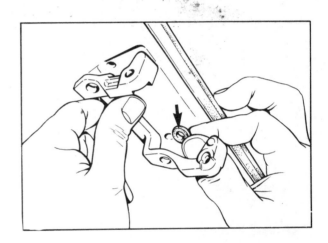

Fig. L:3 Replacing sunroof handle bracket. Note spacer washers arrowed

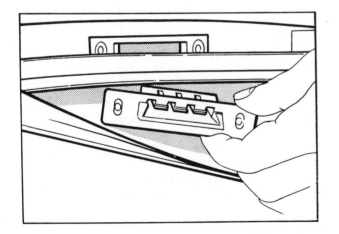

Fig. L:4 Removing the sunroof hinge retainer from roof panel

Fig. L:5 Undo two bolts (arrowed) to detach bonnet hinge

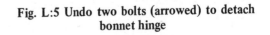

the position of the tailgate striker if necessary.

Tailgate Damper Replacement

1. Open the tailgate and support it in the open position with a length of wood or similar.
2. Remove the screw and spacer assemblies holding the ends of the damper to the tailgate and pillar brackets. Remove the damper.
3. Apply a suitable grease to the pivots at each end of the damper.
4. Fit the spacer on to the pivot screw and assemble to the barrel end of the damper. Connect this end to the pillar bracket.
5. Assemble the other end of the damper to the tailgate in a similar manner (Fig. L:11).

BUMPERS. . . . . [5]

Removal - Front

1. From inside the wheel arches, remove the nut from the inner bracket (Fig. L:12) and the screw from the wrap round portion at each end of the bumper.
2. Remove the bumper complete with mounting brackets.

Installation

1. Cut a piece of sealing strip to sit over each welded stud on the inner mounting brackets.
2. Fit the bumper in place, making sure the spacers are correctly located at the wrap round end brackets.
3. Refit the securing nuts and screws from inside the wheel arches.

Overrider - Removal

1. Remove the bumper as described previously.
2. Remove the overrider retaining screw at the base of the overrider and then slacken the upper clamp bolt (Fig. L:13).
3. Lift the overrider from the bumper.

Installation

Installation of the overrider is a reversal of the removal procedure, making sure the clamps are correctly located over the bumper rim.

Removal - Rear

1. Open the tailgate and lift out the load space subfloor.
2. Remove the number plate lamps from the bumper as described under GENERAL ELECTRICS.
3. Remove the nut and washer assemblies from the studs on the inner mounting bracket.
4. Remove the sealing material from the inner quarter panel cutouts to expose the screw and washer assemblies holding the wrap round ends of the bumpers in place (Fig. L:14).

5. Remove the screws and washers and lift away the bumper.

Installation

1. Cut sealing washers from sealing strip and apply them to the threaded studs on the inner bumper brackets and make sure the spacers are correctly located on the wrap round end brackets.
2. Insert the studs on the inner brackets through the holes in the back panel and loosely secure with the nuts and washers.
3. Secure the wrap round ends of the bumper with the screw and washer assemblies, making sure that the sealing washer on each screw is placed against the body. Replace the sealing material in the quarter panel cutouts.
4. Refit the subfloor and number plate lamps.

DOOR HANDLES. . . . . [6]

Outer Door Handle - Removal

1. Remove the door trim pad as described later in this chapter. Remove the PVC water proof shield.
2. Prise off the clip holding the handle rod to the door batch lever and disengage the rod from the lever.
3. Remove the two screws holding the handle assembly to the door and then remove the handle complete with operating rod (Fig. L:15).
4. Unhook the operating rod from the handle lever.

Installation

1. If a new handle is being fitted, push a new bush into the end of the handle lever. Softening it in hot water first will aid installation.
2. Fit the operating rod, after first dipping the end in petroleum jelly. Insert the curved end of the road through the bush so that the hooked end points to the rear after assembly.
NOTE: Operating rods used with LH locks and handles are marked with red paint.
3. Refit the handle to the door, securing with only one screw at the forward fixing point.
4. Lift the handle to give access to the rear fixing point and insert and tighten the rear mounting screw. Then fully tighten the front screw.
5. Reconnect the operating rod to the lever at the door catch, securing it with the spring clip.
6. Replace the PVC weatherseal and then the door trim pad.

Window Winder Handle - Removal

1. Carefully prise the plastic cap from the regulator shaft end of the handle.
2. Remove the screw holding the handle to the regulator shaft and lift off the handle complete with bezel (Fig. L:16).

Installation

1. With the window closed, fit the bezel and handle to

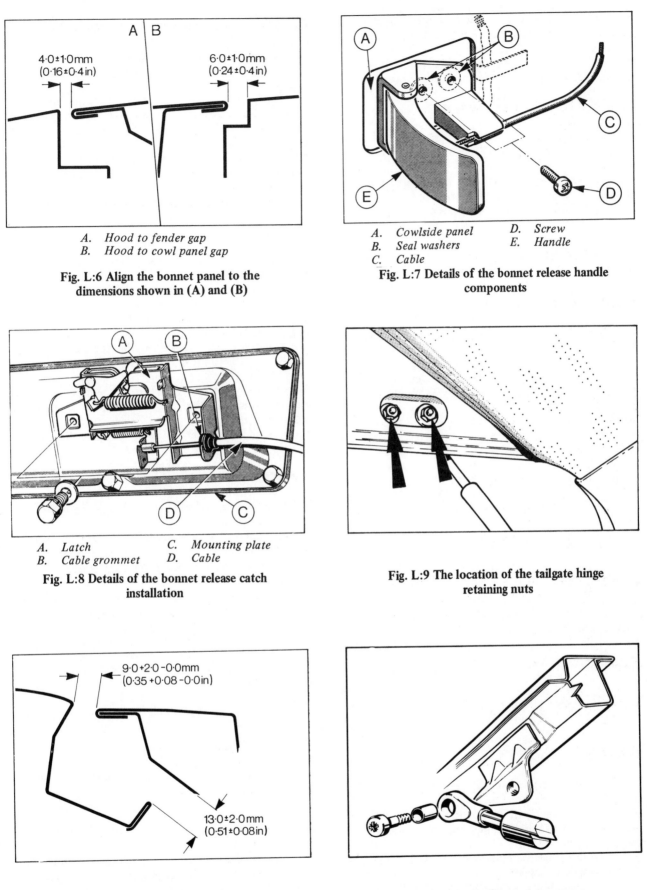

A. Hood to fender gap
B. Hood to cowl panel gap

Fig. L:6 Align the bonnet panel to the dimensions shown in (A) and (B)

A. Cowlside panel   D. Screw
B. Seal washers   E. Handle
C. Cable

Fig. L:7 Details of the bonnet release handle components

A. Latch   C. Mounting plate
B. Cable grommet   D. Cable

Fig. L:8 Details of the bonnet release catch installation

Fig. L:9 The location of the tailgate hinge retaining nuts

Fig. L:10 Adjust the tailgate to align to the dimensions shown

Fig. L:11 Details of the tailgate damper attachment

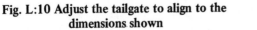

the regulator shaft in a position to match that of the handle on the opposite door. Refit and tighten the retaining screw.

2. Align the stubs on the circular plastic insert with the cutouts in the shaft end of the handle and press it home.

Door Pull Handle - Replacement

1. Using a screwdriver, carefully prise the end covers from the handle (Fig. L:17) to expose the mounting screws.

2. Remove the screw from each end of the handle and lift the handle away from the door trim pad.

3. Replacement is a reversal of the removal procedure.

TRIM PANELS.........................[7]

Door Panel - Removal (Fig. L:18)

1. On Ghia variants only, unscrew the button from the private lock rod and then with a screwdriver or similar flat bladed tool, carefully prise the trim capping retaining clips from their locations and remove the capping.

2. Remove the door window regulator handle as described previously.

3. Remove the door pullhandle as described previously or, if a combined armrest doorpull is fitted, remove that in the following manner: On L models, the rectangular armrest is secured by two screws only which are located on the underside of the rest. The more luxurious models have an armrest with an upswept handle. To remove these, remove the two screws to be found underneath the rest and then twist the rest through 90° at the peg location at the end of the handle. This will allow the peg to be removed.

4. Carefully prise the door catch remote control bezel from its retaining lugs.

5. Feel around the edge of the trim panel to locate the retaining clips and then carefully prise them free of their locations in the door panel. Ideally, a forked tool should be used for this purpose, but if care is taken it is possible to remove them with a screwdriver blade or similar tool (Fig. L:19). When all the clips have been sprung from their locations, remove the door trim pad. If fitted, remove the pocket by releasing its mounting screws from the rear of the trim pad.

Installation

1. Replace any trim clips that were broken on removal of the panel.

2. Refit the door trim pocket (if fitted) and then refit the trim panel to the door, pushing home each of its retaining clips.

3. Refit the remote control bezel, armrest/door pull and window regulator handle.

4. Refit the door trim capping on Ghia models along with the private lock rod button.

Cowl Side Panel - Replacement (Fig. L:20)

1. Remove the screws securing the scuff plate in the area of the trim and also prise off the door aperture weather seal in the area of the trim.

2. Bend the retaining tang clear of the upper edge of the trim panel and then prise out the two clips to remove the panel. Make sure the clips are correctly located in their cutouts in the trim panel.

NOTE: Before removing the trim panel on the driver's side of the car, the bonnet release cable and bracket must be removed from the cowl.

3. Replacement is a reversal of the removal procedure.

Rear Quarter Panel - Removal

1. Disconnect the parcel shelf lifting loops from the tailgate. Depress the top edge of each shelf support bracket and withdraw the brackets and shelf from the rear seat back anchors.

2. Remove the rear seat backrest and cushion as described later in this chapter.

3. Remove the rearmost screw from the scuff plate.

4. Remove the front screw from the parcel shelf support bracket (Fig. L:21).

5. Carefully prise the trim panel upper clips from their locations and pull the panel forwards to disengage the parcel shelf support.

6. Carefully prise the remaining retaining clips free and remove the trim panel.

Installation

1. Make sure the panel securing clips are correctly located in the trim panel.

2. Position the bottom of the panel first by knocking home the retaining clips with a soft headed mallet. Only strike the panel in the area of the clips otherwise damage will result.

3. Position the upper part of the trim and knock home the clips. Refit the parcel shelf support bracket screw.

4. Refit the scuff plate screw and then replace the removed components in the reverse order of removal.

Luggage Compartment Panel - Replacement (Fig. L:22)

1. Release the panel retaining rivet in the rear lower corner by pushing and twisting it through 90°.

2. Pull the panel rearwards to disengage it from the quarter trim panel.

3. Pull the panel downwards to disengage it from the body side rail and remove the panel.

4. Replacement is a reversal of the removal procedure.

Rear Wheelhouse Cover - Removal (Ghia)

1. Remove the rear parcel shelf, luggage compartment panel, rear quarter panel, rear seat back and cushion as described previously.

2. Pull the shock absorber upper mounting cover from

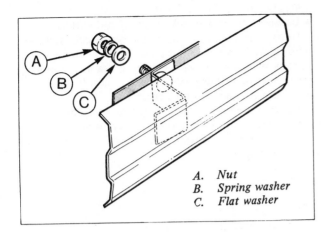

A. Nut
B. Spring washer
C. Flat washer

Fig. L:12 Details of the front bumper centre
bracket attachment

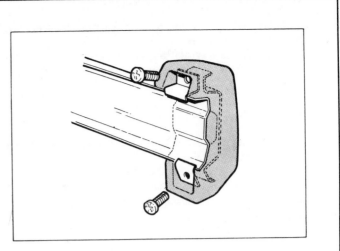

Fig. L:13 The overrider is attached to the
bumper by two screws as shown

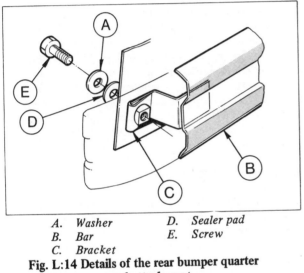

A. Washer   D. Sealer pad
B. Bar   E. Screw
C. Bracket

Fig. L:14 Details of the rear bumper quarter
panel attachment

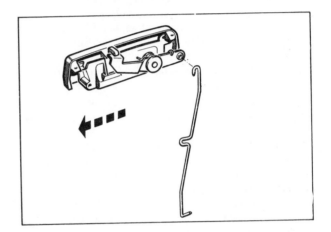

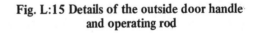

Fig. L:15 Details of the outside door handle
and operating rod

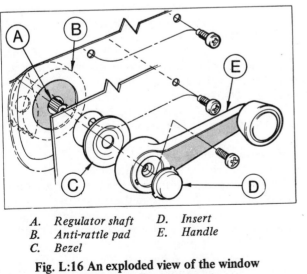

A. Regulator shaft   D. Insert
B. Anti-rattle pad   E. Handle
C. Bezel

Fig. L:16 An exploded view of the window
winder handle components

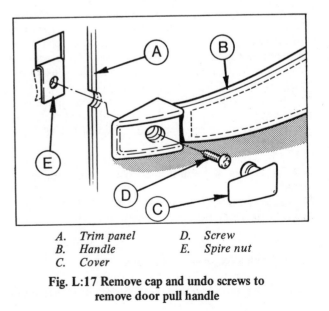

A. Trim panel   D. Screw
B. Handle   E. Spire nut
C. Cover

Fig. L:17 Remove cap and undo screws to
remove door pull handle

its flange and remove the seat latch striker by removing the single retaining screw.

3. Remove the rear subfloor and drill out the two rivets holding the rear of the cover to the floor. Remove the cover.

Installation

1. Apply adhesive to the area of the inner quarter panel as shown in Fig. L:23.

Allow five minutes for the adhesive to cure.

2. Fit the wheelhouse cover, making sure the fit is good around the rear seat striker bracket. Press the flange on to the adhesive.

3. Secure the rear end of the cover to the floor with blind rivets.

4. Replace the remaining components in the reverse order of removal.

Tailgate Panel Trim - Replacement (Fig. L:24)

1. Using a large screwdriver or similar flat bladed tool, carefully prise the panel trim retaining clips from their locations in the door inner panel and remove the trim.

2. Replacement is a reversal of the removal procedure.

DOOR LOCKS .... [8]

Door Remote Control - Removal (Fig. L:25)

1. Remove the door trim pad as described previously. Pull off the PVC weather seal.

2. Unclip the remote control operating rod from the lever on the catch. Push the rod retaining clip out of its aperture in the door inner panel.

3. Remove the two screws holding the remote control handle to the door inner panel and withdraw the handle and operating rod. Disconnect the rod from the handle.

Installation

1. Fit the operating rod to the handle by inserting its curved end into the handle lever. Note that operating rods for use with LH handles are marked with red paint.

2. Slide the retainer over the free end of the rod and position it on the grease section. Insert the handle and rod assembly into the door.

3. Loosely secure the handle with the mounting screws.

4. Connect the free end of the operating rod to the appropriate lever on the door catch, securing it with the spring clip.

5. Adjust the position of the retainer on the operating rod if necessary and pull it into its cutout in the door inner panel.

6. Slide the remote control handle as far to the rear as it will go and fully tighten the mounting screws.

7. Replace the PVC sheet and door trim pad.

Door Lock Assembly - Removal

1. Remove the door trim pad as described previously

and locally remove the PVC weather shield.

2. Unscrew the private lock operating rod button.

3. Unclip the remote control, exterior handle and lock cylinder rods from their appropriate levers at the lock.

4. Remove the three screws holding the lock assembly in place and manoeuvre the assembly until it is possible to remove it through the door aperture.

5. Remove the private lock operating rod from its lever. Prise the spring clips from the latch lever bushes.

6. Remove the three white bushes and one black bush from the latch.

Installation

1. Insert a black bush into the private lock latch lever and similarly push three white bushes into the remaining three latch levers.

2. Fit the spring clips to the three white bushes (silver clips for RH and black for LH).

3. Dip the curved end of the private lock rod into petroleum jelly and fit it to the black bush.

4. With the latch in the open position, guide it into place in the door, making sure the private latch operating rod is placed through the grommet in the upper edge of the door inner panel. Align the latch in the door pillar aperture and mount the assembly with the three screws.

5. Connect the exterior handle, lock cylinder and remote control operating rods to the appropriate levers on the latch and snap home the retaining clips.

6. Replace the PVC weathershield and refit the door trim pad, etc.

Door Lock Striker - Removal

Slacken the striker locknut and unscrew the striker, locknut and washer from the retainer caged on the reverse of the door pillar.

Installation

1. Fit the washer to the threaded end of the striker so that its cone apex is adjacent to the nut face. Screw the striker into the retainer, but do not tighten the locknut.

2. Open and close the door, moving the striker each time until satisfactory door closing is achieved.

3. Tighten the locknut.

As a check on the correct positioning of the door striker, the specified final assembly dimension between the striker centreline and the centreline of the door latch upper rivet is 0.6 in (15 mm) (Fig. L:26).

Door Lock Barrel - Removal (Fig. L:27)

1. Remove the door trim pad as described previously and locally remove the PVC weathershield.

2. Prise the spring clip from the end of the lock barrel rod and disconnect the rod from the latch lever.

3. Pull the lock cylinder retainer downwards and remove the lock cylinder and barrel assembly from the door together with the operating rod.

4. Note the relative positions of the end cap, cylinder spring and lever and remove the screw from the end of the

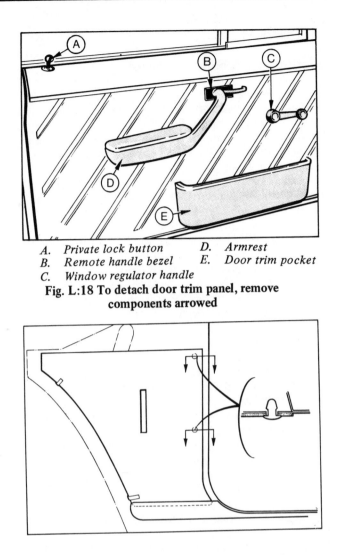

A. Private lock button   D. Armrest
B. Remote handle bezel   E. Door trim pocket
C. Window regulator handle

Fig. L:18 To detach door trim panel, remove components arrowed

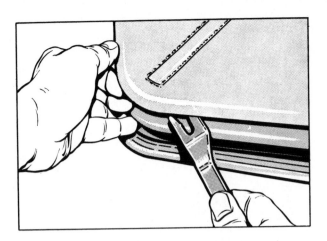
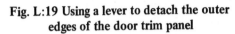

Fig. L:19 Using a lever to detach the outer edges of the door trim panel

Fig. L:20 The location of the cowl side panel attachment clips

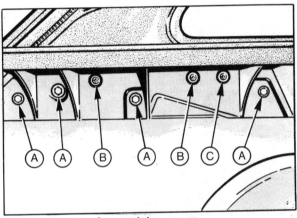

A. Bracket retaining screws
B. 'C' pillar trim panel retaining screws
C. Quarter trim panel capping screw

Fig. L:21 Undo the screws and bolts (arrowed) to detach rear parcel shelf support bracket

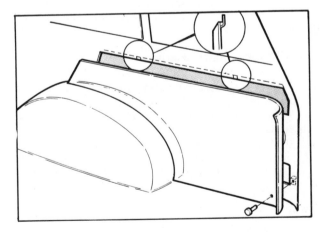

Fig. L:22 Removing the luggage compartment side trim panel

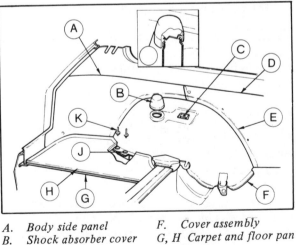

A. Body side panel   F. Cover assembly
B. Shock absorber cover   G, H Carpet and floor pan
C. Rear seat latch bracket   J. Washer
D. Quarter trim panel   K. Pop rivet
E. Adhesive location

Fig. L:23 Details of the wheelhouse cover panel attachment points

cylinder.

5. Lift off the end cap, disengage the lever and remove them together with the spring.

6. Insert the key and remove the barrel from the cylinder.

Installation

1. Making sure the O ring seal is correctly located in the cylinder housing groove, fit the key into a new barrel and insert it into the cylinder. Make sure the plug under the barrel head locates in the cylinder groove to allow free rotation of the key. Fit the spring, crossing the legs over the lug on the cylinder.

2. Refit the lever and rod assembly, locating the end cap so that its tang locates between the legs of the spring.

3. Refit the locking screw and washer, making sure that the key is free to turn through 90° on either side of the central position.

4. Fit the pad over the lock cylinder barrel and under the cylinder flange, aligning the cutouts in the pad with the lugs on the housing.

5. Refit the lock cylinder assembly to the door making sure the lever faces the front of the car. Align the barrel and, from inside the door, fit the retaining spring clip. Slide it upwards around the cylinder and tap it lightly into place with a mallet.

6. Replace the PVC weathershield and door trim pad.

Tailgate Lock Assembly - Removal (Fig. L:28)

1. Remove the tailgate trim panel as described previously.

2. Release the clip holding the latch operating lever to the plastic cam on the lock cylinder.

3. Remove the three screws holding lock assembly in place and remove the assembly complete with operating rod.

Installation

Installation is a reversal of the removal procedure.

Tailgate Lock Barrel - Removal (Fig. L:29)

1. Remove the tailgate trim panel as described previously.

2. Remove the clip holding the operating rod to the plastic cam on the cylinder.

3. Slide the retainer along so that the large aperture in the end clears the lock barrel and withdraw the lock cylinder and barrel from the tailgate.

Installation

1. Slide the pad over the cylinder, aligning the cutouts in the pad with the lugs on the cylinder housing.

2. Insert the cylinder assembly into the tailgate and secure it with the retainer, tapping the latter lightly into place with a mallet.

3. Reconnect the latch operating rod to the plastic cam with the spring clip and then replace the tailgate trim pad.

WINDOWS . . . . [9]

Door Quarter Window - Removal

1. Using a screwdriver and a suitable pad to prevent damage to the paintwork carefully remove the inner and outer belt weatherstrips (Fig. L:30).

2. Remove the door trim pad as described previously and peel off the PVC weathershield. Wind the window down as far as it will go.

3. Remove the two screws securing the dividing channel to the door. The upper one can be found by pulling down the silent channel. The lower one is secured to a bracket on the door inner panel (Fig. L:31).

4. Pull the dividing channel upwards and backwards at an angle of 45° to remove it from the door.

5. Remove the glass from the weatherstrip.

6. Remove the clip or clips holding the lower front triangular portion of the weatherstrip to the door and then prise the weatherstrip clear of the door.

Installation

1. Refit the glass to the weatherstrip and then lubricate the latter to aid installation in the door. Do not allow the soap to contaminate the adhesive pad at the front of the weatherstrip otherwise it will not adhere to the door. Make sure the glass and weatherstrip are pushed as far forward as they will go and then remove the backing from the adhesive pad, sticking it to the door. Fit new retaining clips, pushing them through the rubber into the door.

2. Refit the dividing channel, guiding it around the door glass and positioning it approximately.

3. Secure the two ends of the channel with the screws and washers.

4. If necessary, push the vertical section of the moulding upwards to achieve an acceptable mitre joint at the rear upper corner.

5. Refit the PVC weathershield and door trim pad.

6. Refit the inner and outer belt weatherstrips, noting that if the original strips are to be used the adhesive area of each should be covered with double sided tape prior to fitting.

Door Window Glass - Removal

1. Remove the door trim pad as described previously and peel off the PVC weathershield.

2. Remove the door quarter window as described previously.

3. Slide the door glass to disengage it from the regulator arm. Hold the regulator arm clear of the glass and remove the glass through the top of the door, passing inboard of the window frame.

Installation

1. Tilt the glass at the front and insert it into the door. Fit the regulator arm into the door glass channel at the same time engaging the glass in the rear silent channel.

2. Refit the door quarter window.

NOTE: If the PVC weathershield is torn or badly distort-

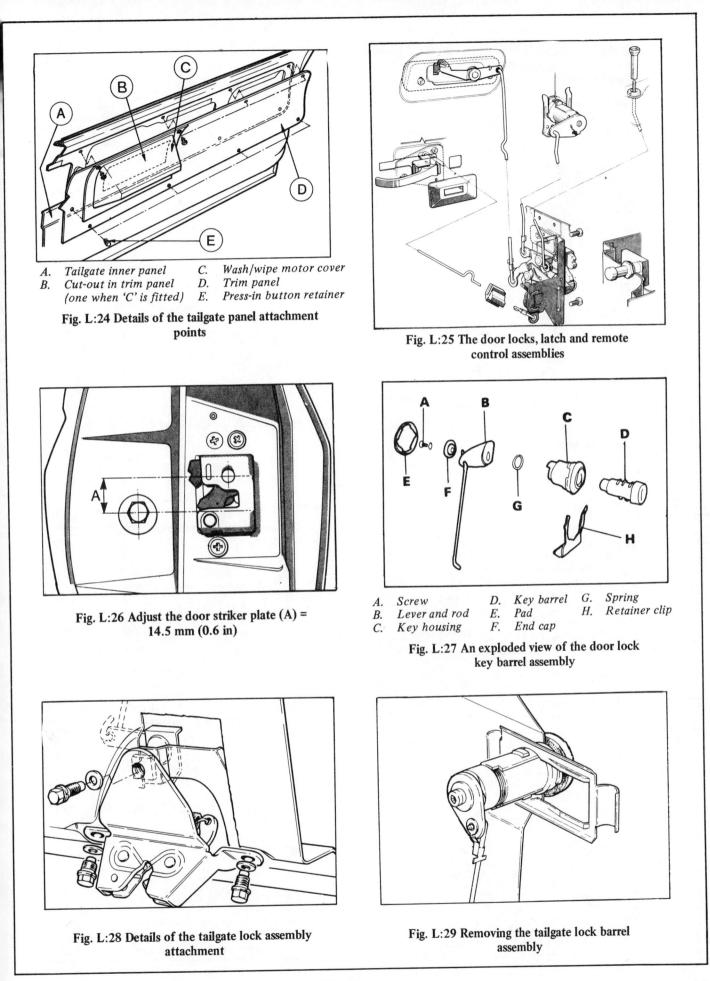

A. Tailgate inner panel
B. Cut-out in trim panel
(one when 'C' is fitted)
C. Wash/wipe motor cover
D. Trim panel
E. Press-in button retainer

Fig. L:24 Details of the tailgate panel attachment points

Fig. L:25 The door locks, latch and remote control assemblies

Fig. L:26 Adjust the door striker plate (A) = 14.5 mm (0.6 in)

A. Screw
B. Lever and rod
C. Key housing
D. Key barrel
E. Pad
F. End cap
G. Spring
H. Retainer clip

Fig. L:27 An exploded view of the door lock key barrel assembly

Fig. L:28 Details of the tailgate lock assembly attachment

Fig. L:29 Removing the tailgate lock barrel assembly

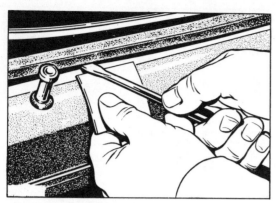

Fig. L:30 Method of removing the door belt inner weatherstrip

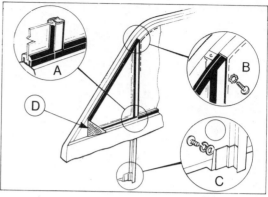

A.   Dividing channel C. · Lower fixing
B.   Upper fixing screw D. Adhesive pad

Fig. L:31 Details of the quarter window assembly fitting

Fig. L:32 Undo the screws to detach the window winder regulator from the door

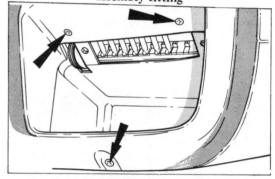

Fig. L:33 The location of the side pocket retaining screws (arrowed)

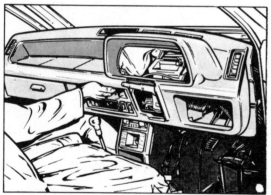

Fig. L:34 Removing the complete fascia panel from the bulkhead

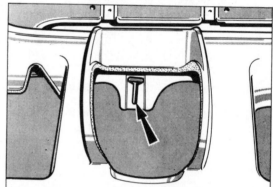

Fig. L:35 Make sure cut out in fascia panel locates over peg on column bracket

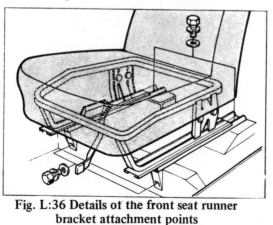

Fig. L:36 Details of the front seat runner bracket attachment points

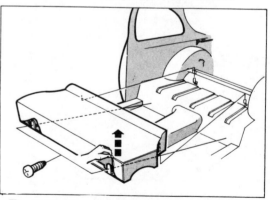

Fig. L:37 Removing the rear seat cushion from attachment points

ed it must be replaced.

3.   Remove all traces of the old PVC together with the adhesive by cleaning with white spirit. Dry the door inner panel with a clean cloth. Apply double sided adhesive tape 0.25 in (6 mm) in from the edge of the inner panel so that the trim pad clip holes are covered. Make sure all joints in the tape are overlapped and then peel off the backing. Using the trimpad as a template, cut out a new PVC weathershield, cutting 0.2 in (5 mm) in from the edge of the trim pad.

4..   Apply the sheet to the door, working from the top and down the sides, push the lower edge into the door slot then press the sides into position working upwards from the bottom edge. Make sure there are no wrinkles or bubbles at the bottom or sides of the sheet and that the sheet completely covers the tape. Cover the slot and lower edge of the seal with tape.

5.   Refit the door trim panel and inner and outer belt weatherstrips.

Door Window Winder Regulator - Removal

1.   Remove the door trim pad and PVC weatherseal.
2.   Wind the window as necessary so that the regulator and bracket assembly can be seen through the lower cutout in the door inner panel.
3.   Remove the four screws from the regulator pivot plate (Fig. L:32) and then push the plate into the shell to disengage the shaft from the door panel.
4.   Slide the regulator arm rearwards to disengage it from the door glass channel.
5.   Push the window upwards and remove the regulator assembly through the lower door aperture.

Installation

Installation is a reversal of the removal procedure.

FASCIA PANEL ASSEMBLY . . . . [10]

Removal

1.   Remove the steering wheel, steering column shroud, choke cable, indicator switches and the instrument cluster as described under the appropriate headings.
2.   Carefully prise the upper air vent from its location to expose the upper retaining screw. Remove the screw.
3.   Remove the lower retaining screw from its location just above the centre console.
4.   On Ghia variants remove the three screws from the driver's side pocket (Fig. L:33) and push the pocket complete with fuse block and rheostat clear of the crash pad.
5.   Remove the four nuts from the steering column support bracket.
6.   Remove the single screw from each end of the crash pad adjacent to the door pillar.
7.   Ease the complete crash pad assembly forwards sufficiently to gain access to the rear of the switch cluster (Fig. L:34). Remove the wiring plugs.
8.   Release the heater controls as described under GENERAL ELECTRICS.
9.   From behind the crash pad, pull off the face level vent hoses and then lift the pad from the car.

Installation

1.   Rest the crash pad on the belt rail and reconnect the face level vent air hoses.
2.   Push the pad approximately into position and refit the heater controls and the wiring plugs to the various switches.
3.   Make sure the cutout in the pad (Fig. L:35) is located over the peg on the steering column bracket and then refit the bracket to the dash panel and steering column.
4.   Replace the side and centre crash pad retaining screws and then the remaining components in the reverse order of removal.

CENTRE CONSOLE . . . . [11]

Removal

1.   Remove the gearlever knob, pull the gaiter up off the console and slide it from the gearlever.
2.   Remove the four screws holding the console in place and lift the console from the tunnel.
3.   If fitted, remove the clock and radio.

Installation

This is a reversal of the removal procedure.

SEATS . . . . [12]

Front Seats - Removal & Installation

1.   Slide the seat as far forwards as it will go to expose the rear bolts holding the seat slide to the floorpan. Remove the bolts (Fig. L:36).
2.   Slide the seat to the rear and remove the forward slide mounting bolts.
3.   Lift out the seat.
4.   Installation is a reversal of the removal procedure, noting that the front slide bolts should be tightened before the rear ones.

Rear Seat - Removal & Installation

1.   Unlatch the seat back and pull the spring pins from each rear seat back pivot. Press the pivot bushes from their body panel brackets and slide them along the pivots until clear of the brackets. Lift the seat back away.
2.   Remove the two screws holding the front edge of the seat cushion to the kick panel. Unhook the cushion from the retaining tabs and lift it out of the car (Fig. L:37).
3.   Installation is a reversal of the removal procedure, noting that to insert the seat back pivot spring pins it is necessary to insert one spring pin first and then push the seat back sideways until the spring pin is hard against the pivot bush. Fit the spring pin in the opposite pivot, selecting the pin hole nearest the bush face. If necessary, slacken the seat back latch retaining screws. Adjust the latch to suit the position of the striker and then retighten the screws.

Accessories

AERIAL . . . . [1]

Installation

1. Mark and then drill a 7/8 in dia hole in the top of the offside (driver's side) front wing to the dimensions shown in Fig. M:1. Clean the area around the underside of the hole to bright metal to ensure a good earth contact.
2. Fit the aerial to the wing panel in the order shown in Fig. M:6.
3. Drill a 7/8 in dia hole through the bulkhead kick panel at a point indicated by a small depression.
4. Feed the aerial lead through the panel into the car interior, using a grommet from the installation kit.
5. Apply sealing compound to the underside of the aerial fitting to prevent corrosion at this point.

SPEAKER. . . . . [2]

Installation

1. Remove the rear seat and the driver's side rear quarter trim panel as detailed in the BODY FITTINGS chapter.
2. Align the speaker grille fixing holes with the perforated speaker area on the trim panel.
3. Secure the speaker and the grille to the trim panel with the screws supplied in the fitting kit.
4. Connect the leads to the speaker and route the lead either under the carpet or through the side sill box section to the radio position.
5. Refit the rear quarter trim panel and the rear seat as detailed in the BODY FITTINGS chapter.

STEREO SPEAKERS . . . . [3]

Installation

Provision is made for the fitting of stereo speakers on the Fiesta as both rear quarter panels are perforated at the speaker mounting points. Fit the speakers following the operations detailed in the previous section for single speaker applications.

RADIO INSTALLATION . . . . [4]

Fiesta Models Without Centre Console

1. Attach the clip nuts to the support plate then temporarily fit it to the console unit supplied in the fitting kit, using the screws provided.
2. Position the console unit centrally on the floorpan tunnel under the lower fascia panel.
3. Holding the support plate in position on the floor, carefully remove the console.
4. Using the support plate as a template, drill four 1/8 in dia holes through into the floorpan.
5. Secure the support plate to the floorpan, using one of the screws provided, to secure the earth lead.
6. Assemble the speaker and outer bezel to the console, and connect the leads to the speaker terminals.
7. Fix the self-adhesive foam strip to the front edge of the console.
8. Connect the fused supply lead to the spare (Yellow) terminal located behind the ignition switch.
9. Connect the speaker lead, aerial lead and power supply lead to the radio.
10. Turn the ignition key to the Accessory position, then switch on the radio and tune it to a weak signal on the 250 metres (1.2 MHz) waveband. Adjust the aerial trimming screw - located adjacent to the tuning knob - to obtain maximum volume.
11. Turn the ignition key to the off position and remove the radio control knobs, escutcheons and trim plates.
12. Fit the radio to the console and refit the escutcheons, trim plates and knobs in the reverse order of removal.
13. Position the console on the support plate and secure with the screws provided.
14. Attach the loose end of the earth lead to the radio using the bolt and washers provided in the kit.

Fiesta Models Fitted With Centre Console

1. Remove the centre console, secured by four screws located at the positions shown in Fig. M:2.
2. Connect the radio supply lead to the (Yellow) spare terminal on the terminal block behind the ignition switch, then route the lead the radio position.
3. Connect the speaker, aerial and power supply leads

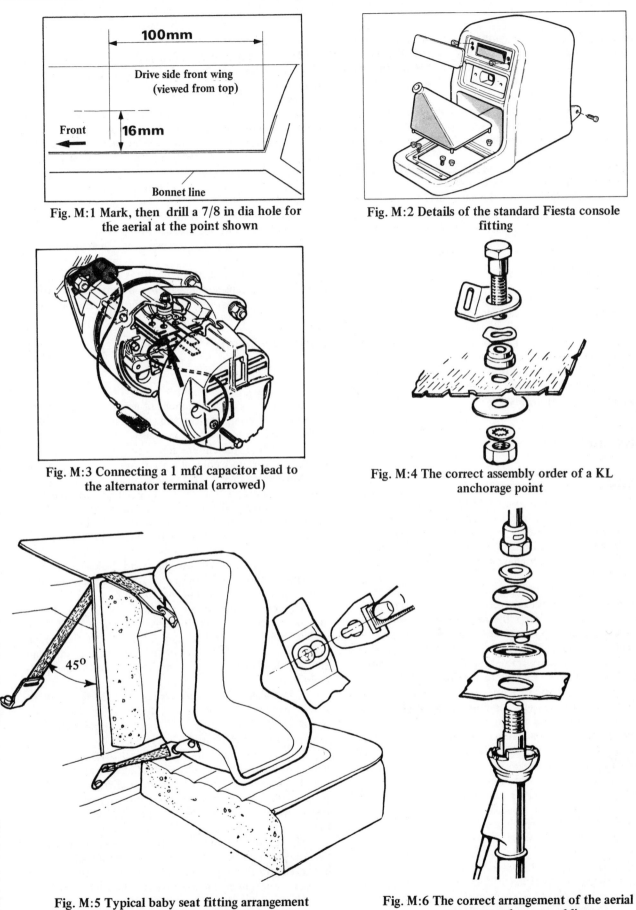

Fig. M:1 Mark, then drill a 7/8 in dia hole for the aerial at the point shown

100mm

Drive side front wing
(viewed from top)

Front

16mm

Bonnet line

Fig. M:2 Details of the standard Fiesta console fitting

Fig. M:3 Connecting a 1 mfd capacitor lead to the alternator terminal (arrowed)

Fig. M:4 The correct assembly order of a KL anchorage point

45°

Fig. M:5 Typical baby seat fitting arrangement and belt anchorage points

Fig. M:6 The correct arrangement of the aerial components when assembling

to the radio. Switch on the ignition to the Accessory position and the radio, tuning it to a weak signal on the 250 metres (1.2 MHz) waveband. Adjust the aerial trimming screw - located adjacent to the tuning knob - to obtain maximum volume. Switch off ignition.

4. Remove the radio position blanking plug from the console and fit the radio in position, refitting the escutcheons, trim plates and knobs in the reverse order of removal.

5. Attach the radio rear support bracket to the console and the radio together with the earth lead.

6. Secure the other end of the earth lead to the heater fixing bolt.

7. Refit the console assembly to the floorpan in the reverse order of removal.

Radio Suppression

1. Connect a 1 Mfd capacitor to the battery supply lead on ignition coil. Fit the capacitor under one of the coil mounting bolts, also the earth lead which is supplied in the fitting kit. The other end of the earth lead should be mounted under the bolt securing the air filter assembly.

2. Connect a 1 Mfd capacitor to the output terminal of the alternator and secure the capacitor to the alternator as shown in Fig. M:3 (Lucas type).

BABY SEAT . . . . [5]

Only by fitting a safety seat or harness, secured firmly to the car structure, can a child have a good chance of surviving a severe road accident without injury. Furthermore with the child safely in position at the rear of the car a driver can concentrate on the road with less distraction, while the child can enjoy the ride in safety and comfort.

There are many types of baby seat and cot restraints on the market and it is essential to the child's safety that a unit is fitted which meets the required safety standards. KL Jeenay Safety Systems are BSI approved and are generally accepted as being among the best on the market.

Baby or child seats are normally suitable for children aged from six to nine months to children aged five years. KL Jeenay safety seats or harnessess can, if necessary, be fitted two or three abreast, doubling up anchor plates at anchorage points where necessary.

Most cars have two or three built in anchorage points for each seating position. These are usually concealed behind the trim or soundproofing and plugged or grommetted. Always use the existing points, even if it means doubling up on an existing rear adult safety belt, using longer bolts (supplied in KL kit).

A general guide to fitting is as follows:

1. If anchorage points have to be drilled, it should be stressed that only fixed parts of the steel structure should be used. The size of the holes should be 1/16 in Always check the position of petrol tank, brake fluid pipes, electrical wiring, spare wheel and other obstructions

before drilling.

2. The two upper straps must make an angle of at least 45° inside view with the car's back seat. Use both wheel arches if required. Ensure that the two slot slide adjuster is near the end of the webbing.

3. When fitting anchorage points refer to Fig. M:4 for correct order of assembly. This is important.

4. Fit the four restraint strap assemblies to the anchorage points using short straps for the bottom of the seat and obviously the long straps for the top.

5. Adjust the seat straps to keep the safety seat as high as possible (Fig. M:5).

6. Attach the lower straps to the seat and adjust the webbing to suit, without overtightening.

7. To remove the seat, press into car squab and remove the lower lugs first.

8. Adjust the harness straps to fit as tightly as comfortable. The lap straps should rest low over the bony part of the hip. Always ensure that the crotch strap is used.

SOUNDPROOFING . . . . [6]

In any car a certain amount of noise is transmitted to the passenger compartment and, if of a high enough level, can not only be annoying, but also tiring on long journeys. Therefore, the elimination or reduction of this noise is desirable for more enjoyable motoring.

Noise can come from a variety of sources, the engine, tyres drumming on the road, the exhaust, wind rushing round the body, vibration of the steel panels, etc. By insulating the body, a large proportion of this noise can be eliminated. Sound Service (Oxford) Ltd., of Witney, Oxon, are leading manufacturers of car soundproofing materials, and their kit for the Ford Fiesta contains a variety of different materials, each designed specifically to reduce or eliminate certain types of noise.

The kit comprises several pieces of Sound Barrier Mat, which is a heavy layer of Plastisol with a black shiny surface bonded to a thick layer of foam material. These pieces are cut to shape and intended to fit the bulkhead area and toe boards, keeping out a lot of engine compartment noise.

Acousticell foam panels are provided, again cut to shape, to fit the floor areas and the underside of the parcel shelf. These keep out a lot of road noise and generally help to insulate the body.

In addition, there are pads that fit beneath the bonnet, mastic strips to seal all bulkhead holes and grommets, tape to reduce wind noise round door apertures and damper pads that are made from a stiff, self adhesive material which, when stuck to large unsupported panels, reduces the drumming and vibrations they give off.

The installation of the kit necessitates the removal of the seats and carpets, etc., and following installation, all lights, electrical components, etc., should be checked for correct operation to ensure that no wires have been dislodged.

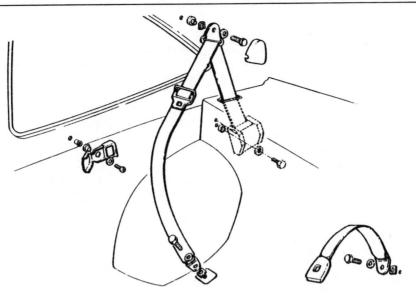

Fig. M:7 Details of the Fiesta rear seat belt mounting points

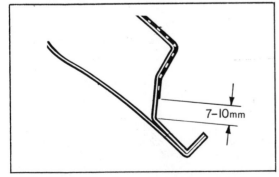

Fig. M:8 Flat the roof paintwork by hand particularly the gutter channel shown

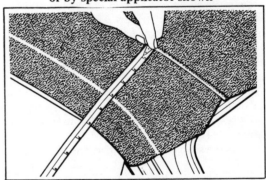

Fig. M:9 Spread the adhesive, either by hand or by special applicator shown

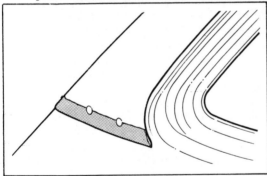

Fig. M:10 Position masking tape across rear body pillar moulding location holes

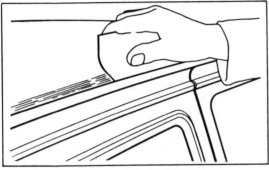

Fig. M:11 Checking the alignment of roof covering between seam and gutter channel

7–10mm

Fig. M:12 Trim the roof covering around the tailgate aperture to the dimension shown

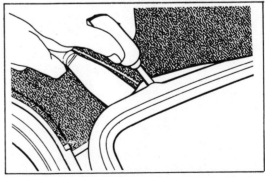

Fig. M:13 Using a blunt tool to lip the roof covering under the windscreen rubber

Accessories

REAR SEAT BELTS...................[7]

Provision is made in the rear of the Fiesta for the fitting of rear seat passenger seat belts. The belt mounting points are shown in Fig. M:7.

To fit the bolts, first remove the rear seat cushion as detailed in the BODY FITTINGS chapter. Fit the belt to the points shown in Fig. M:7, following the instructions supplied with the belt kit.

VINYL ROOF COVERING ....[8]

Fitting

The following instructions are applicable to the fitting of a FORD or other proprietary vinyl roof kit.

1. Remove the trim strip (if fitted) from the roof gutter rail.
2. Using an electric sanding tool or coarse grit wet-or-dry paper, remove the gloss from the roof paintwork to give a key for the adhesive.
3. Carefully flat the paintwork along the area of the roof gutter rail. (Fig. M:8).
4. Place the vinyl roof covering in position, making sure that the outer edges fully overlap the roof extremities, then place chalk mark on the vinyl covering and the window glass, at the front and rear also the sides. This will ensure that the covering can be correctly positioned when the adhesive has been applied.
5. Place the vinyl covering, with the outer appearance surface facing down, on sheets of newspaper on a flat surface.
6. Apply the adhesive to the inside, making sure that it is evenly speed, either using a hand spreading tool or special applicator as shown in Fig. M:9 and allow to dry.
7. Apply a strip of masking tape to the rear body pillar so that the edge of the tape runs across the centre of the holes as shown in Fig. M:10.
8. Place the vinyl covering in position on the roof so that the chalk marks made previously, are aligned. Check that the seam is equal in relation to the roof guttering rail on either side (Fig. M:11).
9. Clamp the sides of the vinyl covering to the gutter rail

mid-way along its length.

10. Fold the front section of the vinyl covering back level with the gutter rail clamps, then coat the front half of the roof with adhesive.
11. Fold the front section of the vinyl cover back carefully in place and smooth it down to a wrinkle free finish. Note that this will be easier to accomplish with two people doing the job.
12. Repeat the procedure on the rear section of the roof, smoothing it down particularly at the fold area between the front and rear sections.
13. Recheck the covering alignment and adjust if necessary before removing the gutter rail clamps.
14. Coat the rear body pillars with adhesive and smooth the covering down to a wrinkle free finish.
15. Pull the covering taut across the side of the roof and smooth it into the gutter rail channel. Trim off the excess material using a sharp knife.
16. Smooth the covering into the tailgate aperture and trim off the edge to the dimension shown in Fig. M:12.
17. Trim the front edge of the covering leaving a ½ in overlap.
18. Using a blunt instrument, lift the rubber edge of the windscreen surround and tuck the covering underneath as shown in Fig. M:13.
19. Flat the paintwork around the tailgate window frame in the same manner as detailed previously for the roof, then coat with adhesive and allow to dry.
20. Coat the vinyl covering backing with adhesive and stick it to the tailgate smoothing it out to obtain a wrinkle free finish.
21. Smooth the covering around the tailgate corner and edge contours and trim it evenly all the way round.
22. Align the moulding retaining clip (if removed) with each pair of holes on either side of the window aperture and secure with Pop rivets. If removed, press the appropriate moulding into place on each retainer.
23. Trim the covering around the window surround rubber leaving a ½ in overlap.
24. Using a blunt instrument, lift the rubber edge of window surround and tuck the covering underneath in a similar manner to that detailed previously for the windscreen.

Tightening Torques

ENGINE

Main bearing caps . . . . .70 lb ft (8.8-10.2 kg m)
Conrod bolts . . . . .22 lb ft (2.6-3.3 kg m)
Rear oil seal carrier . . . . .13 lb ft (1.6-2.0 kg m)
Flywheel . . . . .48 lb ft (6.4-7.0 kg m)
Chain tensioner. . . . . 5.9 lb ft (0.7-0.9 kg m)
Camshaft thrust plate . . . . 3.3 lb ft (0.4-0.5 kg m)
Camshaft sprocket. . . . . .13 lb ft (1.6-2.0 kg m)
Timing cover . . . . 6.3 lb ft (0.7-1.0 kg m)
Water pump . . . . 6.3 lb ft (0.7-1.0 kg m)
Crankshaft pulley . . . . .41 lb ft (5.4-5.9 kg m)
Water pump pulley . . . . 6.3 lb ft (0.7-1.0 kg m)
Alternator to cylinder
    block . . . . .28 lb ft (3.5-4.2 kg m)
Fuel pump . . . . .13 lb ft (1.6-2.0 kg m)
Distributor. . . . . 6.3 lb ft (0.7-1.0 kg m)
Distributor clamp bolt . . . . 2.6 lb ft (0.3-0.4 kg m)
Oil pump. . . . . .13 lb ft (1.6-2.0 kg m)
Oil pump cover. . . . . 7.4 lb ft (0.8-1.2 kg m)
Sump
    stage 1. . . . . 7 lb ft (0.8-1.1 kg m)
    stage 2. . . . . 7 lb ft (0.8-1.1 kg m)
    stage 3. . . . . 7 lb ft (0.8-1.1 kg m)
Sump plug . . . . .18 lb ft (2.1-2.8 kg m)
Oil pressure switch. . . . . .10 lb ft (1.3-1.5 kg m)
Temperature sender . . . . .10 lb ft (1.3-1.5 kg m)
Rocker shaft supports . . . . .27 lb ft (3.4-4.0 kg m)
Cylinder head bolts
    stage 1. . . . . 9 lb ft (1.0-1.5 kg m)
    stage 2. . . . . .33 lb ft (4.0-5.0 kg m)
    stage 3. . . . . .63 lb ft (8.0-9.0 kg m)
    stage 4 (after 10 min). . . . . .77 lb ft (10.0-11.0 kg m)
Rocker cover . . . . 3.3 lb ft (0.4-0.5 kg m)
Exhaust manifold . . . . .17 lb ft (2.1-2.5 kg m)
Inlet manifold. . . . . .13 lb ft (1.6-2.0 kg m)
Carburettor . . . . .14 lb ft (1.7-2.1 kg m)
Thermostat housing. . . . . .14 lb ft (1.7-2.1 kg m)
Fan temperature
    sender. . . . . .21 lb ft (2.7-3.0 kg m)
Spark plugs . . . . .13 lb ft (1.6-2.0 kg m)
Engine mount to block. . . . . . . .66 lb ft (8.0-10.0 kg m)
Engine mount to body . . . . .66 lb ft (8.0-10.0 kg m)
Apron panel
    insulators. . . . . .35 lb ft (4.2-5.2 kg m)
Engine mount to floor
    pan. . . . . .35 lb ft (4.2-5.2 kg m)
Engine mount/support
    insulator . . . . .35 lb ft (4.2-5.2 kg m)
Engine support to
    transmission. . . . . .66 lb ft (8.0-10.0 kg m)

TRANSMISSION

Transmission to engine . . . . .29 lb ft (3.5-4.5 kg m)
Small housing to large
    housing . . . . 18 lb ft (2.5 kg m)
Cover to housing. . . . . .7.2 lb ft (1.0 kg m)

Cap nut (gearshift lock)/
    housing . . . . .21.7 lb ft (3.0 kg m)
Gear/differential housing . . . . . .60 lb ft (7.8-8.6 kg m)
Shift housing to floorpan . . . . . 6.5 lb ft (0.8-1.0 kg m)
Pressure plate to flywheel . . . . . 7 lb ft (0.9-1.1 kg m)
Selector rod mechanism
    Allen screw . . . . .39 lb ft (5.0-6.0 kg m)

FRONT SUSPENSION

Hub retaining nut . . . . . . 180-200 lb ft (24.0-27.0 kg m)
Lower arm pivot bolt . . . . 30-33 lb ft (4.1-4.5 kg m)
Lower arm ball joint clinch
    bolt . . . . 15-18 lb ft (2.0-2.5 kg m)
Lower arm ball joint to lower
    arm. . . . . 40-48 lb ft (5.5-6.5 kg m)
Suspension strut to spindle
    carrier . . . . .74-88 lb ft (10.0-12.0 kg m)
Tie bar to mounting bracket . . 32-40 lb ft (4.4-5.5 kg m)
Tie bar mounting bracket
    to body. . . . . 30-38 lb ft (4.1-5.1 kg m)
Piston rod nut. . . . . 30-38 lb ft (4.1-5.1 kg m)
Top mount retaining
    bolts. . . . . 15-18 lb ft (2.0-2.5 kg m)

STEERING

Steering gear to bulk-
    head . . . . 33-37 lb ft (4.5-5.0 kg m)
Track rod end to steering
    arm. . . . . 18-22 lb ft (2.5-3.0 kg m)
Coupling to pinion spline . . . . 33-41 lb ft (4.5-5.6 kg m)
Steering wheel to steering
    shaft . . . . 20-25 lb ft (2.7-3.4 kg m)
Track rod end locknut . . . . . 42-50 lb ft (5.7-6.8 kg m)
Pinion bearing cover. . . . . . .12.5-17.6 lb ft (1.7-2.4 kg m)
Rack slipper cover . . . . .4.5-6.7 lb ft (0.6-0.9 kg m)
Pinion turning torque. . . . . 5-18 lb in (6.21 kg cm)

REAR AXLE & SUSPENSION

Panhard rod to body bolts. . . . 40-48 lb ft (5.4-6.4 kg m)
Panhard rod to axle bolts . . . . 40-48 lb ft (5.4-6.4 kg m)
Lower arm to body bolts . . . . 40-48 lb ft (5.4-6.4 kg m)
Lower arm to axle bolts . . . . . 40-48 lb ft (5.4-6.4 kg m)
Shock absorber top mounting
    bolts. . . . . 18-22 lb ft (2.5-3.3 kg m)
Shock absorber to axle
    bolts. . . . . 40-48 lb ft (5.4-6.4 kg m)
Carrier plate bolts . . . . 15-18 lb ft (2.0-2.4 kg m)
Stabiliser bar to body nuts . . . 15-18 lb ft (2.0-2.4 kg m)

BRAKES

Caliper to front suspension
    unit . . . . 38-45 lb ft (5.1-6.1 kg m)
Brake pressure control valve
    to bracket . . . . 15-18.5 lb ft (2.0-2.5 kg m)

Index